Goochland County, Virginia

Land Tax Books

1782–1788

Ruth and Sam Sparacio

HERITAGE BOOKS
2021

HERITAGE BOOKS

AN IMPRINT OF HERITAGE BOOKS, INC.

Books, CDs, and more—Worldwide

For our listing of thousands of titles see our website
at
www.HeritageBooks.com

Published 2021 by
HERITAGE BOOKS, INC.
Publishing Division
5810 Ruatan Street
Berwyn Heights, Md. 20740

International Standard Book Number
Paperbound: 978-1-68034-499-8

GOOCHLAND COUNTY, VIRGINIA
LAND TAX BOOKS
1782-1817

(page 1.)

Assignment of all Lands in Goochland County takn by ARCHIBALD PLEA-
SANTS and THOMAS F. BATES, February/March 1782.

Proprietors		No. of Acres	Value	Tax
William FARRER		886	571...10.....0	5...14.....3
Colo. John WOODSON		844	1354.....0.....0	13...10.....9
Matthew WOODSON		1883	1504...10.....0	15.....0.....9
Colo. Richard ADAMS	(Henrico)	1982	1066.....0.....0	10...13.....3
William BLUNKALL		3 1/2	3...10.....0	0.....0.....9
Majr. John WOODSON		535	267...10.....0	2...13.....6
Colo. Thomas HARRIS	(P'tan)	330	432.....0.....0	4.....6.....6
Charles BATES		350	262...10.....0	2...12.....6
Benjamin DARST		100	50.....0.....0	0...10.....0
William POWEL		266	115...10.....0	1.....3.....6
Susannah WOODWARD		500	375.....0.....0	3...15.....0
Philip TINSLEY		50	37...10.....0	0.....7.....6
Elizabeth STODGHILL		28	21.....0.....0	0.....4.....3
Sarah JORDAN		75	75.....0.....0	0...15.....0
John ELLIS	(Henrico)	392	294.....0.....0	2...18.....9
James CURD		440	220.....0.....0	2.....4.....0
John HINES		330	190.....0.....0	1...18.....0
Richard CROUCH	(Henrico)	200	100.....0.....0	1.....0.....0
Thomas SHOEMAKER		200	125.....0.....0	1.....5.....0
William WOODWARD		150	87...10.....0	0...17.....6
Jane VARDER		400	300.....0.....0	3.....0.....0
Samuel ROUNTREE		350	225.....0.....0	2.....5.....0
Robert WADE		97	48...10.....0	0.....9.....9
Randolph ROUNTREE		300	212...10.....0	2.....2.....6
Major Samuel DUVAL		500	450.....0.....0	4...10.....0
Stephen ELLIS		97	97.....0.....0	0...19.....3
Philemon CHILDRES		276	69.....0.....0	0...13.....9
Augustine EASTIN		180	90.....0.....0	0...18.....0
John HUTCHINGS		256 1/2	128.....5.....0	1.....3.....0
Colo. Nathaniel G. MORRIS		400	225.....0.....0	2.....5.....0
Mary & Jane JUDE		536	445.....0.....0	4.....9.....0
Strangeman HUTCHINGS		376	210.....0.....0	2.....2.....0
Major POWERS		180	90.....0.....0	0...18.....0
Richard WADE		73	36...10.....0	0.....7.....4
Pleasant MILLER		278	139.....0.....0	1.....7.....9
Daniel WADE		200	100.....0.....0	1.....0.....0
Revd. Francis HILL		262	98.....5.....0	0...19.....8
Matthew VAUGHAN		800	450.....0.....0	4...10.....0
George HANCOCK		97 1/2	36.....7.....6	0.....7.....6
John REDD		247	98...10.....0	0...19.....9
William BARNETT		200	90.....0.....0	0...18.....0
Athanasius BARNETT	(Louisa)	90 1/2	49.....5.....0	0.....9.....10
James VAUGHAN		362	168...10.....0	1...13.....9

(page 1 contd. Goochland County Land Tax Return for 1782.

Proprietors		No. of Acres	Value	Tax
Susannah BIBB		248	124.....0.....0	1.....4.....9
Matthew RIDDLE		70	24...10.....0	0.....7.....5
Eleanor WILLIS		100	32...10.....0	0.....7.....6

(page 2. Goochland County Land Tax Book for 1782

Proprietors		No. of Acres	Value	Tax
Thomas HARDING		228	114.....0.....0	1.....2.....9
Colo. John SYME	(Hanover)	318	109.....0.....0	1...11.....9
William WOODALL (unable to pay)		63	25.....0.....0	0.....5.....0
Capt. Stockley TOWLES		348 1/2	189...10.....0	1...17.....0
Thomas TOWLES		348 1/2	199.....5.....0	1...19.....0
Anderson PEERS		697 1/2	(blurred)	3.....9.....9
Hezekiah PURYEAR		397 1/1	198...15.....0	1...19.....8
William FORD		200	100.....0.....0	1.....0.....0
Elizabeth FORD		233	116...10.....0	1.....3.....4
John NEAVES		290	132...10.....0	1.....6.....6
Charles JOHNSON		124	49...10.....0	0...10.....0
Thomas CHANCELLOR		125	50.....0.....0	0...10.....0
David ELLIS	(Henrico)	236	118.....0.....0	1.....3.....9
William WEBBER		177	69.....5.....0	0...13.....9
William EDWARDS		80	20.....0.....0	0.....4.....0
Joseph FARRER		100	75.....0.....0	0...15.....0
John FARRER		298	200.....0.....0	2.....0.....0 ·
Colo. John LAPRADE		788	516.....0.....0	5.....3.....3
John JOHNSON		471	235...10.....0	2.....7.....2
Isaac RAGLAND		150	62...10.....0	0...12.....6
Edward WILLIS		160	80.....0.....0	0...16.....0
Elisha LEAKE		818	480...10.....0	4...16.....1
Charles JOHNSON, JUNR.		220	136.....0.....0	1.....1.....0
John F. GRIFFIN		3061	4061.....0.....0	40...12.....3
do. Mr. LEWIS's Tenement		1640	1230.....0.....0	12.....6.....0
Josiah SEAY		95	36.....5.....0	0.....7.....3
Thomas EDWARDS		50	20.....0.....0	0.....4.....0
Obadiah UTLEY		8	0.....4.....0	0.....0.....9
Ann UTLEY		116	45.....0.....0	0.....9.....0
John UTLEY		125	62...10.....0	0...12.....6
William UTLEY		125	62...10.....0	0...12.....6
Hezekiah UTLEY		58	21...15.....0	0.....4.....4
Joseph EVANS		134	50.....5.....0	0...10.....0
Francis EVANS		133 1/2	50.....0.....0	0...10.....0
John GORDON		133	58.....5.....0	0...11.....9
Matthew PLEASANTS		425	412...10.....0	4.....2.....6
James PLEASANTS		500	512...10.....0	5.....2.....6
Judith CHEADLE		299	249...10.....0	2...10.....0
Isaac PLEASANTS		676	900.....0.....0	9.....0.....0
William ROYSTER		543	371...10.....0	3...14.....4
Thomas ROYSTER		200	125.....0.....0	1.....5.....0
Thomas WOODSON		200	150.....0.....0	1...10.....0
Nathaniel WEBSTER		170	67...10.....0	0...13.....6
David WEBSTER		75	48...15.....0	0.....9.....9
John MADDOX		150	62...10.....0	0...12.....6
Robert WINGFIELD		90	45.....0.....0	0.....9.....0

(page 2 contd. Goochland County Land Tax Return for 1782

Proprietors		No. of Acres	Value	Tax
William McCAUL		81	70...10.....0	0...14.....1
Edward REDFORD		208	158.....0.....0	1...11.....9
Milner REDFORD		539	319...10.....0	3.....3...10
Richard SAMPSON		250	112...10.....0	1.....3.....6
Ann COCKE	(Surry)	1567	1433...10.....0	14.....6.....9
Allen COCKE, deced.	(Surry)	1195	1095...10.....0	10...19.....6
Thomas HATCHER		510	305.....0.....0	3.....1.....0
Amos L. MOORE		260	160.....0.....0	1...12.....0
Joseph PLEASANTS		200	100.....0.....0	0...10.....0

(page 3. Goochland County Land Tax Return for 1782

Proprietors		No. of Acres	Value	Tax
Robert PLEASANTS	(Buff)	140	60.....0.....0	0...12.....0
Stephen NOWLAND		150	62...10.....0	0...12.....6
Richard PLEASANTS		368	218.....0.....0	2.....3.....8
Phillip PLEASANTS		121	60...10.....0	0...12.....8
John SAUNDERS		30	15.....0.....0	0.....3.....0
Joseph WOODSON, JUNR.	(Geneto)	225	125.....0.....0	1.....5.....0
Joseph WOODSON, SENR.		222	136.....0.....0	1.....7.....3
Dorothy WATKINS		170	85.....0.....0	0...17.....0
Bartholomew TURNER		200	100.....0.....0	1.....0.....0
Thomas Mann RANDOLPH, Esqr. (Dor.)		1100	1640.....0.....0]	
ditto	(Tuckahoe)	1952	1781.....0.....0]	34.....4.....3
Joseph WILKINS	(Geneto)	429	264.....0.....0]	
ditto	(Little Creek)	270	170.....0.....0]	4.....7.....0
Thomas WATKINS		453	276...10.....0	2...15.....3
John CLARKE		62	23...10.....0	0.....4.....9
Turner CLARKE		90	33...15.....0	0.....6.....9
Jeffry CLARKE		98	39...10.....0	0.....8.....0
Joseph CLARKE		115	43...15.....0	0.....8.....9
Susanna CROUCH		100	50.....0.....0	0...10.....0
Mary ROGERS		17	8...10.....0	0.....1.....9
James HUNNYCUT		287	143...10.....0	1.....8.....9
John LAYNE		50	12...10.....0	0.....2.....6
Peter WALKER	(Geneto)	230	115.....0.....0	1.....3.....0
Benjamin JOHNSON	(do.)	115	57...10.....0	0...11.....6
David JOHNSON	(do.)	115	57...10.....0	0...11.....6
Isham JOHNSON		115	65.....0.....0	0...13.....0
Benjamin WATKINS		238	138.....0.....0	1.....7.....8
John JOHNSON	(Geneto)	271	156.....0.....0	1...11.....3
Henry GRAY		100	50.....0.....0	0...10.....0
John WATKINS		519	281...10.....0	2...17.....0
Capt. Stephen SAMPSON		752	377...10.....0	3...15.....6
Stokes McCAUL		295	147...10.....0	1.....9.....6
Mary MILLER		426	231.....0.....0	2.....6.....3
William WEBBER		340	220.....0.....0	2.....4.....0
Mary FRAIZER		205	102...10.....0	1.....0.....6
Benjamin HUGHES		627	313...10.....0	3.....2.....9
Capt. Gideon HATCHER		360	210.....0.....0	2.....2.....0
John GUERRANT, Gen-		450	275.....0.....0	2...15.....0
Elijah BRUMFIELD		130	65.....0.....0	0...13.....0
Benjamin WOODSON	(Fluvanna)	205	115.....0.....0	1.....3.....0

(page 3 contd. Goochland County Land Tax Return for 1782

Proprietors		No. of Acres	Value	Tax
Benjamin WATKINS, JR.		156	91.....0.....0	0...18.....3
Henry WHITLOW, JR.		50	25.....0.....0	0.....5.....0
Henry WHITLOW, SENR.		99	19...10.....0	0...10.....0
William WILLIS	(of David)	63 1/2	28.....7.....6	0.....5.....9
William NUCKOLS, JR.		121	60...10.....0	0...12.....0
(stained) NUCKOLS		110	55.....0.....0	0...11.....0
Charles NUCKOLS		104	45...10.....0	0.....9.....0
Thomas NUCKOLS		115	50.....0.....0	0...10.....0
Samuel NUCKOLS		115	50.....0.....0	0...10.....0
John GILLIAM	(Pr. Geo.)	500	300.....0.....0	3.....0.....0
William HUGHES	(Hanr.)	115	65.....0.....0	0...13.....0

(page 4. Goochland County Land Tax Return for 1782

Proprietors		No. of Acres	Value	Tax
Giles HARDING		316	164.....0.....0	1...13.....3
John BRUMFIELD		125	62...10.....0	0...12.....6
John WITT	(unable to pay)	17	8...10.....0	0.....1.....9
William POWERS		368	184.....0.....0	0...16.....9
Richard JOHNSON		150	85.....0.....0	0...17.....0
James COCKE		300	150.....0.....0	1...10.....0
Reubin FORD		147	73...10.....0	0...14.....8
William SAUNDERS		25	12...10.....0	0.....2.....6
John DOWDY		122	55...10.....0	0...11.....0
Mary ATKINSON		310	155.....0.....0	1...11.....0
Estate Charles SAMPSON		234	117.....0.....0	1.....3.....4
Joseph LEWIS, JUNR.		407	181.....0.....0	1...16.....3
Rene NAPIER		49	24...10.....0	0.....5.....0
Edward CARTER		34	17.....0.....0	0.....3.....6
Thomas PLEASANTS	(Mercht.)	1578	1626.....0.....0	16...15.....3
Doctor William PASTEUR		700	575.....0.....0	5...15.....0
Francis PLEDGE		50	25.....0.....0	0.....5.....0
William CLARKSON		50	30.....0.....0	0.....6.....0
Estate William PLEDGE, deced.		50	30.....0.....0	0.....6.....0
Archer PLEDGE		50	35.....0.....0	0.....7.....0
John PAYNE, JR.		439	392.....0.....0	3...18.....6
Tucker WOODSON		600	650.....0.....0	6...10.....0
John WOODSON, Gent. (Beaverdam)		665	415.....0.....0]	
do.	(Ferry)	600	387...10.....0]	8.....0.....6
William GEORGE & James ROBERTS		100	75.....0.....0	0...15.....0
David ROSS, Esqr. (Sundry tracts)———		9450	5121...10.....0	51.....4.....3
Edward McBRIDE		200	75.....0.....0	0...15.....0
Thomas OLIVER		273	136...10.....0	1.....7.....4
William RONALD, Esqr.		1170	835.....0.....0	8.....7.....0
Benjamin BRADSHAW		200	75.....0.....0	0...15.....0
John LEWIS		200	100.....0.....0	1.....0.....0
Joseph LEWIS, SENR.		281	140...10.....0	1.....8.....2
Colo. John CURD		609	404...10.....0	4.....1.....0
Elizabeth UNDERWOOD		100	70.....0.....0	0...14.....0
Robert POOR		350	225.....0.....0	2.....5.....0
William HAY	(Richmond)	600	450.....0.....0	4...10.....0
Capt. EDMUND CURD		225	137...10.....0	1.....7.....6
Sarah CURD		211	105...10.....0	1.....1.....1

(page 4 contd. Goochland County Land Tax Return for 1782

Proprietors		No. of Acres	Value	Tax
Thomas COCKE		140	70.....0.....0	0...14.....0
Benjamin COCKE		122	61.....0.....0	0...12.....3
James COCKE		54	27.....0.....0	0.....5.....6
Major John GUERRANT		200	100.....0.....0	1.....0.....0
Joseph POLLARD, Gent.		447	273...10.....0	2...14.....9
Mary PERKINS		161 1/2	80...15.....0	0...16.....1
Molly PERKINS		250	125.....0.....0	1.....5.....0
Estate Walker PERKINS		171 1/2	103...10.....0	1.....0.....0
James MADDOX		600	275.....0.....0	2...15.....0
James GEORGE		100	50.....0.....0	0...10.....0
John SHELTON, Gent.		412	206.....0.....0	2.....1.....3
George UNDERWOOD		526	238.....0.....0	2.....7.....9
Benjamin PERKINS		250	50.....0.....0	0...10.....0
Colo. William FLEMING		780	980.....0.....0	9...16.....0
Elizabeth MEANLY		130	95.....0.....0	0...19.....0
Capt. Joseph SHELTON		1369	754...10.....0	7...11.....0
Martha CARR		499	249...10.....0	2...10.....0
Henry WALMACKER		100	50.....0.....0	0...10.....0
John SHELTON	(Hanr.)	400	200.....0.....0	2.....0.....0

(page 5. Goochland County Land Tax Return for 1782)

Proprietors		No. of Acres	Value	Tax
Nathaniel RAINS		244	111.....0.....0	1.....2.....3
Drury MURRELL		200	75.....0.....0	0...15.....0
John BRADSHAW		450	187...10.....0	1...17.....6
Peter WALKER	(Constable)	116	29.....0.....0	0.....5.....9
Thomas HODGES	(unable to pay)	125	31.....5.....0	0.....6.....3
Benjamin SADLER	(ditto)	100	25.....0.....0	0.....5.....0
William PERKINS		200	75.....0.....0	0...15.....0
Thomas UNDERWOOD, Gent.		600	325.....0.....0	3.....5.....0
Archer PAYNE, Gent.		850	450.....0.....0	4...10.....0
Josias PAYNE, JR.		612	406.....0.....0	4.....1.....3
Colo. George PAYNE		200	100.....0.....0	1.....0.....0
Robert PLEASANTS, JR.		1300	850.....0.....0	8...10.....0
John HUMBER		561	280...10.....0	2...16.....1
Isham RICHARDSON		181	140...10.....0	1.....8.....1
Charles CHRISTIAN		217	133...10.....0	1.....6.....9
John GILLIAM		546	261...10.....0	2...12.....3
Isaac WINSTON	(Hanr.)	735	367...10.....0	3...13.....6
William WHITLOCK		100	37...10.....0	0.....7.....6
William WILLIAMS		500	250.....0.....0	2...10.....0
Thomas DRUMWRIGHT		1030	390.....0.....0	3...18.....0
Ayres LAYNE		155	63...15.....0	0...12.....9
Capt. Humphrey PARRISH		497	177...15.....0	1...15.....6
David GRANTUM		35	16.....5.....0	0.....3.....3
John WALKER		100	20.....0.....0	0.....4.....0
Colo. Jolly PARRISH		735	200.....0.....0	2.....0.....0
Estate Barnett OWEN		100	20.....0.....0	0.....4.....0
William ISBELL		792	252.....0.....0	2...10.....6
Arthur SLAYDEN.		182	45...10.....0	0.....9.....2
Henry LAYNE		100	25.....0.....0	0.....5.....0
John HENDERSON		200	50.....0.....0	0...10.....0

(page 5 contd. Goochland County Land Tax Return for 1782)

Proprietors	No. of Acres	Value	Tax
Mary LAYNE	50	12...10.....0	0.....2.....6
Callam BAILEY	150	37...10.....0	0.....7.....6
John BOWDRY	10	2...10.....0	0.....0.....6
John SLAYDEN	100	25.....0.....0	0.....5....0
William GROOM	100	20.....0.....0	0.....4.....0
William RUTHERFORD	433	141...10.....0	1.....8.....4
Zachariah HAYDEN	660	205.....0.....0	2.....1.....0
Benjamin CRENSHAW	440	160.....0.....0	1...12.....0
William ROBARDS	536	218.....0.....0	2.....3....8
Sarah THOMAS (unable to pay)	160	40.....0.....0	0.....8.....0
Drury HATCHER	5 1/2	1...10.....0	0.....0.....4
Mary TOWLER	200	50.....0.....0	0...10.....0
Matthew LACY	97	28...10.....0	0.....5....9
Jesse LACY	88	26...10.....0	0.....5....3
Benjamin LACY	88	26...10.....0	0.....5....3
Sarah LACY	181	55...10.....0	0...11.....1
William BURGESS	100	25.....0.....0	0.....5.....0
Sherwood PARRISH	162	40...10.....0	0.....8....1
William WALKER	94	24.....0.....0	0.....4...10
Samuel LEMAY	106	26...10.....0	0.....5....3

(page 6. Goochland County Land Tax Return for 1782)

Proprietors	No. of Acres	Value	Tax
William RIGSBY	50	10.....0.....0	0.....2.....0
John PARRISH	121	35...10.....0	0.....7.....0
Aaron PARRISH	121 1/4	30.....0.....0	0.....6.....0
Mary PARRISH	121 1/4	30.....0.....0	0.....6.....0
Booker PARRISH	180	45.....0.....0	0.....9.....0
Armsby CREW	100	30.....0.....0	0.....6.....0
Thomas STAFFORD	540	148...15.....0	1.....9....9
Jesse HODGES	160	55.....0.....0	0...11.....0
Estate Colo. Valentine WOOD	2226	1113.....0.....0	11.....2....8
Samuel PRYOR	400	203...15.....0]	
ditto	75	27...10.....0]	2.....6.....3
Nathaniel CAWLEY	60	30.....0.....0	0.....6.....0
Mary COLEY	100	50.....0.....0	0...10.....0
Susanna COLEY	100	25.....0.....0	0.....5.....0
Ann COLEY	100	50.....0.....0	0...10.....0
Sally COLEY	100	37...10.....0	0.....7....6
Francis COLEY	106	40...15.....0	0.....8.....1
William PRYOR	200	150.....0.....0	1...10.....0
John HILL	150	56.....5.....0	0...11.....4
Thomas B. EADS	136	34.....0.....0	0.....6....9
John WILLIAMS	400	125.....0.....0	1.....5.....0
Stephen G. LETCHER	516	287.....0.....0	2...17....4
Moses PARISH	168	42.....0.....0	0.....8....1
Harrison HARRIS	530	240.....0.....0	2.....8.....0
Mary HIX	300	112...10.....0	1.....2....6
Meshick HIX	450	175.....0.....0	1...16.....0
Daniel POWERS	33 1/2	12.....2.....0	0.....2....6
Francis CLARKE for Mr. DOUGLASS	150	37...10.....0	0.....7....6
Estate Joseph JOHNSON (for ditto)	500	125.....0.....0	1.....5.....0

(page 6 contd. Goochland County Land Tax Return for 1782)

Proprietors		No. of Acres	Value	Tax
Samuel POWEL		350	87...10.....0	0...17.....6
Cornelius TOWLER		190	47...10.....0	0.....9.....6
John WILLIAMSON		200	50.....0.....0	0...10.....0
Thomas POLLOCK		1092 3/4	496.....7.....6	4...19.....4
George PAYNE, JR.		200	68...15.....0	0...13.....9
William S. SMITH		211	93.....0.....0	0...18.....8
Charles MASSIE		300	150.....0.....0	1...10.....0
John PARRISH		561	182.....0.....0	1...16.....6
Ann MICHEL		291	95...10.....0	0...19.....6
David MARTIN		235	92...10.....0	0...18.....6
Paul MEACHUM		295	98...15.....0	0...19.....9
Major Jonas PAYNE		800	400.....0.....0	4.....0.....0
William CHEEK		232	83.....0.....0	0...16.....9
Jennings PULLAM		47	14.....5.....0	0.....2...10
John FARISH		100	37...10.....0	0.....7.....6
Martin MIMS		50	17...10.....0	0.....3.....6
Benjamin SALMONDS		250	75.....0.....0	0...15.....0
Robert CARDIN		200	62...10.....0	0...12.....6
Benjamin MOSBY		200	62...10.....0	0...12.....6
Robert PAGE		133	58.....5.....0	0...11.....9
William MICHEL	/Gent./	865	467...15.....0	4...11.....8

(page 7. Goochland County Land Tax Return for 1782)

Proprietors		No. of Acres	Value	Tax
William PAGE		133	66...10.....0	0...13.....3
William MILLER		300	137...10.....0	1.....7.....6
Thomas MILLER		296	124.....0.....0	1.....4.....9
John PERKINS		277	213...10.....0	2.....2.....8
William BRITT		850	246...15.....0	2.....9.....4
Francis HOUCHINGS		117	41...15.....0	0.....8.....4
Charles HOUCHINGS		117	41...15.....0	0.....8.....4
John CLEMENTS		116	41...10.....0	0.....8.....3
John BRITT		245	111.....5.....0	1.....2.....3
James ALLEN		175	50.....0.....0	0...10.....0
Lewis WILBERN		100	25.....0.....0	0.....5.....0
James HOLEMAN		275	100.....0.....0	1.....0.....0
William HODGES		100	30.....0.....0	0.....6.....0
John LOVELL		343	71...10.....0	0...14.....4
Dabney WADE		300	116.....5.....0	1.....3.....4
Estate William WADE		215	95.....0.....0	0...19.....0
David ALVIS		50	12...10.....0	0.....2.....6
Thomas RIDDLE		435	158...15.....0	1...11.....9
Gideon MIMS		360	165.....0.....0	1...13.....0
David MIMS		315	144.....5.....0	1.....8.....3
Elizabeth MEMINS		50	18...15.....0	0.....3.....9
Shadrach VAUGHAN		913	456...10.....0	4...11.....3
Estate of Jesse PAYNE, deced.		597 1/2	311...10.....0	3.....2.....4
George PAYNE, SR.		977	488...10.....0	4...17.....9
John PAYNE, SR.		2053	1013...10.....0	10.....2.....9
John K. READ		408	204.....0.....0	2.....0.....9
David CRENSHAW		238	90.....0.....0	0...18.....0
John WOODSON	(Meadow)	300	150.....0.....0	1...10.....0

(page 7 contd. Goochland County Land Tax Return for 1782)

Proprietors		No. of Acres	Value	Tax
John SALMONDS		150	50.....0.....0	0...10.....0
William HOLEMAN		990	247...10.....0	2.....9....6
William BOWMAN		100	25.....0.....0	0.....5.....0
Charles RICE		175	62...10.....0	0...12.....6
John HOPKINS		1650	662...10.....0	6...12.....6
Thomas POOR		525	162...10.....0	1...12.....6
Abraham POOR		200	75.....0.....0	0...15.....0
Colo. John MASTERS		700	300.....0.....0	3.....0.....0
Edward MATTHEWS		870	398.....0.....0	3...19.....8
Stephen GRANGE		80	35.....0.....0	0.....7.....0
William THURSTON		122	55...10.....0	0...11.....1
John THURSTON		110	47...10.....0	0.....9.....6
Hugh FRENCH		100	47...10.....0	0.....9.....6
William PROPHET		30	12...10.....0	0.....2.....6
Stephen DAVIS		265	116.....5.....0	1.....3.....3
Henry NASH	(Fluvana)	100	40.....0.....0	0.....8.....0
John DAVIS	(Hanover)	100	45.....0.....0	0.....9.....0
Esther THURSTON	(unable to pay)	53	14.....5.....0	0.....2...10

(page 8. Goochland County Land Tax Return for 1782)

Proprietors	No. of Acres	Value	Tax
Armiger LILLY	400	100.....0.....0	1.....0.....0
Pleasant ADKINS	65	26...10.....0	0.....5.....3
William WILBERN	200	40.....0.....0	0.....8.....0
Ichabod DANIEL	200	70.....0.....0	0...14.....0
Samuel RICHARDSON	536	234.....0.....0	2.....6.....2
Benjamin JOHNSON	140	60.....0.....0	0...12.....0
Joseph PACE	150	57...10.....0	0...11.....6
William JOHNSON	250	100.....0.....0	1.....0.....0
John PACE	130	40.....0.....0	0.....8.....0
William PACE	200	75.....0.....0	0...15.....0
Stephen CROUCH	200	50.....0.....0	0...10.....0
Ann MERRIAN	400	100.....0.....0	1.....0.....0
Henry TUGGLE	100	25.....0.....0	0.....5.....0
Horatio TURPIN	1200	425.....0.....0	4.....5.....0
Bryant CONLEY	150	50.....0.....0	0...10.....0
Colo. Robert LEWIS	565	241.....5.....0	2.....8.....3
Mary LEWIS	1030	865.....0.....0	8...13.....0
Robert GILLAM	691 3/4	2264...10.....0	22...13.....0
Thomas JEFFERSON, Esquire	942	1330...10.....0	13.....6.....0
Archibald JARRETT	353	101...10.....0	1.....0.....3
do.　　for JENNINGS	201	50.....5.....0	0...10.....0
Bowler COCKE, Esquire	1634	1607.....0.....0	16.....1.....0
Estate of Colo. John LEE, deced.	350	100.....0.....0	1.....0.....0
Japheth TOWLER	275	87...10.....0	0...17.....6
Samuel COSBY	225	62...10.....0	0...12.....6
John STRONG	137 1/2	68...15.....0	0...15.....9
Nathan STRONG	97 1/2	48...15.....0	0.....9.....9
Estate of Colo. Tarlton FLEMING, deced	1900	2350.....0.....0	23...10.....0
Edmund DUKE	230	65.....0.....0	0...13.....0
Thomas RANDOLPH, Esqr.	3000	1802...10.....0	18.....0.....6
Benjamin CLOPTON	200	100.....0.....0	1.....0.....0

(page 8 contd. Goochland County Land Tax Return for 1782)

Proprietors	No. of Acres	Value	Tax
William LEWIS	100	25.....0.....0	0.....5.....0
John PHILPOTT	100	25.....0.....0	0.....5.....0
Walter CLOPTON	220	110.....0.....0	1.....2.....3
John BOLLING, Esqr.	1801	1071.....0.....0	10...14.....3
Thomas BOLLING	3500	4072.....0.....0]	
do. (Island)	500	2000.....0.....0]	60...14.....6
Clairborne BRADSHAW	138	69.....0.....0	0...13.....9
James CLEMENTS	179	70.....0.....0	0...14.....0
Charles JOHNSON	200	87...10.....0	0...17.....6
Thomas ELDRIDGE	303	151...10.....0	1...10.....4
John WILLIAMS	250	100.....0.....0	1.....0.....0
David ENGLAND	80	30.....0.....0	0.....6.....0
William A. ENGLAND	139	59...15.....0	0...12.....0

(page 9. Goochland County Land Tax Return for 1782)

Proprietors	No. of Acres	Value	Tax
Wright MOURLAND	100	42...10.....0	0.....8.....6
Lewis HERNDON	300	125.....0.....0	1.....5.....0
Roger CARREL	83	20...15.....0	0.....4.....2
John HERNDON	199	90.....0.....0	0...18.....0
David MULLINS	197	98...10.....0	0...19.....8
Capt. Henry MULLINS	400	175.....0.....0	1...15.....0
George RICHARDSON	1612	678.....0.....0	6...15.....8
John HOPPER	210	92...10.....0	0...18.....6
Edward SCRUGGS (unable to pay)	100	37...10.....0	0.....7.....6
Lucy HODGES	50	15.....0.....0	0.....3.....0
Benjamin PAGE	100	37...10.....0	0.....7.....6
James THOMAS	110	27...10.....0	0.....5.....6
Estate of John TOWLER	62 1/2	15...10.....0	0.....3.....0
Major HANCOCKE	80	32...10.....0	0.....6.....6
John MULLINS	350	137...10.....0	1.....7.....6
Gideon CAWTHON	220	90.....0.....0	0...18.....0
Sarah BRADSHAW	69	30.....0.....0	0.....6.....0
John COX	100	37...10.....0	0.....7.....6
Edward COX	100	45.....0.....0	0.....9.....0
Capt. Josias LEAKE	800	400.....0.....0	4.....0.....0
Benjamin EAST	121 1/2	60.....0.....0	0...12.....0
John PREWIT	240	105.....0.....0	1.....1.....0
Judith CARTER (unable to pay)	100	30.....0.....0	0.....6.....0
William WHITFIELD	105	26.....5.....0	0.....5.....0
Capt. Robert SMITH	40	20.....0.....0	0.....4.....0
Archibald PLEASANTS	299	249.....0.....0	2.....9.....6
Thomas F. BATES	500	427.....0.....0	4.....5.....4

25 days service in the above business ending March the 23d 1782

ARCHD. PLEASANTS   ]
THO: F. BATES   ] Commrs.

Copy   Test G. PAYNE, Cl Cur

(page 10.)

A State of the Land Tax in Goochland County for the Sheriff's Collection November 1st 1783

Proprietors Names		Quantity of Land	Price	Amt. Land	Tax
Colo. Richard ADAMS	(Henrico)	1982	8/9	267.....2.....6	13.....0.....2
Mary ATKINSON		310	8/6	125.....5...10	1...17.....8
James ALLEN		175	7/8	67.....1.....8	1.....0.....2
Daniel ALVIS		50	4/1	10.....4.....2	0.....3.....1
Pleasant ADKINS		65	6/7	21.....7...11	0.....6.....6
William ANDERSON	(Hanover)	1500	8/	600.....0.....0	9.....0.....0
Charles BATES		350	12/1	211.....9.....2	3.....3.....6
William BARNETT		200	7/5	72...10.....0	1.....1.....9
Susanna BIBB		248	8/1	100.....4.....8	1...10.....2
Athanasias BARNETT	(Louisa)	98 1/2	do.	39...16.....3	0...12.....0
Elijah BRUMFIELD		130	do.	52...10...10	0...15...10
John BRUMFIELD		125	do.	50...10.....5	0...15.....2
Benjamin BRADSHAW		200	6/1	60...16.....8	0...18.....3
John BRADSHAW		450	6/9	151...17.....6	2.....5.....7
Callam BAILEY		150	4/1	30...12.....6	0.....9.....3
John BOWDRY		10	do.	2.....0...10	0.....0.....8
William BURGESS		100	do.	20.....8.....4	0.....6.....2
John BOLLING, Esqr.		1891	9/8	913...19.....8	13...14.....3
Thomas BOLLING, Esqr.,		4000		4905.....5.....0	73...11...11
Claibourne BRADSHAW		138	8/1	55...16.....6	0...16.....9
Sarah BRADSHAW		69	7/2	24...14.....6	0.....7.....5
Thomas Fleming BATES		500	13/10	345...16.....8	5.....3.....9
William BLUNKALL		3 1/2	16/2	2...16.....7	0.....0.....6
James BENNETT		200	6/	60.....0.....0	0.....9.....0
William BRITT		850	4/9	201...17.....0	3.....0.....7
John BRITT		245	7/4	89...16.....8	1.....7.....0
William BOWMAN		100	4/1	20.....8.....4	0.....6.....2
Gideon BOWLES		350	6/8	116...13.....4	1...13.....9
James CURD		440	8/1	177...16.....8	2...13.....5
Richard CROUCH	(Henrico)	200	do.	80...16.....8	1.....4.....3
Philemon CHILDERS		276	4/1	66.....7.....0	0...16...11
Thomas CHANCELLOR		125	6/6	40...12.....6	0...12.....3
Judith CHEADLE	(Caroline)	299	13/6	201...16.....6	3.....0.....7
Daniel CLARKE		100	6/1	30.....2.....4	0.....9.....2
Ann COCKE	(Surry)	1567	14/10	1162.....3...10	17.....8.....8
Allen COCKE, deced.	(do.)	1195	14/11	891.....5.....5	13.....7.....5
John CLARKE		62	6/2	19.....2.....4	0.....5.....9
Turner CLARKE		90	6/1	27.....7.....6	0.....8.....3
Jeffry CLARKE		94	6/7	32.....5.....2	0.....9.....9
Joseph CLARKE		115	6/3	30...18.....9	0.....9.....4
Susanna CROUCH		100	8/1	40.....8.....4	0...12.....2
James COCKE		300	do.	121.....5.....0	1...16.....5
Edward CARTER		34	do.	13...14...10	0.....4.....2
William CLARKSON		50	9/9	24.....7.....6	0.....7.....4
Colo. John CURD		609	10/9	327.....6.....9	4...18.....3
Capt. Edmund CURD		225	9/11	111...11.....3	1...13.....6
Sarah CURD		211	8/1	56...11.....2	0...15...10
Benjamin COCKE		122	do.	49.....6.....2	0...14..10

(page 11. Goochland County Land Tax Return for 1783

Proprietors Names		Quantity of Land	Price	Amt. of Land	Tax
James COCKE	(P.tan)	54	8/1	21...16.....6	0.....6.....7
Thomas COCKE		140	do.	56...11.....8	0...17.....0
Martha CARR		499	do.	201...13.....7	3...0.....7
Charles CHRISTIAN		217	10/	108...10.....0	1.....2.....7
Benjamin CRENSHAW		440	5/11	130.....3.....4	1...19.....1
Armsby CREW		100	4/10	24.....3.....4	0.....7.....3
Nathaniel CAWLEY		60	8/1	24.....5.....0	0.....7.....4
Mary COLEY.		100	do.	40.....8.....4	0...12.....2
Susanna COLEY		100	4/1	20.....8.....4	0.....6.....2
Ann COLEY		100	8/1	40.....8.....4	0...12.....2
Sally COLEY		100	6/1	30.....8.....4	0.....9.....2
Francis COLEY		106 1/2	6/3	33.....2.....6	0...10.....0
Francis CLARKE for Mr. DOUGLASS		150	4/1	30...12.....6	0...10.....3
William CHEEK	(Henrico)	232	5/10	67...13.....4	1...0.....4
Robert CARDIN		200	5/1	50...16.....8	0...15.....3
John CLEMENTS		116	5/10	33...16.....8	0...10.....2
Stephen CROUCH		200	5/1	50...16.....8	0...15.....3
Bryant CONLEY		150	5/5	40...12.....6	0...12.....3
Bowler COCKE, Esqr.	(Henrico)	1634	15/11	1300.....7...10	19...10.....2
Samuel COSBY		225	4/5	50...12.....6	0...15.....3
Walter CLOPTON		220	8/1	88...18.....4	1.....6.....9
James CLEMENTS		179	6/4	56...13.....8	0...17.....1
Roger CARREL		83	4/1	16...18...11	0.....5.....2
Gideon CAWTHON		220	6/8	73.....6.....8	1.....2...11
John COX		100	6/11	30.....8.....4	0.....9.....2
Edward COX		100	7/3	36.....5.....0	0...10...11
Judith CARTER		100	4/10	24.....3.....4	0.....7.....3
David CRENSHAW		238	6/2	73.....7.....8	1.....2.....1
Benjamin CLOPTON		200	8/1	80...16.....8	1.....4.....3
Turner CHRISTIAN		235	6/2	72.....7.....0	1.....1.....8
George CROWDAS		100	7/	35.....0.....0	0...10.....6
Benjamin DARST		100	8/1	40.....8.....4	0...12.....2
Major Samuel DUVAL	(Henrico)	500	14/6	362...10.....0	5.....9.....9
John DOWDY		122	7/5	45.....4...10	0...13.....7
Thomas DRUMWRIGHT		1030	6/2	317...11.....8	4...15.....4
Stephen DAVIS		265	7/2	94...19.....2	1.....8.....6
John DAVIS	(Hanover)	100	7/3	36.....5.....0	0...10...11
Ichabod DANIEL		200	5/8	56...13.....4	0...17.....0
Capt. Edmund DUKE	(P.tan)	230	4/7	52...14.....2	0...15...10
Revd. William DOUGLAS		500	6/1	152.....1.....8	2.....5.....8
David DAVIS		100	7/	35.....0.....0	0...10.....6
Noton DICKESON		400	do.	70.....0.....0	1.....1.....0
Susanna DAVIS		200	do.	35.....0.....0	0...10.....6
John ELLIS	(Henrico)	392	12/1	236...16.....8	3...11.....0
Stephen ELLIS		97	16/2	78.....8.....2	1.....3.....7
Augustin EASTIN		180	8/1	72...15.....0	1.....1...10
David ELLIS		236	do.	95.....7.....8	1.....8.....8
William EDWARDS		80	4/1	16.....6.....8	0.....4...11
Joseph EVANS		134	6/1	40...15.....2	0...12.....3
Francis EVANS		133 1/2	5/5	36.....3.....2	0...10...11

(page 11 contd. Goochland County Land Tax Return for 1783)

Proprietors Names		Quantity of Land	Price	Amt. of Land	Tax
Thomas B. EADS		136	4/1	27...15.....4	0.....8.....4

(page 12. Goochland County Land Tax Return for 1783)

Proprietors Names		Quantity of Land	Price	Amt. of Land	Tax
Thomas ELDRIDGE		303	8/1	122.....9.....3	1...16.....9
David ENGLAND		80	6/1	24.....6.....8	0.....7.....4
William A. ENGLAND		139	7/	48...13.....0	0...14.....8
Benjamin EAST		121 1/2	8/1	49.....2.....2	0...14.....9
Thomas EDWARDS		50	6/6	16.....5.....0	0.....4...11
Thomas EMMERSON		100	do.	17...10.....0	0.....5.....3
Henry EMMERSON		240	do.	45.....0.....0	0...13.....6
Thomas EMMERSON, JR.		100	do.	17...10.....0	0.....5.....3
William FARRAR, Gent.		886	10/5	461.....9.....2	6...18.....6
John FARRAR		298	10/9	160.....3.....6	2.....8.....1
William FORD		200	8/1	80...16.....8	1.....4.....3
Elizabeth FORD		233	do.	94.....3.....5	1.....8.....4
Joseph FARRAR		100	12/1	60.....8.....4	0...18.....2
Mary FRAYSER		205	8/1	82...17.....1	1.....4...11
Reuben FORD		147	do.	59.....8.....3	0...17...10
John FARISH		100	8/1	34...11.....8	0...10.....5
Estate Colo. Tarlton FLEMING, deced.		1900	20/2	1915...16.....3	28...14.....9
Honble. William FLEMING, Esqr.		780	20/4	793.....0.....0	11...17...11
John FURLONG		100		17...10.....0	0.....5.....2
John FARISH		100	6/1	30.....8.....4	0.....9.....2
John Tayloe GRIFFIN, Esqr.		3061	21/5	3277...16.....5	49.....3.....5
do. for Mr. LEWIS's Tenement		640		992.....0.....0	14...17.....8
John GORDEN		133	7/5	47...13.....2	0...14.....4
Henry GRAY		100	8/1	40.....8.....4	0...12.....2
John GUERRANT, Gent.		450	9/11	223.....2.....6	3.....7.....0
John GILLAM	(Pr. Geo.)	500	9/9	243...15.....0	3...13.....2
Capt. William GEORGE		75	8/1	30.....6.....3	0.....9.....1
do. Court House		100	12/1	60.....8.....4	0...18.....2
Major John GUERRANT		200	8/1	80...16.....8	1.....4.....3
James GEORGE		100	do.	40.....8.....4	0...12.....2
John GILLAM		546	7/9	211...11.....6	3.....3.....6
David GRANTHAM		35	7/6	13.....2.....6	0.....4.....0
William GROOM		100	3/3	16.....5.....0	0.....4...11
Robert GILLAM	(Pr. Geo.)	691 3/4		1827.....7.....6	27.....8...3]
do. for Mrs. JEFFERSON's Dower		330		871...15.....0	13.....1...6]
Stephen GRANGE		80	7/2	28...13.....4	0.....8.....8
Estate James GEORGE, deced.		150	6/	45.....0.....0	0...13.....6
Anselm GEORGE		175	4/	35.....0.....0	0...10.....6
John GILBERT		150	3/6	26.....5.....0	0.....7...11
Daniel GRUBBS		250	do.	43...15.....0	0...13.....2
Colo. Thomas HARRIS	(P.tan)	330	21/	346...10.....0	5.....4.....0
John HINES		330	9/4	154.....0.....0	2.....6.....3
John HUTCHINS		256 1/2	8/1	130...13.....5	1...11.....2
Strangeman HUTCHINS		370	9/2	171.....2.....6	2...11.....5
Revd. Francis HILL		262	6/1	73...13...10	1.....3...11

(page 12 contd. Goochland County Land Tax Return for 1783)

Proprietors Names		Quantity of Land	Price	Amt. of Land	Tax
Thomas HARDING		228	8/1	92.....3.....0	1.....7.....8
Capt. THOMAS HATCHER		510	9/9	248...12.....6	3...14.....8

(page 13. Goochland County Land Tax Return for 1783)

Proprietors Names		Quantity of Land	Price	Amt. of Land	Tax
James HUNNICUTT		287	8/1	115...19...11	1...14...10
Benjamin HUGHES		627	do.	253.....8.....3	3...16.....1
Capt. Gideon HATCHER		360	9/7	172...10.....0	2...11.....9
William HUGHES	(Hanover)	115	9/2	52...14.....2	0...15...10
Giles HARDING		316	8/	134.....6.....0	2.....0.....4
William HAY, Esqr.		600	12/1	362...10.....0	5.....8.....1
John HENDERSON		200	4/1	40...16.....8	0...12.....3
John HUMBER		561	8/1	226...14.....9	3.....8.....1
Zachariah HADEN		660	5/1	167...15.....0	2...10.....4
Drury HATCHER		5 1/2	4/5	1.....4.....9	0.....0.....5
Jesse HODGES		160	5/7	44...13.....4	0...13.....5
John HILL	(Amherst)	150	6/1	46...12.....6	0...13.....9
Harrison HARRIS		530	7/4	194.....6.....8	2...18.....4
Mary HICKS		300	6/1	91.....5.....0	1.....7.....5
Mesheck HICKS		450	6/4	142...10.....0	2.....2.....9
Francis HOUCHINS		117	5/10	34.....2.....6	0...10.....3
Charles HOUCHINS		117	do.	34.....2.....6	0...10.....3
James HOLEMAN		275	5/11	81.....7.....1	1.....4.....5
William HODGES		100	4/10	24.....3.....4	0.....7.....3
Capt. William HOLEMAN		990	4/1	202.....2.....6	3.....0.....8
Colo. John HOPKINS		1650	6/7	543.....2.....6	8.....3.....0
Lewis HERNDON		300	6/9	101.....5.....0	1...10.....5
John HOPPER		210	7/2	75.....5.....0	1.....2.....7
Lucy HODGES		50	4/10	12.....1.....8	0.....3.....8
Major HANCOCKE		80	6/7	26.....6.....8	0.....7...11
George HANCOCKE		97 1/2	6/2	30.....1.....3	0.....9.....1
Thomas HODGES		50	5/1	12...14.....2	0.....3.....9
John HOLLAND		272 1/2	7/3	98...13...10	1.....9.....8
William HICKS		125	do.	45.....6.....3	0...13.....9
James HOWARD		136	do.	54.....6.....0	0...16.....4
John HOWARD		166	6/	49...10.....0	0...14...11
Anthony HADEN	(Fluvana)	400	4/	80.....0.....0	1.....4.....0
Nathaniel HOLLAND		200	7/3	72...10.....0	1.....1.....9
Mary & Jane JUDE		536	13/6	361...16.....0	5.....8.....7
John JOHNSON	(O.)	471	8/1	190.....7.....3	2...17.....6
Charles JOHNSON, JR.		220	11/5	125...11.....8	1...17.....9
Benjamin JOHNSON	(Geneto)	115	8/1	46.....9.....7	0...14.....0
David JOHNSON	(do.)	115	do.	46.....9.....7	0...14.....0
Isham JOHNSON		115	9/2	62...14.....2	0...15...10
John JOHNSON	(Geneto)	271	9/4	126.....9.....4	1...18.....0
Richard JOHNSON		150	9/2	68...15.....0	1.....0.....8
William ISBELL		792	5/7	221.....2.....0	3.....6.....4
Estate Joseph JOHNSON for Mr. DOUGLASS		500	4/1	102.....1.....8	1...10.....8
Benjamin JOHNSON	(Byrd)	140	7/	49.....0.....0	0...14.....9

(page 14. Goochland County Land Tax Return for 1783)

Proprietors Names	Quantity of Land	Price	Amt. of Land	Tax
Honble. Thomas JEFFESON, Esqr.	612	8/1	247.....7.....0	3...13.....1
William JOHNSON	250	6/1	76.....0...10	1.....2...10
Archibald JARRETT	353	4/9	83...16.....9	1.....5.....2
do. for JENNINGS	201	4/1	41.....0.....9	0...12.....4
Devereux JARRETT	290	do.	59.....4.....9	0...17...10
David JARRETT	250	do.	51.....0...10	0...15.....4
Charles JOHNSON	200	7/2	71...13.....4	1.....1.....6
Sarah JORDAN	75	16/2	60...12.....6	0...18.....3
John JOHNSON (of Joseph)	100	4/	20.....0.....0	0.....6.....0
John JONES	100	do.	20.....0.....0	0.....6.....0
Daniel JOHNSON (of Charles)	150	do.	30.....0.....0	0.....9.....0
John LAPRADE	788	10/3	420.....5.....4	6.....6.....1
Capt. Elisha LEAKE	818	9/7	301...19.....2	5...17.....8
John LAYNE	50	4/1	10.....4.....2	0.....3.....1
John LEWIS (Cardmaker)	200	8/1	80...16.....8	1.....4.....3
Ayres LAYNE	155	6/8	51...13.....4	0...15.....6
Henry LAYNE	100	4/1	20.....8.....4	0.....6.....2
Mary LAYNE	50	do.	10.....4.....2	0.....3.....1
Matthew LACY	97	4/10	23.....8...10	0.....7.....1
Jesse LACY	88	4/11	21...12.....8	0.....6.....6
Benjamin LACY	88	do.	21...12.....8	0.....6.....6
Sarah LACY	181	5/	45.....5.....0	0...13.....7
Samuel LAMAY	106	4/1	21...12...10	0.....6.....6
Stephen G. LETCHER	516	8/1	208...11.....0	3.....2.....6
John LOVELL	343	8/1	138...12.....7	2.....1.....8
Armiger LILLY (Fluvanna)	400	4/1	81...13.....4	1.....4.....6

(notation between John Lovell and Armiger Lilly, "too high.")

Proprietors Names	Quantity of Land	Price	Amt. of Land	Tax
Colo. ROBERT LEWIS	565	7/	197...15.....0	2...19.....6
Mary LEWIS (deced)	1030	13/6	695.....5.....0	10.....8.....7
Estate of John LEE, deced.	350	4/8	81...13.....4	1.....4.....4
William LEWIS (R.C.)	100	4/1	20.....8.....4	0.....6.....2
Capt. Josiah LEAK	800	8/1	323.....6.....8	4...17.....0
Joseph LEWIS, JR.	407	7/3	147...10.....9	2.....4.....4
Joseph LEWIS, SENR., deced.	281	8/1	113...11.....5	1...14.....1
Joseph LOWRY	200		35.....0.....0	0...10.....6
Matthew LOWRY	400	4/	80.....0.....0	1.....4.....0
Colo. Nathaniel G. MORRIS	400	9/1	181...13.....4	2...14.....6
John MADDOX	150	6/9	50...12.....6	0...15.....3
William McCAUL	81	14/1	57.....0.....7	0...17.....2
Amos L. MOORE	260	10/	130.....0.....0	1...19.....0
Stokes McCAUL	295	8/1	119.....4.....7	1...15...10
Mary MILLER	426	8/10	188.....3.....0	2...16.....6
Edward McBRIDE	200	6/1	60...16.....8	0...18.....3
James MADDOX	600	7/5	222...10.....0	3.....6.....9
Elizabeth MEANLY	130	11/9	76.....7.....6	1.....2...11
Drury MURRELL	200	6/1	60...16.....8	0...18.....3
Charles MASSIE	300	8/1	121.....5.....0	1...16.....5

(page 15. Goochland County Land Tax Return for 1783)

Proprietors Names	Quantity of Land	Price	Amt. of Land	Tax
Ann MITCHELL	291	6/5	93.....7.....3	1.....8.....5
David MARTIN	235	do.	75.....7...11	1.....2.....8
Paul MEACHUM	295	5/6	81.....2.....6	1.....4.....5
Martin MIMS	50	5/8	14.....3.....4	0.....4.....3
Benjamin MOSBY	200	5/1	50...16.....8	0...15.....3
William MITCHELL, Gent.	865 1/2	8/1	349...12.....1	5.....4...11
Capt. William MILLER	300	7/5	111.....5.....0	1...13.....4
Thomas MILLER	296	6/10	101.....2.....8	1...10.....5
Gideon MIMS	360	7/5	133...10.....0	2.....0...10
David MIMS	315	do.	116...16.....3	1...15.....1
Elizabeth MIMS	250	7/3	90...12.....6	1.....7.....3
Sarah MIMS	50	6/1	15.....4.....2	0.....4.....7
John MARTIN	700	6/2	215...16.....8	3.....4.....9
Edward MATTHEWS	873	7/5	322...12.....6	4...16...10
Ann MERRIAN	400	4/1	81...13.....4	1.....4.....6
Wright MOURLAND	100	6/11	34...11.....8	0...10.....5
Capt. David MULLINS	197	8/1	79...12.....5	1.....3...11
Capt. Henry MULLINS	400	7/2	143.....6.....8	2.....3.....0
John MULLINS, deced.	350	6/5	112.....5...10	1...13.....4
Thomas MASSIE (Overseer)	289	7/	101.....3.....0	1...10.....3
Samuel MOSS	200	4/	40.....0.....0	0...12.....0
William MARTIN	400	6/	120.....0.....0	1...16.....0
Majr. Thomas MASSIE, (Frederick)	2285	do.	685...10.....0	10.....5.....9
John MOSS	75	8/	30.....0.....0	0.....9.....0
John MOSS, JR.	200	8/1	80...16.....8	1.....4.....3
William MASSIE	223	7/3	80...16.....9	1.....4.....3
Capt. Nathaniel MASSIE	/485 3/4	8/	474.....6.....0	7.....2.....3
James NOWELL	400	6/	120.....0.....0	1...16.....0
Samuel NUCKOLS	115	7/2	41.....4.....2	0...12.....5
John NEAVES	290	7/5	107...10...10	1...12.....4
Stephen NOWLAND	150	6/9	50...12.....6	0...15.....3
Rene NAPIER	49	8/1	19...16.....1	0.....6.....0
Henry NASH (Fluvanna)	100	6/6	32...10.....0	0.....9.....9
William NUCKOLS, JR.	121	8/4	48...18.....1	0...14.....9
Pouncy NUCKOLS	110	do.	44.....9.....2	0...13.....5
Charles NUCKOLS	104	7/2	37.....5.....4	0...11.....3
Thomas NUCKOLS	115	do.	41.....4.....2	0...12.....5
Thomas OLIVER	273	8/1	110.....6...10	1...13.....2
Estate Barnett OWEN, deced.	100	3/3	16.....5.....0	0.....4...11
William POWELL	266	7/2	95.....6.....4	1.....8.....8
Major POWERS	180	8/1	72...15.....0	1.....2...10
Anderson PEERS	697 1/2	do.`	281...18.....2	4.....4.....7
Hezekiah PURYEAR	397 1/2	do.	160...13.....2	2.....8.....3
Matthew PLEASANTS	425	15/8	332...18.....4	4...19...11
James PLEASANTS	500	16/7	414...11.....8	6.....4.....5
Isaac PLEASANTS	676	21/6	726...14.....0	10...18.....1
Joseph PLEASANTS	200	8/1	80...16.....8	1.....4.....3
Robert PLEASANTS (Buff.)	140	7/	49.....0.....0	0...14.....9

(page 16. Goochland County Land Tax Return for 1783)

Proprietors Names	Quantity of Land	Price	Amt. of Land	Tax
Richard PLEASANTS	368	8/11	164.....1.....4	2.....9.....3
Philip PLEASANTS	121	8/1	48...18.....0	0...14.....9
William POWERS	368	do.	148...14.....8	2.....4.....8
Thomas PLEASANTS (Mercht.)	1578	16/9	1321...11.....6	19...16.....6
Doctor William PASTEUR (York)	700	13/4	466...13.....4	7.....0.....0
Francis PLEDGE	50	8/1	20.....4.....2	0.....6.....1
Estate of William PLEDGE, deced.	50	9/9	24.....7.....6	0.....7.....4
Archer PLEDGE	50	11/5	28...10...10	0.....8.....7
John PAYNE, JR.	439	14/5	316.....8...11	4...15.....0
Robert POOR	350	10/5	182.....5...10	2...14.....9
Joseph POLLARD, Gent.	447	9/11	221...12.....9	3.....6.....6
Mary PERKINS	161 1/2	8/1	65.....5.....6	0...19.....7
Molly PERKINS	250	do.	101.....0...10	1...10.....4
Estate of Walker PERKINS	171 1/2	9/10	84.....6.....5	1.....5.....4
Benjamin PERKINS	250	3/3	40...12.....6	0...12.....3
William PERKINS	200	6/1	60...16.....8	0...18.....3
Archer PAYNE, Gent.	850	8/7	364...15...10	5.....9.....6
Josias PAYNE, JR.	612	10/9	328...19.....0	4...18.....9
Colo. George PAYNE (Glebe)	200	8/1	80...16.....8	1.....4.....3
Robert PLEASANTS, JR. (Henrico)	1300	10/7	687...18.....4	10.....6.....5
Colo. Jolly PARISH, deced.	735	4/6	165.....7.....6	2.....9.....8
Sherwood PARISH	162	4/4	33.....1.....6	0...10.....0
Joel PARISH	121	4/10	29.....4...10	0.....8...10
Aaron PARISH	121 1/4	4/1	24...15.....2	0.....7.....6
Mary PARISH	121 1/4	do.	24...15.....2	0.....7.....6
Booker PARISH	180 1/4	do.	36.....6.....1	0...11.....1
Samuel PRYOR	400	8/3	165.....0.....0	2...19.....6]
do.	75	5/11	22.....3.....9	0.....6.....8]
William PRYOR	200	12/1	120...16.....8	1...16.....3
Moses PARISH	168	4/1	34.....6.....0	0...10.....4
Daniel POWERS	33 1/2	5/11	9...18.....3	0.....3.....0
Samuel POWELL	350	4/1	71.....9.....2	1.....1.....6
Thomas POLLOCK	1092 3/4	7/3	397.....2.....6	5...18...11
George PAYNE, JR. (O.K.)	200	5/7	55...16.....8	0...16.....9
John PARISH	564	5/3	148.....1.....0	2.....4.....5
Majr. Josias PAYNE	800	8/1	323.....6.....8	4...17.....0
Jennings PULLAM	47	5/	11...15.....0	0.....3.....7
Robert PAGE	133	7/2	47...13.....2	0...14.....4
William PAGE	133	8/1	53...15.....1	0...16.....2
John PERKINS	477	12/5	296.....2.....9	4...18...11
Estate of Jesse PAYNE, deced.	597 1/2	8/5	251.....9.....0	3...15.....6
George PAYNE, SENR.	977	8/1	394...17.....5	5...18.....6
Colo. John PAYNE	2053	8/	821.....4.....0	12.....6.....5
Thomas POOR	525	5/1	133.....8.....9	2.....0.....1
Abraham POOR	200	6/1	60...16.....8	0...18.....3
William PROPHET	30	6/9	10.....2.....6	0.....3.....1
Joseph PACE	150	6/3	46...17.....6	0...14.....1

(page 17. Goochland County Land Tax Return for 1783)

John PACE	130	5/	32...10.....0	0.....9.....9
William PACE	200	6/1	60...16.....8	0...18.....3

(page 17 contd. Goochland County Land Tax Return for 1783)

Proprietors Names		Quantity of Land	Price	Amt. of Land	Tax
John PHILPOTT		100	4/1	20.....8.....4	0.....6.....2
Benjamin PAGE		100	6/1	30.....8.....4	0.....9.....2
John PREWIT		240	7/2	86.....0.....0	1.....5...10
Archibald PLEASANTS		299	13/6	201...16.....6	3.....0.....7
Capt. Humphrey PARISH		497	5/10	144...19.....2	2.....3.....6
George PRIDDY		250	6/	75.....0.....0	1.....2.....6
Anderson PARISH		170	3/3	27...12.....6	0.....8.....3
William PARISH		250	7/	87...10.....0	1.....6.....3
Samuel ROUNTREE		350	10/5	182.....5...10	2...14.....9
Randolph ROUNTREE		300	11/4	171.....5.....0	2...11.....5
John REDD		247	6/6	80.....5.....6	1.....4.....1
Matthew RIDDLE		70	7/	24...10.....0	0.....7.....5
Isaac RAGLAND		150	6/9	50...12.....6	0...15.....3
William ROYSTER, Gent.		543	11/1	300...18.....3	4...10.....4
Thomas ROYSTER		200	10/1	100...16.....8	1...10.....3
Edward REDFORD		208	12/4	128.....5.....4	1...18.....6
Milner REDFORD		539	9/8	260...10.....4	3...18.....2
Colo. Thomas M. RANDOLPH		1100	24/1	1324...11.....8	19...17.....5]
do.	(Tuckahoe)	1952	14/9	1439...12.....0	21...11...11]
Mary ROGERS		17	8/1	6...17.....5	0.....1.....1
David ROSS, Esqr.		9450	8/10	4173...15.....0	62.....2.....2
William RONALD, Esqr.		1170	11/7	677...12.....6	10.....3.....4
Nathaniel RAINE		244	7/5	90.....9.....8	1.....7.....2
Isham RICHARDSON		181	12/6	113.....2.....6	1...14.....0
William RUTHERFORD		433	5/4	115.....9.....4	1...14.....8
William ROBARDS		536	6/7	176.....8.....8	2...13.....0
William RIGSBY		50	3/3	8.....2.....6	0.....2.....6
Thomas RIDDLE		485	5/11	128...13.....9	1...18.....8
Doctor John K. READ		408	8/1	164...18.....0	2.....9.....6
Charles RICE		175	5/10	51.....0...10	0...15.....4
Capt. Samuel RICHARDSON		536	7/2	192.....1.....4	2...17.....8
Thomas RANDOLPH, Esqr.		3000	9/9	1462...10.....0	21...18.....9
George RICHARDSON		1612	6/10	550...15.....4	8.....5.....3
William ROBARDS, JR.		265	6/	79...10.....0	1.....3...11
Elizabeth STODGHILL		28	12/1	16...18.....4	0.....5.....1
Thomas SHOEMAKER		200	10/1	100...16.....8	1...10.....3
Colo. John SYME	(Hanover)	318	8/1	128...10.....6	1...18.....7
Josiah SEAY		85	6/3	29...13.....9	0.....8...11
John SAUNDERS		30	8/1	10.....2.....1	0.....3.....8
Capt. Stephen SAUNDERS		752	8/2	307.....1.....4	4...12.....1
William SAUNDERS		25	8/1	10.....2.....1	0.....3.....1
Estate of Charles SAMPSON		234	do.	94...11.....6	1.....8.....5
John SHELTON, Gent.		412	do.	166...10.....4	2...10.....0
Capt. Joseph SHELTON		1369	9/	616.....1.....0	9.....4...10
John SHELTON	(Hanover)	400	8/1	161...13.....4	2.....8.....6
Benjamin SADLER		100	4/1	20.....8.....4	0.....6.....2
Arthur SLAYDEN		182	do.	37.....3.....2	0...11.....2

(page 18. Goochland County Land Tax Return for 1783)

Proprietors Names		Quantity of Land	Price	Amt. of Land	Tax
John SLAYDEN		100	4/1	20.....8.....4	0.....6.....2
William L. SMITH		211	7/2	75...12.....2	1.....5.....9
Benjamin SALMONDS		250	4/10	60.....8.....4	0...18.....2
John SALMONDS		150	5/5	40...12.....6	0...12.....3
John STRONG		137 1/2	8/1	55...11.....6	0...16.....9
Edward SCRUGGS		100	6/1	30.....8.....4	0.....9.....2
Capt. Robert SMITH	(P.tan)	40	8/1	16.....3.....4	0.....4...11
Richard SAMPSON		250	7/3	90...12.....6	1.....7.....3
Philip TINSLEY		50	12/1	30.....4.....2	0.....9.....1
Capt. Stockley TOWLES		348 1/2	8/6	148.....2.....3	2.....4.....6
Thomas TOWLES, Esqr.		348 1/2	9/4	162...12.....8	2.....8...10
Bartholomew TURNER		200	8/1	80...16.....8	0...18.....3
Sarah THOMAS		100	4/1	32...13.....4	0.....9...10
Mary TOWLER		200	do.	40...16.....8	0...12.....3
Cornelius TOWLER		190	do.	38...15...10	0...11.....8
William THURSTON		122	7/5	45.....4...10	0...13.....7
John THURSTON		110	7/1	38...19.....2	0...11.....9
Esther THURSTON		53	4/5	11...14.....1	0.....3.....7
Henry TUGGLE		100	5/1	25.....8.....4	0.....7.....8
Horatio TURPIN		1200	5/9	345.....0.....0	5.....3.....6
Japheth TOWLER		275	5/2	71.....0...10	1.....1.....4
James THOMAS		110	4/1	24...10.....0	0.....7.....5
John TOWLER		62 1/2	do.	12...15.....3	0.....3...10
Reuben THURSTON		53	5/	13.....5.....0	0.....4.....1
Benjamin THACKER		100	3/3	16.....5.....0	0.....5.....0
Obadiah UTLEY		8	8/1	3.....4.....8	0.....1.....0
Ann UTLEY		116	6/4	36...14.....8	0...11.....1
John UTLEY		125	8/1	50...10.....5	0...15.....2
Hezekiah UTLEY		58	6/1	17...12...10	0.....5.....4
Elizabeth UNDERWOOD		100	11/5	57.....1.....8	0...17.....2
George UNDERWOOD		526	7/4	192...17.....4	2...17...11
Thomas UNDERWOOD, Gent.		600	8/9	262...10.....0	3...18.....9
William UTLEY		125	8/1	50...10.....5	0...15.....3
Jane VAIDEN		400	12/1	241...13.....4	3...12.....6
Matthew VAUGHAN, Gent.		800	9/1	363.....6.....8	5.....9.....0
James VAUGHAN		362	7/7	137.....5.....2	2.....1.....3
Shadrach VAUGHAN		913	8/1	369.....0.....1	5...10.....9
Estate of JOHN WOODSON		844	25/10	1090.....3.....4	16.....7.....1
Matthew WOODSON		1883	12/11	1216.....2.....1	18.....4...10
Majr. Joseph WOODSON		535	8/1	216.....4.....7	3.....4...11
Susanna WOODWARD		500	12/1	302.....1.....8	4...10.....8
William WOODWARD		150	9/5	70...12.....6	1.....1.....3
Robert WADE		97	8/1	39.....4.....1	0...11...10

(page 19. Goochland County Land Tax Return for 1783)

| Richard WADE | | 297 | 9/7 | 142.....6.....2 | 2.....2.....9 |
| John WADE | | 73 | 8/1 | 29...10.....1 | 0.....8...11 |

(page 19 contd. Goochland County Land Tax Return for 1783)

Proprietors Names		Quantity of Land	Price	Amt. of Land	Tax
Pleasant WILLIS		278	8/1	112.....7.....2	1...13.....9
Daniel WADE		200	do.	80...16.....8	1.....4.....3
Eleonar WILLIS		100	6/1	30.....8.....4	0.....9.....2
William WOODALL		63	6/6	20.....9.....6	0.....6.....2
William WEBBER	(Preacher)	177	6/4	56.....1.....0	0...16...10
Edward WILLIS		160	8/1	64...13.....4	0...19.....5
Thomas WOODSON		200	12/1	120...16.....8	1...16.....3
Nathaniel WEBSTER		170	6/6	55.....5.....0	0...16.....7
David WEBSTER		75	10/6	39...17.....6	0...12.....0
Robert WINGFIELD		90	8/1	36.....7.....6	0...10...11
Joseph WOODSON, JR.	(Geneto)	225	9/	101.....5.....0	1...10.....5
Joseph WOODSON, SR., deced (do.)		222	10/	111.....0.....0	1...13.....4
Dorothy WATKINS		170	8/1	68...14.....2	1.....0.....8
Joseph WATKINS		429	10/	214...10.....0	3.....4.....5]
do	(Little Creek)	270	10/3	138.....7.....6	2.....1...7]
Thomas WATKINS		453	8/1	183.....1.....9	2...15.....0
Peter WALKER	(Geneto)	230	do.	92...19.....2	1.....7...11
Benjamin WATKINS		238	9/5	112.....1.....2	1...13.....8
John WATKINS		519	8/11	231.....7.....9	3.....9.....6
William WEBBER		340	10/6	178...10.....0	2...13.....7
Benjamin WOODSON	(Fluvanna)	205	9/1	93.....2.....1	1.....8.....0
Benjamin WATKINS, JR.		156	9/5	73.....9.....0	1.....2.....1
Henry WHITLOW, JR.		50	8/1	20.....4.....2	0.....6.....1
Henry WHITLOW, SENR.		99	do.	40.....0.....3	0...12.....1
William WILLIS	(of D.)	63 1/2	7/3	23.....0.....5	0.....6...11
John WITT		17	8/1	6...17.....5	0.....5.....1
Tucker WOODSON		600	17/8	530.....0.....0	7...19.....0
John WOODSON	(C. Ferry)	600	10/5	312...10.....0	4...13.....9]
do.	(Beaverdam)	665	10/1	335.....5.....5	5.....0...7]
Henry WALMACK		100	8/1	40.....8.....4	0...12.....2
Peter WALKER	(Constable)	116	4/1	23...13.....8	0.....7.....2
Isaac WINSTON	(Hanover)	735	8/1	297.....1.....3	4.....9.....2
William WHITLOCK		100	6/1	30.....8.....4	0.....9.....2
William WILLIAMS, deced.		500	8/1	202.....1.....8	3.....0.....8
John WALKER		100	3/3	16.....5.....0	0.....4...11
William WALKER		94	4/2	19...11.....8	0.....5...11
Thomas WAFFORD		540	4/6	121...10.....0	1...16.....6
Estate Colo. Valentine WOOD, deced.		2226	8/1	899...13.....6	13.....9...11
John WILLIAMS	(D. C.)	400	5/1	101...13.....4	1...10.....6
John WILLIAMSON		200	4/1	40...16.....8	0...12.....3
Lewis WILBOURNE		100	do.	20.....8.....4	0.....6.....2
Dabney WADE		300	6/3	93...15.....0	1.....8.....2
Estate of William WADE		215	7/3	77...18.....9	1.....3.....5
John WOODSON	(Meadow)	300	8/1	121.....5.....0	1...16.....5

(page 20. Goochland County Land Tax Return for 1783)

Proprietors Names	Quantity of Land	Price	Amt. of Land	Tax
William WILBOURNE	200	3/3	32...10.....0	0.....9.....9
John WILLIAMS, JR.	250	6/6	81.....5.....0	1.....4.....5
William WHITFIELD	105	4/1	21.....8.....9	0.....6.....6
James WILLIAMS	10	7/	3...10.....0	0.....0...11
Solomon WILLIAMS	103	do.	36.....1.....0	0...10...10

(page 20 contd. Goochland County Land Tax Return for 1783)

Proprietors Names	Quantity of Land	Price	Amt. of Land	Tax
Philip WILLIAMS	200	6/	60.....0.....0	0...18.....0
Capt. Samuel WOODSON	368	8/1	148...14.....8	2.....4.....9
Capt. John WARE	925	6/6	300...12.....6	4...10.....2
Ann YOUNGER	100	3/3	16.....5.....0	0.....4...11

October 30th 1783.

ARCHD. PLEASANTS   ]
THOS: F. BATES   ]   Commrs.

Novr. 12th 1783. Rec'd of the Commrs. of the Land Tax the Sheriff's Collecting List, being a duplicate of this, amounting to the above sum of twelve hundred sixty one pounds and eight pence.
L. 1261.....0.....9

MATTHEW VAUGHAN Dep. Sheriff
for JOHN HOPKINS, Sheriff

(page 21)
Sundry Tracts of Land & Taxes omitted in the List sent up.

	Acres Land	Tax
William ANDERSON	1500	9.....0.....0
Gideon BOWLES	350	1...13.....9
Turner CHRISTIAN	235	1.....1.....8
George CROWDAS	100	0...10.....6
David DAVIS	100	0...10.....6
Noton DICKERSON	400	1.....1.....0
Susanna DAVIS	200	0...10.....6
Thomas EMMERSON	100	0.....5.....3
Henry EMMERSON	240	0...13.....6
Thomas EMMERSON, JR.	100	0.....5.....3
John FURLONG	100	0.....5.....3
Estate of James GEORGE, deced.	150	0...13.....6
Andrew GEORGE	175	0...10.....6
John GILBERT	150	0.....7...11
Daniel GRUBBS	250	0...13.....2
John HOLLAND	272 1/4	1.....9.....8
William HICKS	125	0...13.....9
James HOWARD	136	0...16.....4
John HOWARD	166	0...14...11
Anthony HADEN	400	1.....4.....0
Nathaniel HOLLAND	200	1.....1.....9
John JOHNSON	100	0.....6.....0
John JONES	100	0.....6.....0
Daniel JOHNSON	150	0.....9.....0
Joseph LOWRY	200	0...10.....6
Matthew LOWRY	400	1.....4.....0
Thomas MASSIE (Overseer)	289	1...10.....3
Samuel MOSS	200	0...12.....0
William MARTIN	400	1...16.....0
Majr. Thomas MASSIE	2285	10.....5.....9
John MOSS	75	0.....9.....0

(page 21 contd. Sundry Tracts of Land & Taxes omitted in the List sent up for 1783)

		Acres of Land	Tax
John MOSS, JR.		200	1.....4.....3
William MASSIE		223	1.....4.....3
Capt. Nathaniel MASSIE		1185 3/4	7.....2.....3
George PRIDDY		250	1.....2.....6
Anderson PARISH		170	0.....8.....3
William PARISH		250	1.....6.....3
William ROBARDS, JR.		265	1...3...11
Reubin THURSTON		53	0.....4.....1
Benjamin THACKER		100	0.....5.....0
William UTLEY		125	0...15.....3
James WILLIAMS		10	0.....0...11
Solomon WILLIAMS		103	0...10...10
Philip WILLIAMS		200	0...18.....0
Capt. Samuel WOODSON		368	2.....4.....9
Capt. John WARE		925	4...10.....2
Ann YOUNGER		100	0.....4...11
John PERKINS	(Short Qty.)	200	2.....7.....3
James NOWELL	(do.)	300	1.....7.....0

14576 acres Land & Tas L. 68...11.....0

Besides the above ommissions which are inserted in this List, there are many errors in the valuation, which the Commissoners are not allowed to rectify.

T. F. BATES

(page 22.)

A State of the Land Tax in Goochland County for the Sheriff's Collection
May 1, 1784.

Proprietors		Quantity of Land	Price	Amt. of Land	Tax
Colo. Richard ADAMS	(Henrico)	1982	8/9	867.....2.....6	13.....0.....2
Mary ADKINSON		310	8/1	125.....5...10	1...17.....8
James ALLEN		175	4/7	34...16.....3	0.....7.....6
David ALVIS		50	4/1	10.....4.....2	0.....3.....1
Pleasant ADKINS		65	6/7	21.....7...11	0.....6.....6
William ANDERSON, Esqr.	(Hanover)	1500	8/	600.....0.....0	9.....0.....0
Charles BATES		350	12/1	211...9.....2	3...3...6
William BARNETT		200	7/6	72...10.....0	1.....1.....9
Susanna BIBB		248	8/1	100.....4.....8	1...10.....2
John BLACKWELL		98 1/2	do.	39...16.....3	0...12.....0
Elijah BRUMFIELD	(of WATKINS)	200	10/3	102...10.....0	1...10.....9
John BRUMFIELD		125	8/1	50...10.....5	0...15.....2
John BRADSHAW		450	6/9	151...17.....6	2.....5.....7
Callam BAILEY		150	4/1	30...12.....6	0.....9.....3
John BOWDRY		10		2.....0...10	0.....0.....8

(page 22 contd. Goochland County Land Tax Return for 1784)

Proprietors		Quantity of Land	Price	Amt. of Land	Tax
William BURGESS		100	4/1	20.....8.....4	0.....6.....2
John BOLLING, Esqr.		1891	9/8]		
PREWIT's Tenement		149	7/2]	1967.....7.....6	14...10.....3
Thomas BOLLING, Esqr.		4000		1906.....5.....0	73...11...11
Clairbourne BRADSHAW		138	8/1	55...15.....6	0...16.....9
Sarah BRADSHAW		69	7/2	24...14.....6	0.....7.....5
Thomas F. BATES		500	13/10	345...16.....8	5.....3.....9
William BLUNKALL		3 1/2	16/2	2...16.....7	0.....0...11
James BENNETT	(Henrico)	200	6/1	60.....0.....0	0...18.....0
William BRITT		850	4/9	201...17.....0	3.....0.....7
Capt. John BRITT		245	7/4	89...16.....8	1.....7.....0
William BOWMAN		100	4/1	20.....8.....4	0.....6.....2
Gideon BOWLES		350	6/8	116...13.....4	1...13.....9
William BUSBY	(of A. Parish)	50	4/1	10.....4.....2	0.....3.....1
James CURD		440	8/1	177...16.....8	2...13.....5
Richard CROUCH	(Henrico)	200	do.	80...16.....8	1.....4.....3
Philemon CHILDERS		276	4/1	56.....7.....0	0...16...11
Thomas CHANCELLOR		125	6/6	40...12.....6	0...12.....3
Judith CHEADLE	(Caroline)	299	13/6	201...16.....6	3.....0.....7
Daniel CLARKE		100	6/1	30.....8.....4	0.....9.....2
Ann COCKE	(Surry)	1567	14/10	1162.....3...10	17.....8.....8
Allen COCKE, deced)	(do.)	1195	14/11	891.....5.....5	13.....7.....5
John CLARKE		62	6/2	19.....2.....4	0.....5.....9
Turner CLARKE		90	6/1	27.....7.....6	0.....8.....3
Jeffry CLARKE		98	6/7	32.....5.....2	0.....9.....9
Joseph CLARKE		115	6/3	30...18.....9	0.....9.....4
Susanna CROUCH		100	8/1	40.....8.....4	0...12.....2
James COCKE		300	do.	121.....5.....0	1...16.....5
Edward CARTER		34	do.	13...10.....4	0.....4.....2
William CLARKSON		50	9/9	24.....7.....6	0.....7.....4
Colo. John CURD		609	10/9	327.....6.....9	4...18.....3
Capt. Edmund CURD		225	9/11	111...11.....3	1...13.....6
Sarah CURD		211	8/1	56...11.....8	1.....5.....8
Benjamin COCKE		122	do.	49.....6.....2	0...14...10
James COCKE	(P.tan)	64	do.	21...16.....6	0.....6.....7

(page 23. Goochland County Land Tax Return for 1784)

Thomas COCKE		140	8/1	56...11.....8	0...17.....0
Martha CARR		499	do.	201...13.....7	3.....0.....7
George CHRISTIAN		217	10/	108...10.....0	1...12.....7
Benjamin CRENSHAW		440	5/11	130.....3.....4	1...19.....1
Armsby CREW		100	4/10	24.....3.....4	0.....7.....3
Nathaniel CAWLEY		60	8/1	24.....5.....0	0.....7.....4
Mary COLEY		100	do.	40.....8.....4	0...12.....2
Susanna COLEY		100	4/1	20.....8.....4	0.....6.....2
Ann COLEY		100	8/1	40.....8.....4	0...12.....2
Sally COLEY		100	6/1	30.....8.....4	0.....9.....2
Francis COLLEY		106 1/2	6/3	33.....2.....6	0...10.....0
Francis CLARKE	for Mr. DOUGLAS	150	4/1	30...12.....6	0.....9.....3
William CHEEK	(Henrico)	232	5/10	67...13.....4	1.....0.....4

(page 23 contd. Goochland County Land Tax Return for 1784)

Proprietors		Quantity of Land	Price	Amt. of Land	Tax
John CLEMENTS		116	5/10	33...16.....8	0...10.....2
Stephen CROUCH		200	5/1	50...16.....8	0...15.....3
Bryant CONLEY		150	5/5	40...12.....6	0...12.....3
Bowler COCKE, Esqr.	(Henrico)	1434	15/11	1141.....4.....6	17...2.....5
Samuel COSBY		225	4/5	50...12.....6	0...15.....3
Walter CLOPTON		220	8/1	88...18.....4	1.....6.....9
James CLEMENTS		179	6/4	56...13.....8	0...17.....1
Roger CARRELL		83	4/1	16...18...11	0.....5.....2
Gideon CAWTHON		220	6/8	73.....6.....8	1.....2...11
John COX		100	6/1	30.....8.....4	0.....9.....2
Edward COX		100	7/3	36.....5.....0	0...10...11
Judith CARTER		100	4/10	24.....3.....4	0.....7.....3
David CRENSHAW		238	6/2	73.....7.....8	1.....2.....1
Benjamin CLOPTON		200	8/1	80...16.....8	1.....4.....3
Turner CHRISTIAN		235	6/2	72.....7.....0	1.....1.....8
George CROWDAS		100	7/	35.....0.....0	0...10.....6
Benjamin DARST		100	8/1	40.....8.....4	0...12.....2
John DOWDY		122	7/5	45.....4...10	0...13.....7
Thomas DRUMWRIGHT		1030	6/2	317...11.....8	4...15.....4
Stephen DAVIS		265	7/2	94...19.....2	1.....8.....6
John DAVIS	(Hanover)	100	7/3	36.....5.....0	0...10...11
Ichabod DANIEL		200	5/8	56...13.....4	0...17.....0
Capt. Edmund DUKE	(P.tan)	230	4/7	52...14.....2	0...15...10
Revd. William DOUGLAS		500	6/1	152.....1.....8	2.....5.....8
David DAVIS		100	7/	35.....0.....0	0...10.....6
Noton DICKINSON		400	3/6	70.....0.....0	1.....1.....0
Susanna DAVIS		200	do	35.....0.....0	0...10.....6
John ELLIS	(Henrico)	392	12/1	236...16.....8	3...11.....0
Stephen ELLIS		97	16/2	78.....8.....2	1.....3.....7
Augustin EASTIN		180	8/1	72...15.....0	1.....1...10
David ELLIS		236	do.]		
do A. PEERS's Tenement		138 1/2	do.]	151.....7.....3	2.....5.....6
William EDWARDS		80	4/1	16.....6.....8	0.....4...11
Joseph EVANS		134	6/1	40...15.....2	0...12.....3
Francis EVANS		133 1/2	5/5	36.....3.....2	0...10...11
Thomas ELDRIDGE		303	8/1	122.....9.....3	1...16.....9
David ENGLAND		80	6/1	24.....6.....8	0.....7.....4

(page 24. Goochland County Land Tax Return for 1784)

William A. ENGLAND		139	7/	48...13.....0	0...14.....8
Benjamin EAST		121 1/2	8/1	49.....2.....2	0...14.....9
Thomas EDWARDS		50	6/6	16.....5.....0	0.....4...11
Thomas EMMERSON		100	do.	17...10.....0	0.....5.....3
Henry EMMERSON		240	do.	45.....0.....0	0...13.....6
Thomas EMMERSON, JR.		100	do.	17...10.....0	0.....5.....3
William FARRAR, Gent.		886	10/5	461.....9.....2	6...18.....6
John FARRAR		298	10/9	160.....3.....6	2.....8.....1
William FORD		200	8/1	80...16.....8	1.....4.....3

(page 24 contd. Goochland County Land Tax Return for 1784)

Proprietors		Quantity of Land	Price	Amt. of Land	Tax
Elizabeth FORD		233	8/1	94.....3.....5	1.....8.....4
Joseph FARRAR		100	12/1	60.....8.....4	0...18.....2
Mary FRAYSER		205	8/1	82...17.....1	1.....4...11
Reubin FORD		147		59.....8.....3	0...17...10
John FARISH		100	6/1	30.....8.....4	0.....9.....2
Estate of Colo. Tarlton FLEMING, deced.		1900	20/3	1915...16.....8	28...14.....9
Honble. William FLEMING, Esqr.		390	20/4	396...10.....0	5...19.....0
Colo. Charles FLEMING		390	do.	396...10.....0	5...19.....0
John FURLONG		100	3/6	17...10.....0	0.....5.....3
Joseph R. FARRAR		400	12/1	241...13.....4	3...12.....6
Hugh FRENCH		100	6/11	34...11.....8	0...10.....5
John Tayloe GRIFFIN, Esqr.		3311		3902.....6.....5	48...10...10
John GORDEN		133	7/2	47...13.....2	0...14.....4
Henry GRAY		100	8/1	40.....8.....4	0...12.....2
John GUERRANT, Gent.		450	9/11	223.....2.....6	3.....7.....0
John GILLAM	(Pr. Geo.)	500	9/9	243...15.....0	3...13.....2
Capt. William GEORGE		75	8/1	]	
do for SALMOND's Tenement		250	4/10	] 90...14.....7	1.....7.....3
JOHN GRAY		85	10/3	44.....8.....4	0...13.....6
Majr. John GUERRANT		200	8/1	80...16.....8	1.....4.....3
James GEORGE		100	do.	40.....8.....4	0...12.....2
John GILLAM		546	7/9	211...11.....6	3.....3.....6
David GRANTHAM		35	7/6	13.....2.....6	0.....4.....0
William GROOM		100	3/3	16.....5.....0	0.....4...11
Robert GILLAM, Esqr.	(Pr. Geo.)	1021 3/4		2699.....2.....6	40.....9.....9
Stephen GRANGE		80	7/2	28...13.....4	0.....8.....8
Estate of James GEORGE, deced.		150	6/	45.....0.....0	0...13.....6
Anselm GEORGE		175	4/	35.....0.....0	0...10.....6
John GILBERT		150	3/6	26.....5.....0	0.....7...11
Daniel GRUBBS		250	do.	43...15.....0	0...13.....2
John HYLTON		411	10/9	220...18.....3	3.....6.....3
David HUDSON, WOODSON's land		368	8/1	148...14.....8	2.....4.....9
John HUSON, PULLAM's land		47	5/	11...15.....0	0.....3.....7
Capt. Thomas HATCHER		510	9/9	248...12.....6	3...14.....8
James HUNNICUTT		287	8/1	115...19...11	1...14...10
Benjamin HUGHES		627	do.	253.....8.....3	3...16.....1
Capt. Gideon HATCHER		360	9/7	172...10.....0	2...11.....9

(page 25. Goochland County Land Tax Return for 1784)

Proprietors		Quantity of Land	Price	Amt. of Land	Tax
William HUGHES,	(Hanover)	115	9/2	52...14.....2	0...15...10
Giles HARDING		316	8/6	134.....6.....0	2.....0.....4
William HAY, Esqr.		600	12/1	362...10.....0	5.....8.....1
John HENDERSON		200	4/1	40...16.....8	0...12.....3
John HUMBER		561	8/1	226...14.....9	3.....8.....1
Zachariah HADEN		660	5/1	167...15.....0	2...10.....4
Drury HATCHER		5 1/2	4/6	1.....4.....9	0.....0.....5
John HODGES		160	5/7	44...13.....4	0...13.....5
John HILL	(Amherst)	150	6/1	45...12.....6	0...13.....9
Harrison HARRIS		530	7/4	194.....6.....8	2...18.....4

(page 25 contd. Goochland County Land Tax Return for 1784)

Proprietors		Quantity of Land	Price	Amt. of Land	Tax
Mary HICKS		300	6/1	91.....5.....0	1.....7.....5
Meshick HICKS		450	6/4	142...10.....0	2.....2.....9
Francis HOUCHINS		117	5/19	34.....2.....6	0...10.....3
Charles HOUCHINS, JR.		117	do	34.....2.....6	0...10.....3
James HOLMAN		275	5/11	81.....7.....1	1.....4.....5
William HODGES		100	4/10	24.....3.....4	0.....7.....3
Capt. William HOLMAN		590	4/1	120.....9.....2	1..16.....2
Colo. John HOPKINS		1650	6/7	543.....2.....6	8.....3.....0
Lewis HERNDON		300	6/9	101.....5.....0	1...10.....5
John HERNDON		199	7/4	72...19.....4	1.....1...11
John HOPPER		210	7/2	75.....5.....0	1.....2.....7
Lucy HODGES		50	4/10	12.....1.....8	0.....3.....8
Major HANCOCKE		97 1/2	6/2	30.....1.....3	0.....9.....1
Thomas HODGES		50	5/1	12...14.....2	0.....3.....9
John HOLLAND		272 1/4	7/3	98...13...10	1.....9.....8
William HICKS		125	do.	45.....6.....3	0...13.....9
James HOWARD		436	do.	54.....6.....0	0...16.....4
John HOWARD		166	6/	49...10.....0	0...14...11
Anthony HADEN	(Fluvanna)	400	4/	80.....0.....0	1.....4.....0
Nathaniel HOLLAND		200	7/3	72...10.....0	1.....1.....9
Mary JUDE		268	13/6	180...18.....0	2...14.....4
John JOHNSON	(O.)	471	8/1	190.....7.....3	2...17.....6
Charles JOHNSON		124	6/6	40.....6.....0	0...12.....2
Charles JOHNSON, JR.		220	11/5	125...11.....8	1...17.....9
David JOHNSON	(Geneto)	115	8/1	46.....9.....7	0...14.....0
Isham JOHNSON	(do.)	115	9/2	52...14.....2	0...15...10
John JOHNSON	(do.)	271	9/4	126.....9.....4	1...18.....0
Richard JOHNSON		150	9/2	68...15.....0	1.....0.....8
William ISBELL		792	5/7	221.....2.....0	3.....6.....4
Estate of Joseph JOHNSON for Mr. DOUGLAS		500	4/1	102.....1.....8	1...10.....8
Benjamin JOHNSON	(Byrd)	140	7/	49.....0.....0	0...14.....9
William JOHNSON		250	6/1	76.....0...10	1.....2...10
Honble. Thomas JEFFERSON, Esqr.		612	8/1	247.....7.....0	3...13.....1
Archibald JARRETT		353	4/9	83...16.....9	1.....5.....2
do. for JENNINGS		201	4/1	41.....0.....9	0...12.....4
Devereux JARRETT		290	do.	59.....4.....9	0...17...10
David JARRETT		250	do.	51.....0...10	0...15.....4
Charles JOHNSON		200	7/2	71...13.....4	1.....1.....6

(page 26. Goochland County Land Tax Return for 1784)

Proprietors		Quantity of Land	Price	Amt. of Land	Tax
Sarah JORDAN		75	16/2	60...12.....6	0...18.....3
John JOHNSON	(of Joseph)	100	4/	20.....0.....0	0.....6.....0
John JONES		100	do.	20.....0.....0	0.....6.....0
Daniel JOHNSON	(of Charles)	150	do.	30.....0.....0	0.....9.....0
John LAPRADE		788	10/8	420.....5.....4	6.....6.....1
Capt. Elisha LEAKE		818	9/7	391...19.....2	5...17.....8
John LAYNE		50	4/1	10.....4.....2	0.....3.....1
John LEWIS (Cardmaker)		200	8/1	80...16.....8	1.....4.....3
Ayres LAYNE		155	6/8	51...13.....4	0...15.....6

(page 26 contd. Goochland County Land Tax Return for 1784)

Proprietors	Quantity of Land	Price	Amt. of Land	Tax
Henry LAYNE	100	4/1	20.....8.....4	0.....6.....2
Mary LAYNE	50	do.	10.....4.....2	0.....3.....1
Matthew LACY	97	4/10	23.....8...10	0.....7.....1
Jesse LACY	88	4/11	21...12.....8	0.....6.....6
Benjamin LACY	88	do.	21...12.....8	0.....6.....6
Sarah LACY	181	5/	45.....5.....0	0...13.....7
Samuel LAMAY	106	4/1	21...12...10	0.....6.....6
John LOVELL	343	3/4	57.....3.....4	0...17.....3
Armiger LILLY	400	4/1	81...13.....4	1.....4.....6
Colo. Robert LEWIS (Old Tract)]	565	7/		
do. of BYRD Tenement]	1030	13/6	893.....0.....0	13.....8.....1
Estate of John LEE, deced.	350	4/8	81...13.....4	1.....4.....4
William LEWIS (R.C.)	100	4/1	20.....8.....4	0.....6.....2
Capt. Josiah LEAKE	800	8/1	323.....6.....8	4...17.....0
Joseph LEWIS, JR.	407	7/3	147...10.....9	2.....4.....4
Estate of Joseph LEWIS, SENR., deced.	281	8/1	113...11.....5	1...14.....1
Joseph LOURY	200	3/6	35.....0.....0	0...10.....6
Matthew LOURY	400	4/	80.....0.....0	1.....4.....0
Joseph MAY0, Esqr. (Henrico)	500	14/6	362...10.....0	5.....9.....9
Colo. Nathaniel G. MORRIS	400	9/1	181...13.....4	2...14.....6
John MADDOX	150	6/9	50...12.....6	0...15.....3
William McCAUL	81	14/1	57.....0.....7	0...17.....2
Amos L. MOORE	260	10/	130.....0.....0	1...19.....0
Stokes McCAUL	295	8/1	119.....4.....7	1...15...10
Mary MILLER	426	8/10	188.....3.....0	2...16.....6
Edward McBRIDE	200	6/1	60...16.....8	0...18.....3
James MADDOX	335	6/8	111...13.....4	1...13.....6
Elizabeth MEANLEY	130	11/9	76.....7.....6	1.....2...11
Drury MURRELL	200	6/1	60...16.....8	0...18.....3
Charles MASSIE	300	8/1	121.....6.....0	1...16.....5
Ann MITCHELL	291	6/5	93.....7.....3	1.....8.....0
David MARTIN	235	do.	75.....7...11	1.....2.....8
Paul MEACHUM	295	5/6	81.....2.....6	1.....4.....5
Benjamin MOSBY	200	5/1	50...16.....8	0...15.....3
William MITCHELL, Gent.	865 1/2	8/1	349...12.....1	5.....4...11
Capt. William MILLER	300	7/5	111.....5.....0	1...13.....4
Thomas MILLER	296	6/10]		
do. RICHARDSON's Tenement	181	12/6]	214.....5.....2	3.....4.....6
Capt. William MERIWETHER (Louisa)	516	8/1	208...11.....0	3.....2.....6
Gideon MIMS	360	7/5	133...10.....0	2.....0...10
David MIMS	215	do.	116...16.....3	1...15.....1

(page 27. Goochland County Land Tax Return for 1784)

Proprietors	Quantity of Land	Price	Amt. of Land	Tax
Elizabeth MIMS	250	7/3	90...12.....6	1.....7.....3
Sarah MIMS	50	6/1	15.....4.....2	0.....4.....7
John MARTIN	700	6/2	215...16.....8	3.....4.....9
Edward MATTHEWS	873	7/5	322...12.....6	4...16...10
Ann MERRIAN	400	4/1	81...13.....4	1.....4.....6
Wright MOURLAND	100	6/11	34...11.....8	0...10.....5
Capt. David MULLINS	197	8/1	79...12.....5	1.....3...11

(page 27 contd. Goochland County Land Tax Return for 1784

Proprietors		Quantity of Land	Price	Amt. of Land	Tax
Capt. Henry MULLINS		400	7/2	143.....6.....8	2.....3.....0
Estate of John MULLINS, deced.		350	6/5	112.....5...10	1...13.....4
Thomas MASSIE	(Overseer)	289	7/	101.....3.....0	1...10.....3
Samuel MOSS		200	4/	40.....0.....0	0...12.....0
William MARTIN		400	6/	120.....0.....0	1...16.....0
Major Thomas MASSIE		2285	do.	685...10.....0	10.....5.....9
John MOSS		75	8/	30.....0.....0	0.....9.....0
John MOSS, JR.		200	8/1	80...16.....8	1.....4.....3
William MASSIE		223	7/3	80...16.....9	1.....4.....3
Capt. Nathaniel MASSIE		1185 3/4	8/	474.....6.....0	7.....2.....3
Thomas NOWELL		100	6/	30.....0.....0	0.....9.....0
James NOWELL		300	do.	90.....0.....0	1.....7.....0
Samuel NUCKOLS		115	7/2	41.....4.....2	0...12.....5
John NEAVES		290	7/5	107...10...10	1...12.....4
Stephen NOWLAND		150	6/9	50...12.....6	0...15.....3
Rene NAPIER		49	8/1	19...16.....1	0.....6.....0
Henry NASH,	(Fluvanna)	100	6/6	32...10.....0	0.....9.....9
William NUCKOLS, JR.		121	8/1	48...18.....1	0...14.....9
Pouncey NUCKOLS		110	do.	44.....9.....2	0...13.....5
Charles NUCKOLS		104	7/2	37.....5.....4	0...11.....3
Thomas NUCKOLS		115	do.	41.....4.....2	0...12.....5
Thomas OLIVER		273	8/1	110.....6...10	1...13.....2
Estate of Barnett OWEN		100	3/3	16.....5.....0	0.....4...11
Samuel PARSONS		490	15/	367...10.....0	5...10.....3
John PRICE	(Henrico)	268	13/6	180...18.....0	2...14.....4
William PAYNE		201	10/9	108.....0.....9	1...12.....6
Estate of Colo. Jolly PARISH		735	4/5	165.....7.....6	2.....9.....8
William POWELL		266	7/2	95.....6.....4	1.....8.....8
Major POWERS		180	8/1	72...15.....0	1.....2...10
Anderson PEERS		559	do.	226...18.....7	3.....7.....9
Hezekiah PURYEAR		397 1/2	do.]		
do. HUTCHINS's Tenement		256 1/2	do.]	290.....6.....7	3...19.....6
Matthew PLEASANTS		425	8/1	171...15.....5	2...11.....6
James PLEASANTS, Gent.		500	16/7	414...11.....8	6.....4.....5
Isaac PLEASANTS		676	21/6	726...14.....0	10...18.....1
Joseph PLEASANTS		200	8/1	80...16.....8	1.....4.....3
Robert PLEASANTS	(Buff.)	140	7/	49.....0.....0	0...14.....9
Richard PLEASANTS		368	8/11	164.....1.....4	2.....9.....3
Philip PLEASANTS		121	8/1	48...18.....0	0...14.....9
William POWERS		368	do.	148...14.....8	2.....4.....8
Thomas PLEASANTS, (Mercht.)		1578	16/9	1321...11.....6	19...16.....6
Doctor William PASTEUR	(York)	700	13/4	466...13.....4	7.....0.....0

(page 28. Goochland County Land Tax Return for 1784)

Francis PLEDGE		50	8/1	20.....4.....2	0.....6.....1
Estate of William PLEDGE, deced.		50	9/9	24.....7.....6	0.....7.....4
Archer PLEDGE		50	11/5	28...10...10	0.....8.....7
John PAYNE, JR.		439	14/5	316.....8...11	4...15.....0

(page 28 contd. Goochland County Land Tax Return for 1784)

Proprietors	Quantity of Land	Price	Amt. of Land	Tax
Robin POOR	350	10/5	182.....5...10	2...14.....9
Joseph POLLARD, Gent.	447	9/11	221...12.....9	3.....6.....6
Mary PERKINS	161 1/2	8/1	65.....5.....6	0...19.....7
Molly PERKINS	250	do.	101.....0...10	1...10.....4
William PERKINS	200	6/11	60...16.....8	0...18.....3
Willam PERKINS, JR. of ROBARDS	265	6/	79...10.....0	1.....3...11
Estate of Walker PERKINS	171 1/2	9/10	84.....6.....5	1.....5.....4
Benjamin PERKINS	250	3/3	40...12.....6	0...12.....3
Archer PAYNE, Gent.	850	8/7	364...15...10	5.....9.....6
Colo. George PAYNE (Glebe)	200	8/1	80...16.....8	1.....4.....3
Robert PLEASANTS, JR. (Henrico)	1300	10/7	687...18.....4	10...6.....5
Sherwood PARISH	162	4/1	33.....1.....6	0...10.....0
Joel PARISH	121	4/10	29.....4...10	0.....8...10
Aaron PARISH	71 1/4	4/1	14...11.....0	0.....4.....5
Mary PARISH	121 1/4	do.	24...15.....2	0.....7.....6
Booker PARISH	180 1/4	do.	36.....6.....1	0...11.....1
Samuel PRYOR	475		187.....3.....9	3.....6.....2
William PRYOR	200	12/1	120...16.....8	1...16.....3
Moses PARISH	168	4/1	34.....6.....0	0...10.....4
Daniel POWERS	33 1/2	5/11	9...18.....3	0.....3.....0
Samuel POWELL	350	4/1	71.....9.....2	1.....1.....6
Thomas POLLOCK	1092 3/4	7/3]		
do. for Courthouse	100	12/1]	457.....5...10	6...17.....1
Estate of George PAYNE, JR. deced. (O.K.)	200	5/7	55...16.....8	0...16.....9
John PARISH	564	5/3	148.....1.....0	2.....4.....5
Major Jonas PAYNE	800	8/1	323.....6.....8	4...17.....0
Robert PAGE	133	8/1	63...15.....1	0...16.....2
John PERKINS	477	7/4]		
do. MIMS's Tenement	50	5/8]	189.....1.....4	2...16.....9
Estate of Jesse PAYNE, deced.	597 1/2	8/5	251.....9.....0	3...15.....6
Capt. Joseph PAYNE	977	8/1	394...17.....5	5...18.....6
Colo. John PAYNE	2053	8/	821.....4.....0	12...6.....5
Thomas POOR	525	5/1	133.....8.....9	2.....0.....1
Abram POOR	200	6/1	60...16.....8	0...18.....3
William PROPHET	30	6/9	10.....2.....6	0.....3.....1
Joseph PACE	150	6/3	46...17.....6	0...14.....1
John PACE	130	5/	32...10.....0	0.....9.....9
William PACE	200	6/1	60...16.....8	0...18.....3
John PHILPOTT	100	4/1	20.....8.....4	0.....6.....2
Benjamin PAGE	100	6/1	30.....8.....4	0.....9.....2
John PREWIT	91	7/2	32...12.....2	0.....9...10
Archibald PLEASANTS	299	13/6	201...16.....6	3.....0.....7
Capt. Humphrey PARISH	497	5/10	144...19.....2	2.....3.....6

(page 29. Goochland County Land Tax Return for 1784)

Proprietors	Quantity of Land	Price	Amt. of Land	Tax
George PRIDDY	250	6/	75.....0.....0	1.....2.....6
Anderson PARISH	170	3/3	27...12.....6	0.....8.....3
William PARISH	250	7/	87...10.....0	1.....6.....3
Samuel ROUNTREE	350	10/5	182.....5...10	2...14.....9
Randolph ROUNTREE	300	11/5	171.....5.....0	2...11.....5

(page 29 contd. Goochland County Land Tax Return for 1784

Proprietors		Quantity of Land	Price	Amt. of Land	Tax
John REDD		247	6/6	80.....5.....6	1.....4.....1
Matthew RIDDLE		70	7/	24...10.....0	0.....7.....5
Isaac RAGLAND		150	6/9	50...12.....6	0...15.....3
William ROYSTER, Gent.		543	11/1	300.....8.....3	4...10.....4
Thomas ROYSTER		200	10/1	100...16.....8	1...10.....3
Edward REDFORD		208	12/4	128.....5.....4	1...18.....6
Milner REDFORD		539	9/8	260...10.....4	3...18.....2
Colo. Thomas M. RANDOLPH, Esqr. Tuckahoe	1952	14/9]			
do.	Dover	1100	24/1]	2764.....3.....8	41.....9.....4
Mary ROGERS		17	8/1	6...17.....5	0.....1.....1
David ROSS, Esqr.		9450	8/10]		
do.	HOLMAN's Tenement	400	4/1]	4255.....8.....4	63.....6.....8
William RONALD, Esqr.		1170	11/7]		
do.	BRADSHAW's Tenement	200	6/1]	738.....9.....2	11.....1.....7
Nathaniel RAINE		244	7/5	90.....9.....8	1.....7.....2
William RUTHERFORD		433	5/4	115.....9.....4	1...14.....8
William RIGSBY		50	3/3	8.....2.....6	0.....2.....6
Thomas RIDDLE		435	5/11	128...13.....9	1...18.....8
Doctor John K. READ		408	8/1	164...18.....0	2.....9.....6
Charles RICE		175	5/10	51.....0...10	0...15.....4
Capt. Samuel RICHARDSON		536	7/2	192.....1.....4	2...17.....8
Thomas RANDOLPH, Esqr.		3000	9/9	1462...10.....0	21...18.....9
George RICHARDSON		1612	6/10	550...15.....4	8.....5.....3
Elizabeth STODGHILL		28	12/1	16...18.....4	0.....5.....1
Thomas SHOEMAKER		200	10/1	100...16.....8	1...10.....3
Colo. John SYME	(Hanover)	318	8/1	128...10.....6	1...18.....7
Josiah SEAY		95	6/3	.29...13.....9	0.....8...11
John SAUNDERS		30	8/1	12.....2.....6	0.....3.....8
Capt. Stephen SAMPSON		752	8/2	307.....1.....4	4...12.....1
William SAUNDERS		25	8/1	10.....2.....1	0.....3.....1
Estate of Charles SAMPSON		234	do.	94...11.....6	1.....8.....5
John SHELTON, Gent.		412	do.]		
do for James MADDOX's Tenement		50	9/10]	191.....2.....0	2.....7.....5
Capt. Joseph SHELTON,	(Louisa)	1369	9/	616.....1.....0	9.....4...10
John SHELTON	(Hanover)	400	8/1	161...13.....4	2.....8.....6
Benjamin SADLER		100	4/1	20.....8.....4	0.....6.....2
Arthur SLAYDEN		182	do.	37.....3.....2	0...11.....2
John SLAYDEN		100	do	20.....8.....4	0.....6.....2
William L. SMITH		211	7/2	75...12.....2	1.....5.....9
John STRONG		137 1/2	8/1	55...11.....6	0...16.....9
Nathan STRONG		137 1/2	do.	55...11.....6	0...16.....9
Edward SCRUGGS		100	6/1	30.....8.....4	0.....9.....2
Capt. Robert SMITH	(P.tan)	40	8/1	16.....3.....4	0.....4...11
Richard SAMPSON		250	7/3	90...12.....6	1.....7.....3
Philip TINSLEY		50	12/1	30.....4.....2	0.....9.....1
Capt. Stokley TOWLES		348 1/2	8/6	148.....2.....3	2.....4.....6

(page 30. Goochland County Land Tax Return for 1784)

Proprietors	Quantity of Land	Price	Amt. of Land	Tax
Thomas TOWLES, Esqr.	348 1/2	9/4	162...12.....8	2.....8...10

(page 30 conts. Goochland County Land Tax Return for 1784)

Proprietors		Quantity of Land	Price	Amt. of Land	Tax
Bartholomew TURNER		200	8/1	80...16.....8	1.....4.....3
Sarah THOMAS		160	4/1	32...13.....4	0.....9...10
Mary TOWLER		200	do.	40...16.....8	0...12.....3
Cornelius TOWLER		190	do.	38...15...10	0...11.....8
William THURSTON		122	7/5	45.....4...10	0...13.....7
John THURSTON		110	7/1	38...19.....2	0...11.....9
Esther THURSTON		53	4/5	11...14.....1	0.....3.....7
Henry TUGGLE		100	5/1	25.....8.....4	0.....7.....8
Horation TURPIN		1200	5/9	345.....0.....0	5.....3.....6
James THOMAS		110	4/1	24...10.....0	0.....7.....6
John TOWLER		62 1/2	do.	12...15.....3	0.....3...10
Reuben THURSTON		53	5/	13.....5.....0	0.....4.....1
Benjamin THACKER		100	3/3	16.....5.....0	0.....5.....0
William UTTLEY		125	8/1	50...10.....5	0...15.....3
Obadiah UTTLEY		8	do.	3.....4.....8	0.....1.....0
Ann UTTLEY		116	6/4	36...14.....8	0.....4.....1
John UTTLEY		125	8/1	50...10.....5	0...15.....3
Hezekiah UTTLEY		58	6/1	17...12...10	0.....5.....4
Elizabeth UNDERWOOD		100	11/5	57.....1.....8	0...17.....2
George UNDERWOOD		526	7/4	192...17.....4	2...17...11
Thomas UNDERWOOD, Gent.		600	8/9	262...10.....0	3...18.....9
Estate of James UNDERWOOD, deced.		215	6/8	71...13.....4	1.....1.....6
Matthew VAUGHAN, Gent.		800	9/1	363.....6.....8	5.....9.....0
James VAUGHAN		362	7/7	137.....5.....2	2.....1.....3
Shadrach VAUGHAN		913	8/1	369.....0.....1	5...10.....9
Charles WADDELL Mr. HILL's land		262	6/1	79...13...10	1.....3...11
Richard WALMACK MILLER's		150	5/5	40...12.....6	0...12.....3
Colo. John WOODSON		844	25/10	1090.....3.....4	16.....7.....1
Matthew WOODSON		1883	12/11	1216.....2.....1	18.....4...10
Major Joseph WOODSON		535	8/1	216.....4.....7	3.....4 11
Susanna WOODWARD		500	12/1	302.....1.....8	4...10.....8
William WOODWARD		150	9/5	70...12.....6	1.....1.....3
Robert WADE		97	8/1	39.....4.....1	0...11...10
Richard WADE		297	9/7	142.....6.....2	2.....2.....9
John WADE		73	8/1	29...10.....1	0.....8...11
Pleasant WILLIS		278	8/1	112.....7.....2	1...13.....9
Daniel WADE		200	do.	80...16.....8	1.....4.....3
Eleanor WILLIS		100	6/1	30.....8.....4	0.....9.....2
William WOODALL		63	6/6	20.....9.....6	0.....6.....2
William WEBBER	(Preacher)	177	6/5	56.....1.....0	0...16...10
Edward WILLIS		160	8/1	64...13.....4	0...19.....5
Thomas WOODSON		200	12/1	120...16.....8	1...16.....3
Nathaniel WEBSTER		170	6/6	55.....5.....0	0...16.....7
David WEBSTER		75	10/6	39...17.....6	0...12.....0
Robert WINGFIELD		90	8/1	36.....7.....6	0...10...11
Joseph WOODSON, JR.	(Geneto)	225	9/	101.....5.....0	1...10.....5
Estate of Joseph WOODSON, SENR., deced		222	10/	111.....0.....0	1...13.....4
Foster WEBB, Esqr.	(New Kent)	475		150...17.....6	2.....5.....7
Dorothy WATKINS		170	8/1	68...14.....2	1.....0.....8

(page 30 contd. Goochland County Land Tax Return for 1784)

Proprietors		Quantity of Land	Price	Amt. of Land	Tax
Joseph WATKINS		429	10/]		
do. Ben JOHNSON's Tenement		115	8/1]	260...19.....7	3...18.....5

(page 31. Goochland County Land Tax Return for 1784)

Proprietors		Quantity of Land	Price	Amt. of Land	Tax
Thomas WATKINS		453	8/1]		
do. BRUMFIELD's Tenement		130	do]	235...12.....7	3...10...10
Peter WALKER	(Geneto)	230	do.	92...19.....2	1.....7...11
Benjamin WATKINS		238	9/5	112.....1.....2	1...13.....8
John WATKINS		519	8/11	231.....7.....9	3.....9.....6
William WEBBER		340	10/6	178...10.....0	2...13.....7
Benjamin WOODSON	(Fluvanna)	205	9/1	93.....2.....1	1.....8.....0
Benjamin WATKINS, JR.		156	9/5	73.....9.....0	1.....2.....1
Henry WHITLOW, JR.		50	8/1	20.....4.....2	0.....6.....1
Henry WHITLOW, SENR.		99	do.	40.....0.....3	0...12.....1
William WILLIS (of D.)		63 1/2	7/3	23.....0.....5	0.....6...11
John WITT.		17	8/1	6...17.....5	0.....2.....0
Tucker WOODSON		600	17/8	530.....0.....0	7...19.....0
John WOODSON	(C. Ferry)	1265		647...15.....5	9...14.....4
Henry WALMACK		100	8/1	40.....8.....4	0...12.....2
Peter WALKER	(Constable)	116	4/1	23...13.....8	0.....7.....2
Isaac WINSTON	(Hanover)	735	8/1	297.....1.....3	4.....9.....2
William WHITLOCK		100	6/1	30.....8.....4	0.....9.....2
Drury WILLIAMS		500	8/1	202.....1.....8	3.....0.....8
John WALKER		100	3/3	16.....5.....0	0.....4...11
William WALKER		94	4/2	19...11.....8	0.....5...11
Thomas WAFFORD		540	4/6	121...10.....0	1...16.....6
Estate of Colo. Valentine WOOD, deced.		2226	8/1]		
do. for ROBARD's Tenement		536	6/7]	1076.....2.....2	16....( )....( )
William WILLIAMS		50	4/1	10.....4.....2	0.....5....( )
John WILLIAMS	(D.C.)	400	5/1]		
do. of EADES's Tenement		136	4/1]	129.....8.....9	1...18...10
John WILLIAMSON		200	do.	40...16.....8	0...12.....3
Lewis WILBOURNE		100	do.	20.....8.....4	0.....6.....2
Dabney WADE		300	8/1	121.....5.....0	1...16.....5
William WILBOURNE		200	3/3	32...10.....0	0.....9.....9
John WILLIAMS, JR.		250	6/6	81.....5.....0	1.....4.....5
William WHITFIELD		105	4/1	21.....8.....9	0.....6.....6
James WILLIAMS		10	7/	3...10.....0	0.....0...11
Solomon WILLIAMS		103	do.	36.....1.....0	0...10...10
Philip WILLIAMS		200	6/	60.....0.....0	0...18.....0
Capt. John WARE		925	6/6	300...12.....6	4...10.....2
Ann YOUNGER		100	3/3	16.....5.....0	0.....4...11

May 17th. 1784. Rec'd of the Commrs. of the Tax for Goochland County a State of the Land
Tax for the present Collection amounting to Twelve hundred forty four pounds, four shillings, it
being a duplicate of this.
L. 1244.....4.....0   MATT: VAUGHAN, Dep. Shf.
                                                        for JOHN HOPKINS, Shf.

(page 32). Goochland County Land Tax Return for 1784)

Goochland. Return of the Land Tax from Commissioners for the year 1784.

ARCHD. PLEASANTS   ]
THOMAS F. BATES   ] Commrs.

This Return makes the amount to be taxed less then it was in 1783 and does not shew the particulars therefore it is an improper Return.
JNO. P.

(page 33.)

A State of the Land Tax taken in Goochland County for the Sheriff's Collection in specie, &c. July 13th 1785.

Proprietors		Quantity of Land	Price	Amt. of Land	Tax
Colo. Richard ADAMS,	(Henrico)	1982	8/9	867.....2.....6	6...10.....1
Mary ADKINSON		310	8/1	125.....5...10	0...18...10
James ALLEN		175	4/7	34...16.....3	0.....3.....9
David ALVIS		50	4/1	10.....4.....2	0.....1.....7
William ANDERSON, Esqr.	(Hanover)	1500	8/	600.....0.....0	4...10.....0
Charles BATES		350	12/1	211.....9.....2	1...11.....9
William BARNETT		200	7/6	72...10.....0	0...11.....0
Susanna BIBB		248	8/1	100.....4.....8	0...15.....1
John BLACKWELL		98 1/2	do.	39...16.....3	0.....6.....0
Elijah BRUMFIELD		200	10/3	102...10.....0	0...15.....5
John BRUMFIELD		125	8/1	50...10.....5	0.....7.....7
John BRADSHAW		450	6/9	151...17.....6	1.....2...10
Callam BAILEY		150	4/1	30...12.....6	0.....4.....8
John BOWDRY		10	do.	2.....0...10	0.....0.....4
William BURGESS		100	do.	20.....8.....4	0.....3.....1
Colo. John BOLLING		1440		677.....7.....6	5.....1.....8
John BOLLING, JR.		600	9/8	290.....0.....0	2.....3.....6
Thomas BOLLING, Esqr.	(Chesterfield)	4000		4906.....5.....0	35...16.....0
Claibourne BRADSHAW		138	8/1	55...15.....6	0.....8.....5
Sarah BRADSHAW		69	7/2	24...14.....6	0.....3.....9
Thomas F. BATES		500	13/10	345...16.....8	2...11...11
William BLUNKALL		3 1/2	16/2	2...16.....7	0.....0.....6
James BENNETT	(Henrico)	200	6/	60.....0.....0	0.....9.....0
William BRITT		850	4/9	201...17.....6	1...10.....4
Capt. John BRITT		245	7/4	89...16.....8	0...13.....6
William BOWMAN		100	4/1	20.....8.....4	0.....3.....1
Gideon BOWLES		350	6/8	116...13.....4	0...16...11
William BUSBY		50	4/1	10.....4.....2	0.....1.....7
James CURD		440	8/1	177...16.....8	1.....6.....9
Richard CROUCH	(Henrico)	200	do.	80...16.....8	0...12.....2
Philemon CHILDERS		276	4/1	56.....7.....0	0.....8.....6
Thomas CHANCELLOR		125	6/6	40...12.....6	0.....6.....2
Judith CHEADLE		299	13/6	201...16.....6	1...10.....4
Daniel CLARKE		100	6/1	30.....8.....4	0.....4.....7
Ann COCKE	(Surry)	1567	14/10	1162.....3...10	8...14.....4
Estate of Colo. Allen COCKE, deced.		1195	14/11	891.....5.....5	6...13.....9

(page 33 contd. Goochland County Land Tax Return for 1785)

Proprietors		Quantity of Land	Price	Amt. of Land	Tax
John CLARKE		62	6/2	19.....2.....4	0.....2...11
Turner CLARKE		90	6/1	27.....7.....6	0.....4.....2
Estate of Jeffry CLARKE, deced.		98	6/7	32.....5.....2	0.....4...11
Joseph CLARKE		115	6/3	30...18.....9	0.....4.....8
Susanna CROUCH		100	8/1	40.....8.....4	0.....6.....1
James COCKE		300	do.	121.....5.....0	0...18.....3
Edward CARTER		34	do.	13...10.....4	0.....2.....1
William CLARKSON		50	9/9	24.....7.....6	0.....3.....8
Colo. John CURD		609	10/9	327.....6.....9	2.....9.....2
Capt. Edmund CURD		225	9/11	111...11.....8	0...16.....9
Sarah CURD		211	8/1	56...11.....8	0...12...10
Benjamin COCKE		122	do.	49.....6.....2	0.....7.....5
James COCKE	(P.tan)	54		21...16.....6	0.....3.....4

(page 34. Goochland County Land Tax Return for 1785)

Proprietors		Quantity of Land	Price	Amt. of Land	Tax
Thomas COCKE		140	8/1	56...11.....8	0.....8.....0
Martha CARR		499	do.	201...13.....7	1...10....( )
Benjamin CRENSHAW		440	5/11	130.....3.....4	0...19.....7
Armsby CREW		100	4/10	24.....3.....4	0.....3.....8
Nathaniel CAWLEY		60	8/1	24.....5.....0	0.....3.....8
Mary COLEY		100	do.	40.....8.....4	0.....6.....1
Susanna COLEY		100	4/1	20.....8.....4	0.....3.....1
Ann COLEY		100	8/1	40.....8.....4	0.....6.....1
Sally COLEY		100	6/1	30.....8.....4	0.....4.....7
Francis COLEY		106 1/2	6/3	33.....2.....6	0.....5.....0
Francis CLARKE for Mr. DOUGLAS		150	4/1	30...12.....6	0.....9.....3
William CHEEK	(Henrico)	232	5/10	67...13.....4	0...10.....2
Estate of Robert CARDIN, deced.		200	5/1	50...16.....8	0.....7.....8
John CLEMENTS		116	5/10	33...16.....8	0.....5.....1
Stephen CROUCH		200	5/1	50...16.....8	0.....7.....8
Bryant CONLEY		150	5/5	40...12.....6	0.....6.....2
Bowler COCKE, Esqr.	(Henrico)	1509		1165...12.....0	8...14.....9
Samuel COSBY		225	4/6	50...12.....6	0.....7.....8
Walter CLOPTON		220	8/1	88...18.....4	0...13.....5
James CLEMENTS		179	6/4	56...13.....8	0.....8.....7
Roger CARRELL		83	4/1	16...18...11	0.....2.....7
Gideon CAWTHON		220	6/8	73.....6.....8	0...11.....6
John COX		100	6/1	30.....8.....4	0.....4.....7
Edward COX		100	4/10	24.....3.....4	0.....3.....8
David CRENSHAW		239	6/2	73.....7.....8	0...11.....1
Benjamin CLOPTON		200	8/1	80...16.....8	0...12.....2
Judith CARTER		100	4/10	24.....3.....4	0.....3.....8
Turner CHRISTIAN		235	6/2	72.....7.....0	0...10...10
George CROWDAS		100	7/	35.....0.....0	0.....5.....3
Benjamin DARST		100	8/1	40.....8.....4	0.....6.....1
John DOWDY		122	7/5	45.....4...10	0.....6...10
Thomas DRUMWRIGHT		1030	6/2	317...11.....8	2.....7.....8
Stephen DAVIS		265	7/2	94...19.....2	0...14.....3
John DAVIS	(Hanover)	100	7/3	36.....5.....0	0.....5.....6
Ichabod DANIEL		200	5/8	56...13.....4	0.....8.....6

(page   34 contd. Goochland County Land Tax Return for 1785)

Proprietors		Quantity of Land	Price	Amt. of Land	Tax
Reverend William DOUGLAS		500	6/1	152.....1.....8	1.....2...10
David DAVIS		100	7/	35.....0.....0	0.....5.....3
Noton DICKINSON		400	3/6	70.....0.....0	0...10.....6
Susanna DAVIS		200	do.	35.....0.....0	0.....5.....3
John ELLIS	(Henrico)	392	12/1	236...16.....8	1...15.....6
Stephen ELLIS		97	16/2	78.....8.....2	0...11...10
David ELLIS		372 1/2	8/1	151.....7.....3	1.....2.....9
William EDWARDS		80	4/1	16.....6.....8	0.....2.....6
Joseph EVANS		134	6/1	40...15.....2	0.....6.....2
Francis EVANS		133 1/2	5/5	36.....3.....2	0.....5.....6
Thomas ELDRIDGE		203	8/1	82.....0...11	0...12.....3
David ENGLAND		80	6/1	24.....6.....8	0.....3.....8
Benjamin EAST		121 1/2	8/1	49.....2.....2	0.....7.....5
Thomas EDWARDS		50	6/6	16.....5.....0	0.....2.....6
Thomas EMMERSON		100	3/6	17...10.....0	0.....2.....8

(page 35. Goochland County Land Tax Return for 1785)

Proprietors		Quantity of Land	Price	Amt. of Land	Tax
Henry EMMERSON		240	6/6	45.....0.....0	0.....6.....9
Thomas EMMERSON, JR.		100	do	17...10.....0	0.....2.....8
William FARRAR, Gent.		886	10/5	461.....9.....2	3.....9.....3
John FARRAR		298	10/9	160.....3.....6	1.....4.....1
William FORD		200	8/1	80...16.....8	0...12.....2
Elizabeth FORD		233	do.	94.....3.....5	0...14.....2
Joseph FARRAR		100	12/1	60.....8.....4	0.....9.....1
Mary FRAYSER		205	8/1	82...17.....1	0...12.....6
Reuben FORD		147	do.	59.....8.....3	0.....9.....0
John FARISH		100	6/1	30.....8.....4	0.....4.....7
Estate of Colo. Tarlton FLEMING, deced.		1900	20/2	1915...16.....8	14.....7.....5
Honble. William FLEMING, Esqr.		390	20/4	396...10.....0	2...19.....6
Colo. Charles FLEMING		390	do.	396...10.....0	2...19.....6
John FURLONG		100	3/6	17...10.....0	0.....2.....8
Joseph R. FARRAR		400	12/1	241...13.....4	1...16.....3
Hugh FRENCH		100	6/11	34...11.....8	0.....5.....3
John Tayloe GRIFFIN, Esqr.		3311		3902.....6.....5	24.....5.....5
John GORDEN		133	7/2	47...13.....2	0.....7.....2
Henry GRAY		100	8/	40.....8.....4	0.....6.....1
John GUERRANT, Gent.		450	9/11]		
do. of Stephen SAMPSON, Gent.		186	]	334.....2.....6	2...10.....3
John GILLAM	(Pr. Geo.)	500	9/9	243...16.....0	1...16.....7
Capt. William GEORGE		325		90...14.....7	0...13.....8
John GRAY		85	10/3	44.....8.....4	0.....6.....9
Major John GUERRANT		200	8/1	80...16.....8]	
do. of Thomas ELDRIDGE		103	do.	41...12.....7]	
do. of William A. ENGLAND		89	7/	31.....3.....0]	0...19.....6
James GEORGE		100	8/1	40.....8.....4	0.....6.....1
John GILLAM, SENR.		546	7/9	211...11.....6	1...11.....9
David GRANTHAM		35	7/6	13.....2.....6	0.....2.....0
William GROOM		100	3/3	16.....5.....0	0.....2.....6

(page 35 contd. Goochland County Land Tax Return for 1785)

Proprietors		Quantity of Land	Price	Amt. of Land	Tax
Robert GILLAM Esqr.	(Pr. Geo.)	1021 3/4		2699.....2.....6	20.....4...11
Stephen GRANGE		80	7/2	28...13.....4	0.....4.....4
Estate of James GEORGE, deced.		150	6/	45.....0.....0	0.....6.....9
Anselm GEORGE		175	4/	35.....0.....0	0.....5.....3
John GILBERT		150	3/6	26.....5.....0	0.....4.....0
Daniel GRUBBS		250	do.	43...15.....0	0.....6.....7
David HUDSON		368	8/1	148...14.....8	1.....2.....5
John HYLTON		411	10/9	220...18.....3	1...13.....2
John HUSON		47	5/	11...15.....0	0.....1...10
Francis Eppes HARRIS		330	21/	346...10.....0	2...12.....0
John HINES		330	9/4	154.....0.....0	1.....3.....2
Strangeman HUTCHINS		370	9/3	171.....2.....6	1.....5.....9
Thomas HARDING		228	8/1	92.....3.....0	0...13...10
James HUNNICUTT		287	8/1	115...19...11	0...17.....5
Benjamin HUGHES		627	do.	253.....8.....3	1...18.....1
Capt. Gideon HATCHER		360	9/7	172...10.....0	1.....5...11

(page 36. Goochland County Land Tax Return for 1785)

Proprietors		Quantity of Land	Price	Amt. of Land	Tax
William HUGHES	(Hanover)	115	9/2	52...14.....2	0.....7...11
Giles HARDING		316	8/6	134.....6.....0	1.....0.....2
William HAY, Esqr.		600	12/1	362...10.....0	2...14.....1
John HENDERSON		200	4/1	40...16.....8	0.....6.....2
John HUMBER		561	8/1	226...14.....9	1...14.....1
Zachariah HADEN		660	5/1	167...15.....0	1.....5.....2
Drury HATCHER		5 1/2	4/6	1.....4.....9	0.....0.....3
Jesse HODGES		160	5/7	44...13.....4	0.....6.....9
John HILL	(Amherst)	150	6/1	45...12.....6	0.....6...11
Harrison HARRIS		530	7/4	194.....6.....8	1.....9.....2
Mary HICKS		300	6/1	91.....5.....0-	0...13.....9
Mesheck HICKS		450	6/4	142...10.....0	1.....1.....5
Francis HOUCHINS		117	5/10	34.....2.....6	0.....5.....2
Charles HOUCHINS, JR.		117	do.	34.....2.....6	0.....5.....2
James HOLMAN		275	5/11	81.....7.....1	0...12.....3
William HODGES		100	4/10	120.....9.....3	0...18.....1
Colo. John HOPKINS		1650	6/7	543.....2.....6	4.....1.....6
Lewis HERNDON		300	6/9	101.....5.....0	0...15.....3
John HERNDON		199	7/4	72...19.....4	0...11.....0
John HOPPER		210	7/2	75.....5.....0	0...11.....4
Lucy HODGES		50	4/10	12.....1.....8	0.....1...10
Major HANCOCKE		80	6/7	26.....6.....8	0.....4.....0
George HANCOCKE		97 1/2	6/2	30.....1.....3	0.....4.....7
Thomas HODGES		50	5/1	12...14.....2	0.....1...11
John HOLLAND		272 1/4	7/3	98...13...10	0...14...10
William HICKS		125	do.	45.....6.....3	0.....6...11
James HOWARD		136	do.	54.....6.....0	0.....8.....2
John HOWARD		166	6/	49...10.....0	0.....7.....6
Anthony HADEN	(Fluvanna)	400	4/	80.....0.....0	0...12.....0
Nathaniel HOLLAND		200	7/3	72...10.....0	0...10...11
Reverend Francis HILL		262	6/1	79...13...10	0...12.....0

(page 36 contd. Goochland County Land Taxt Return for 1785)

Proprietors		Quantity of Land	Price	Amt. of Land	Tax
John JOHNSON	(0)	471	8/1	190.....7.....3	1.....8.....9
Charles JOHNSON		124	6/6	40.....6.....0	0.....6.....1
Charles JOHNSON, JR.		220	11/5	125...11.....8	0...18...11
David JOHNSON	(Geneto)	115	8/1	46.....9...7	0.....7.....0
John JOHNSON	(do.)	271	9/4	126.....9...4	0...19.....0
Isham JOHNSON	(do.)	115	9/2	52...14.....2	0.....8.....0
Richard JOHNSON		150	do.	68...15.....0	0...10.....4
William ISBELL		792	5/7	221.....2.....0	1...13.....2
Estate of Joseph JOHNSON for DOUGLAS		500	4/1	102.....1.....8	0...15.....4
Estate of Benjamin JOHNSON (Byrd)		140	7/	49.....0.....0	0.....7.....5
William JOHNSON		250	6/1	76.....0...10	0...11.....5
Honble. Thomas JEFFERSON, Esqr.		612	8/1	247.....7.....0	1...16.....7
Archibald JARRETT		353	4/9	83...16.....9	0...12.....7
do. for JENNINGS		201	4/1	41.....0.....9	0.....6.....2
Devereux JARRETT		290	do.	59.....4.....9	0.....8...11
David JARRETT		250	do.	51.....0...10	0.....7.....8
Charles JOHNSON		200	7/2	71...13.....4	0...10.....9

(page 37. Goochland County Land Tax Return for 1785)

Proprietors		Quantity of Land	Price	Amt. of Land	Tax
Sarah JORDAN		75	16/2	60...12.....6	0.....9.....2
John JOHNSON (of Joseph)		100	4/	20.....0.....0	0.....3.....0
John JONES		100	do.	20.....0.....0	0.....3.....0
Daniel JOHNSON (of Charles)		150	do.	30.....0.....0	0.....4.....6
Estate of John LAPRADE		788	10/8	420.....5.....4	3.....3...1
Capt. Elisha LEAKE		818	9/7	391...19.....2	2...18...10
John LAYNE		50	4/1	10.....4.....2	0.....1.....7
John LEWIS (C.Maker)		200	8/1	80...16.....8	0...12.....2
Ayres LAYNE		155	6/8	51...13.....4	0.....7.....9
Henry LAYNE		100	4/1	20.....8.....4	0.....3.....1
Matthew LACY		97	4/10	23...8...10	0.....3.....7
Jesse LACY		88	4/11	21...12.....8	0.....3.....3
Benjamin LACY		88	do.	21...12.....8	0.....3.....3
Mary LAYNE		50	4/1	10...4.....2	0.....1.....7
Sarah LACY		181	5/	45...5.....0	0.....6...10
Samuel LEMAY		106	4/1	21...12...10	0.....3.....3
Armiger LILLY	(Fluvanna)	400	4/1	81...13.....4	0...12.....3
Howell LEWIS		600	7/	221.....7...6	1...13.....4
Colo. Robert LEWIS		995	13/6	671...12.....6	5.....0.....9
Estate of John LEE, deced.		350	4/8	81...13.....4	0...12.....2
William LEWIS	(R.C.)	100	4/1	20.....8.....4	0.....3.....1
Capt. Josiah LEAKE		800	8/1	323.....6.....8	2.....8.....6
Joseph LEWIS		407	7/3	147...10.....9]	
do. his late Father's		281	8/1	113...11.....5]	1...19.....3
Joseph LOWRY		200	3/6	35.....0.....0	0.....5.....3
Matthew LOWRY		400	4/	80.....0.....0	0...12.....0
Stephen G. LETCHER		49	8/1	19...16.....1	0.....3.....0
Joseph MAYO, Esqr.	(Henrico)	500	14/6	362...10.....0	2...14...11
Colo. Nathaniel G. MORRIS		400	9/1	181...13.....4	1.....7.....3
John MADDOX		150	6/9	50...12.....6	0.....7.....8

(page 37 contd. Goochland County Land Tax Return for 1785)

Proprietors	Quantity of Land	Price	Amt. of Land	Tax
William McCAUL	81	14/1	57.....0.....7	0.....8.....7
Amos L. MOORE	260	10/	130.....0.....0	0...19.....6
Stokes McCAUL	295	8/1	119.....4.....7	0...18.....0
Mary MILLER	426	8/10	188.....3.....0	1.....8.....3
Edward McBRIDE	200	6/1	60...16.....8	0.....9.....2
Elizabeth MEANLEY	130	11/9	76.....7.....6	0...11.....6
Reverend Daniel McCAULEY	200	6/1	60...16.....8	0.....9.....2
Charles MASSIE	300	8/1	121.....5.....0	0...18.....3
Ann MITCHELL	291	6/5	93.....7.....3	0...14.....0
David MARTIN	235	do.	75.....7...11	0...11.....4
Paul MEACHUM	295	5/6	81.....2.....6	0...12.....3
Benjamin MOSBY	200	5/1	50...16.....8	0.....7.....8
William MITCHELL, Gent.	865 1/2	8/1	349...12.....1	2...12.....6
Capt. William MILLER	300	7/5	111.....5.....0	0...16.....8
Thomas MILLER	477		214.....5.....2]	
do. CHRISTIAN's Tenement	217	10/	108...10.....0]	2.....8.....7
Capt. William MERIWETHER	516	8/1	208...11.....0	1...11.....3
Gideon MIMS	360	7/5	133...10.....0	1.....0.....5
David MIMS	315	do.	116...16.....3	0...17.....7

(page 38. Goochland County Land Tax Return for 1785)

Proprietors	Quantity of Land	Price	Amt. of Land	Tax
Elizabeth MIMS	250	7/3	90...12.....6	0...13.....8
Sarah MIMS	50	6/1	15.....4.....2	0.....2.....4
John MARTIN	700	6/2	215...16.....8	1...12.....5
Estate of Edward MATTHEWS	582	7/5	215.....1.....8	1...12.....4
Jane MATTHEWS	291	do.	107...10...10	0...16.....2
Ann MERRIAN	400	4/1	81...13.....4	0...12.....3
Wright MOURLAND	100	6/11	34...11.....8	0.....5.....3
Capt. David MULLINS	197	8/1	79...12.....5	0...12.....0
Capt. Henry MULLINS	400	7/2	143.....6.....8	1.....1.....6
Estate of John MULLINS, deced.	350	6/5	112.....5...10	0...16.....8
Thomas MASSIE	289	7/	101.....3.....0	0...15.....2
Samuel MOSS	200	4/	40.....0.....0	0.....6.....0
William MARTIN	400	6/	120.....0.....0	0...18.....0
Major Thomas MASSIE	2285	do.	685...10.....0	5.....2...11
John MOSS	75	8/	30.....0.....0	0.....4.....6
John MOSS, JR.	200	8/1	80...16.....8	0...12.....2
Capt. Nathaniel MASSIE	1185 3/4	8/	474.....6.....0	3...11.....2
Thomas NOWELL	100	6/	30.....0.....0	0.....4.....6
James NOWELL	300	do.	90.....0.....0	0...13.....6
Samuel NUCKOLS	115	7/2	41.....4.....2	0.....6.....3
John NEAVES	290	7/5	107...10...10	0...16.....2
Stephen NOWLIN	150	6/9	50...12.....6	0.....7.....8
Henry NASH (Fluvanna)	100	6/6	32...10.....0	0.....4...11
William NUCKOLS, JR.	121	8/1	48...18.....1	0.....7.....5
Pouncey NUCKOLS	110	do.	44.....9.....3	0.....6.....9
Charles NUCKOLS	104	7/2	37.....5.....4	0.....5.....8
Thomas NUCKOLS	115	do.	41.....4.....2	0.....6.....3
Thomas OLIVER	273	8/1	110.....6...10	0...16.....7
Estate of Barnett OWEN, deced.	100	3/3	16.....5.....0	0.....2.....6

(page 38 contd. Goochland County Land Tax Return for 1785)

Proprietors		Quantity of Land	Price	Amt. of Land	Tax
Samuel PARSONS		523 1/3	15/	392...10.....0	2....18.....9
John PRICE	(Henrico)	268	13/6	180...18.....0	1.....7.....2
William PAYNE		201	10/9	108.....0.....9	0...16.....3
Estate of Capt. Jolly PARISH, deced.		735	4/5	165.....7.....6	1.....4...10
William POWELL		266	7/2	95.....6.....4	0...14.....4
Major POWERS		180	8/1	72...15.....0	0...11.....6
Anderson PEERS		559	do.	225...18.....7	1...13...11
Hezekiah PURYEAR		664	do.	290.....6.....7	1...19.....9
Matthew PLEASANTS		425	do.	171...15.....5	1.....5.....9
James PLEASANTS, Gent.		500	16/7	414...11.....8	3.....2.....3
Isaac PLEASANTS		676	21/6	726...14.....0	5.....9.....1
Joseph PLEASANTS		200	8/1	80...16.....8	0...12.....2
Robert PLEASANTS	(Buff.)	140	7/	49.....0.....0	0.....7.....5
Richard PLEASANTS		368	8/11	164.....1.....4	1.....4.....8
Philip PLEASANTS		121	8/1	48...18.....0	0.....7.....5
William POWERS		368	do.	148...14.....8	1.....2.....4
Thomas PLEASANTS, Mercht.		1578	16/9	1321...11.....6	9...18.....3
Dr. William PASTEUR		700	13/4	466...13.....4	3...10.....0

(page 39. Goochland County Land Tax Return for 1785)

Proprietors		Quantity of Land	Price	Amt. of Land	Tax
Estate of Francis PLEDGE, deced.		50	8/1	20.....4.....2	0.....3.....1
Estate of William PLEDGE, deced.		50	9/9	24.....7.....6	0.....3.....8
Archer PLEDGE		50	11/5	28...10...10	0.....4.....4
John PAYNE.		439	14/5	316.....8...11	2.....7.....6
Robin POOR		350	10/5	182.....5...10	1.....7.....5
Joseph POLLARD, Gent.		447	9/11	221...12.....9	1...13.....3
Mary PERKINS		161 1/2	8/1	65.....5.....6	0.....9...10
Molly PERKINS		250	do.	101.....0...10	0...15.....2
William PERKINS		200	6/1	60...16.....8	0.....9.....2
William PERKINS, JR.		265	6/	79...10.....0	0...12.....0
Estate of Walker PERKINS		171 1/2	9/10	84.....6.....5	0...12.....8
Benjamin PERKINS		250	3/3	40...12.....6	0.....6.....2
Archer PAYNE, Gent.		850	8/7	364...15...10	2...14.....9
Colo. George PAYNE (Glebe)		200	8/1	80...16.....8]	
do. of David ROSS		256	10/	128.....0.....0]	1...11.....4
Robert PLEASANTS, JR. (Henrico)		1300	10/7	687...18.....4	5.....3.....3
Sherard PARISH		162	4/1	33.....1.....6	0.....5.....0
Joel PARISH		121	4/10	29.....4...10	0.....4.....5
Aaron PARISH		71 1/4	4/4	14...11.....0	0.....2.....3
Mary PARISH		121 1/4	4/1	24...15.....2	0.....3.....9
Booker PARISH		180 1/4	do.	36.....6.....1	0.....5.....7
Samuel PRYOR, Gent.		475		187.....3.....9	1...13.....1
William PRYOR		200	12/1	120...16.....8	0...18.....2
Moses PARISH		168	4/1	34.....6.....0	0.....5.....2
Daniel POWERS		33 1/2	5/11	9...18.....3	0.....1.....6
Samuel POWELL		350	4/1	71.....9.....3	0...10.....9
Thomas POLLOCK		1092 3/4	7/3]		
do. Court House		100	12/1]	457.....5...10	3.....8.....7
Estate of George PAYNE, JR deced., (O.K.)		200	5/7	55...16.....8	0.....8.....5
John PARISH		564	5/3	148.....1.....0	1.....2.....3
Major Jonas PAYNE		800	8/1	323.....6.....8	2.....8.....6

(page 39 contd. Goochland County Land Tax Return for 1785)

Proprietors	Quantity of Land	Price	Amt. of Land	Tax
Robert PAGE	133	7/2	47...13.....2	0.....7.....2
William PAGE	133	8/1	53...15.....1	0.....8.....1
John PERKINS	527		189.....1.....4	1.....8.....5
Estate of Jesse PAYNE, deced.	597 1/2	8/5	251.....9.....0]	
do. of Capt. Joseph PAYNE	100	8/1	40.....8.....4]	2.....3...10
Capt. Joseph PAYNE	877	do.	354.....9.....1	2...13.....4
Estate of Colo. John PAYNE, deced.	2053	8/	821.....4.....0	6.....3.....3
Thomas POOR	525	5/1	133.....8.....9	1.....0.....1
Abram POOR	200	6/1	60...16.....8	0.....9.....2
William PROPHET	30	6/9	10.....2.....6	0.....1.....7
Joseph PACE	150	6/3	46...17.....6	0.....7.....1
John PACE	130	5/1	32...10.....0	0.....4...11
William PACE	200	6/1	60...16.....8	0.....9.....2
John PHILPOTT	100	4/1	20.....8.....4	0.....3.....1
Benjamin PAGE	100	6/1	30...8.....4	0.....4.....7
John PREWIT	91	7/2	32.....2.....2	0.....5...11
Archibald PLEASANTS	299	13/6	201...16.....6	1...10.....4
Capt. Humphrey PARISH	497	5/10	144...19.....2	1.....1.....9
Jesse PAYNE of ADKINS	65	6/7	21.....7...11	0.....3.....3
Alexander PARISH from Land Office	250	5/	62...10.....0	0.....9.....5
George PRIDDY	250	6/	75.....0.....0	0...11.....3

(page 40. Goochland County Land Tax Return for 1785)

Proprietors	Quantity of Land	Price	Amt. of Land	Tax
Anderson PARISH	170	3/3	27...12.....6	0.....4.....2
William PARISH	250	7/	87...16.....0	0...13.....2
Josias PAYNE, JR. of MADDOX	335	6/8	111...13.....4	0...16.....9
Estate of William ROUNTREE, deced.	108	10/5	56.....5.....0	0.....8.....6
Samuel ROUNTREE	121	do.	63.....0.....5	0.....9.....6
William ROUNTREE	121	do.	63.....0.....5	0.....9.....6
Randolph ROUNTREE	300	11/5	171.....5.....0	1.....5.....9
John REDD	247	6/6	80.....5.....6	0...12.....1
Matthew RIDDLE	70	7/	24...10.....0	0.....3.....9
Isaac RAGLAND	150	6/9	50...12.....6	0.....7.....8
William ROYSTER, Gent.	543	11/1	300...18.....3	2.....5.....2
Thomas ROYSTER	166 2/3		84.....1.....6	0...12.....5
Edward REDFORD	208	12/4	128.....5.....4	0...19.....3
Milner REDFORD	539	9/8	260...10.....4	1...19.....1
Colo. Thomas M. RANDOLPH	3052		2764.....3.....8	20...14.....8
Mary ROGERS	17	8/1	6...17.....5	0.....0.....7
David ROSS, Esqr.	9594		4166.....8.....4]	
do. for WHITFIELD's Tenement	105	4/1	21...8.....9]	31.....8.....3
William RONALD, Esqr.	1370		738.....9.....2	5...10...10
Nathaniel RAINE	244	7/5	90.....9.....9	0...13.....7
William RUTHERFORD	433	5/4	115.....9.....4	0...17.....4
William RIGSBY	50	3/3	8.....2.....6	0.....1.....3
Thomas RIDDLE	435	5/11	128...13.....9	0...19.....4
Doctor John K. READ	408	8/1	164...18.....0	1.....4.....9
Estate of Charles RICE, deced.	175	5/10	51.....0...10	0.....7.....8
Capt. Samuel RICHARDSON	536	7/2	192.....1.....4	1.....8...10
Thomas RANDOLPH, Esqr.	3000	9/9	1462...10.....0	10...19.....5

(page 40 contd. Goochland County Land Tax Return for 1785)

Proprietors	Quantity of Land	Price	Amt. of Land	Tax
George RICHARDSON	1612	6/10	550...15.....4	4.....2.....8
James ROBARDS (of LOVELL)	343	3/4	57.....3.....4	0.....8.....8
Elizabeth STODGHILL	28	12/1	16...18.....4	0.....2.....7
Thomas SHOEMAKER	200	10/1	100...16.....8	0...15.....2
Colo. John SYME	318	8/1	128...10.....6	0...19.....4
Josiah SEAY	95	6/3	29...13.....9	0.....4.....6
John SAUNDERS	20	8/1	12.....2.....6	0.....1...10
Capt. Stephen SAMPSON	566	do.	266...10.....0	1...19.....8
William SAUNDERS	25	do.	10.....2.....1	0.....1.....7
Estate of Charles SAMPSON	234	do	94...11.....6	0...14.....3
John SHELTON, Gent.	462		191.....2.....0	1.....8.....9
David SHELTON	840		440.....0.....0	3.....6.....0
Joseph SHELTON	529		314...10.....0	2.....7.....3
Major Stephen SOUTHALL	400	8/1	161...13.....4	1.....4.....3
Benjamin SADLER	100	4/1	20.....8.....4	0.....3.....1
Arthur SLAYDEN	182	do.	37.....3.....2	0.....5.....7
John SLAYDEN	100	do.	20.....8.....4	0.....3.....1
William L. SMITH.	211	7/2	75...12.....2	0...12...11
John STRONG	137 1/2	8/1	55...11.....6	0.....8.....5
Nathan STRONG	137 1/2	do.	55...11.....6	0.....8.....5
Edward SCRUGGS	100	6/1	30.....8.....4	0.....4.....7
Estate of Capt. Robert SMITH (P.tan)	40	8/1	16.....3.....4	0.....2.....6
Richard SAMPSON	250	7/3	90...12.....6	0...13.....8
James SAMMONS	230	4/7	52...14.....2	0.....8.....0
Major Robert H. SAUNDERS	330	13/6	222...15.....0	1...13.....5

(page 41. Goochland County Land Tax Return for 1785)

Proprietors	Quantity of Land	Price	Amt. of Land	Tax
Philip TINSLEY	50	12/1	30.....4.....2	0.....4.....7
Capt. Stockley TOWLES	348 1/2	8/6	148.....2.....3	1.....2.....3
Thomas TOWLES, Esqr.	348 1/2	9/4	162...12.....8	1.....4.....5
Bartholomew TURNER	200	8/1	80...16.....8	0...12.....2
Sarah THOMAS	160	4/1	32...13.....4	0.....4...11
Mary TOWLER	200	do.	40...16.....8	0.....6.....2
Cornelius TOWLER	190	do.	38...15...10	0.....5...10
William THURSTON	122	7/5	45.....4...10	0.....6...10
John THURSTON	110	7/1	38...19.....2	0.....5...11
Esther THURSTON	53	4/5	11...14.....1	0.....1...10
Henry TUGGLE	100	5/1	25.....8.....4	0.....3...10
Horatio TURPIN	1200	5/9	345.....0.....0	2...11.....9
James THOMAS	110	4/1	24...10.....0	0.....3.....9
John TOWLER	62 1/2	do.	12...15.....3	0.....1...11
Reuben THURSTON	53	5/	13.....5.....0	0.....2.....1
Benjamin THACKER	100	3/3	16.....5.....0	0.....2.....6
Sarah TIBBS (suppose)	50	7/	31.....3.....0	0.....4.....8
William UTLEY	125	8/1	50...10.....5	0.....7.....8
Obadiah UTLEY	8	do.	3.....4.....8	0.....0.....6
Ann UTLEY	116	6/4	36...14.....8	0.....5.....7
John UTLEY	125	8/1	50...10.....6	0.....7.....8
Hezekiah UTLEY	58	6/1	17...12...10	0.....2.....8

(page 41 contd. Goochland County Land Tax Return for 1785)

Proprietors		Quantity of Land	Price	Amt. of Land	Tax
Elizabeth UNDERWOOD		110	11/5	57.....1.....8	0.....8.....7
George UNDERWOOD		526	7/4	192...17.....4	1.....9.....0
Thomas UNDERWOOD, Esqr.		600	8/9	262...10.....0	1...19.....5
Estate of James UNDERWOOD, deced.		215	6/8	71...13.....4	0...10.....9
Matthew VAUGHAN		800	9/1	363.....6.....8	2...14.....6
James VAUGHAN		362	7/7	137.....5.....2	1.....0.....8
Shadrach VAUGHAN		913	8/1	369.....0.....1	2...15.....5
Richard WALMACK (MILLER's)		150	5/5	40...12.....6	0.....6.....2
Colo. John WOODSON		844	25/10	1090.....3.....4	8.....3.....7
Matthew WOODSON		1883	12/11	1216.....2.....1	9.....2.....5
Major Joseph WOODSON		535	8/1	216.....4.....7	1...12.....6
Susanna WOODWARD		500	12/1	302.....1.....8	2.....5.....4
William WOODWARD		150	9/5	70...12.....6	0...10.....8
Robert WADE		97	8/1	39.....4.....1	0.....5...11
Richard WADE		297	9/7	142.....6.....2	1.....1.....5
John WADE		73	8/1	29...10.....1	0.....4.....6
Pleasant WILLIS		278	do.	112...7.....2]	
do. for Augustin EASTIN's Tenement		180	do.	72...15.....0]	1.....7...10
Daniel WADE		200	do.	80...16.....8	0...12.....2
Eleanor WILLIS		100	6/1	30.....8.....4	0.....4.....7
William WOODALL		63	6/6	20.....9.....6	0.....3.....7
William WEBBER	(Preacher)	177	6/4	56.....1.....0	0.....8.....5
Edward WILLIS		160	8/1	64...13.....4	0.....9.....9
Thomas WOODSON		200	12/1	120...16.....8	0...18.....2
Nathaniel WEBSTER		170	6/6	55.....5.....0	0.....8.....4
Robert WINGFIELD		90	8/1	36.....7.....6	0.....5.....6
David WEBSTER		75	10/6	39...17.....6	0.....6.....0
Joseph WOODSON,	(Geneto)	225	9/	101.....5.....0	0...15.....3
Estate of Joseph WOODSON, deced.		222	10/	111.....0.....0	0...16.....8
Joseph WOODSON, JR.	(Major)	400		150...17.....6	1.....2.....7
Dorothy WATKINS		170	8/1	68...14.....2	0...10.....4
Joseph WATKINS		544		260...19.....7	1...19.....3

(page 42. Goochland County Land Tax Return for 1785)

Thomas WATKINS		583	8/1	235...12.....7	1...15.....5
Peter WALKER	(Geneto)	230	do.	92...19.....2	0...14.....0
Benjamin WATKINS		238	9/5	112.....1.....2	0...16...10
John WATKINS		519	8/11	231.....7.....9	1...14.....9
William WEBBER		340	10/6	178...10.....0	1.....6...10
Benjamin WOODSON	(Fluvanna)	205	9/1	93.....2.....1	0...14.....0
Benjamin WATKINS		156	9/5	73.....9.....0	0...11.....1
Henry WHITLOW, JR.		50	8/1	20.....4.....2	0.....3.....1
Henry WHITLOW, SENR.		99	do.	40.....0.....3	0.....6.....1
William WILLIS (of David)		63 1/2	7/3	23.....0.....5	0.....3.....6
John WITT		17	8/1	6...17.....5	0.....1.....0
Tucker WOODSON		600	17/8	530.....0.....0	3...19.....6
John WOODSON	(C. Ferry)	1265		647...15.....5	4...17.....2
Henry WALMACK		100	8/1	40.....8.....4	0.....6.....1
Peter WALKER	(Constable)	116	4/1	23...13.....8	0.....3.....7

(page 42 contd. Goochland County Land Tax Return for 1785)

Proprietors		Quantity of Land	Price	Amt. of Land	Tax
Isaac WINSTON	(Hanover)	735	8/1	297.....1.....3	2.....4.....7
Drury WILLIAMS		500	do.	202.....1.....8]	
do. for WHITLOCK's Tenement		100	6/1	30.....8.....4]	1...15.....0
John WALKER		100	3/3	16.....5.....0	0.....2...6
William WALKER		94	4/2	19...11.....8	0.....3.....0
Thomas WAFFORD		540	4/6	121...10.....0	0...18.....3
Estate of Colo. Valentine WOOD		2762		1076.....2.....2	8.....1.....6
William WILLIAMS		50	4/1	10.....4.....2	0.....1.....7
John WILLIAMS	(D.C.)	536		129.....8.....8	0...19.....6
John WILLIAMSON		200	4/1	40...16.....8	0.....6.....2
Lewis WILBOURNE		100	do.	20.....8.....4	0.....3.....2
Dabney WADE		300	6/3	93...15.....0	0...14.....1
Estate of William WADE, deced.		215	7/3	77...18.....9	0...11.....9
John WOODSON	(Meadow)	300	8/1	121.....5.....0	0...18.....3
William WILBOURNE		200	3/3	32...10.....0	0.....4...11
John WILLIAMS		250	6/6	81.....5.....0	0...12.....3
James WILLIAMS		10	7/	3...10.....0	0.....0.....6
Solomon WILLIAMS		103	do.	36.....1.....0	0.....5.....6
Philip WILLIAMS		200	6/	60.....0.....0	0.....9.....0
Capt. John WARE		925	6/6	300...12.....6	2.....5.....1
William WOODALL		63	do.	20.....9.....6	0.....3.....1
Ann YOUNGER		100	3/3	16.....5.....0	0.....2...6

                                        THO: F. BATES   ]
                                        ARCHD. PLEASANTS   ] Commrs.

        July 18, 1785. Rec;d of the Commrs. of the Tax, the Sheriff's Collecting List of the Land Tax
in Goochland County amounting to six hundred twenty four pounds, fifteen shillings and 11d specie
also a List; also a List of the Certificate Tax in said County amounting to eight hundred forty three
pounds, nineteen shillings and seven pence

                                        STEPHEN SAMPSON, Shf.

(page 43).

        A State of the Land Tax in Goochland County for the Sheriff's Collection for November 1st
1786.

Proprietors	Quantity of Land	Price	Amt. of Land	Certificate Tax	Specie Tax
Colo. Richard ADAMS, Henrico	1982	8/9	867.....2.....6	8...13.....6	13.....0.....2
Mary ADKINSON	310	8/1	125.....5...10	1.....5.....2	1...17.....8
James ALLEN	175	4/7	34...16.....3	0.....7.....0	0...10.....6
David ALVIS	125	4/1	25...10.....5	0.....5.....2	0.....7.....9
William ANDERSON, London	1500	8/	600.....0.....0	6.....0.....0	9.....0.....0

(page 43 contd. Goochland County Land Tax Return for 1786

Proprietors	Quantity of Land	Price	Amt. of Land	Certificate Tax	Specie Tax
John BOWLES (of J. WILLIAMS)	151 1/4		37.....5.....0	0.....7.....6	0...11.....3
Charles BATES	350	12/1	211.....9.....2	2.....2.....4	3.....3.....6
William BARNETT	200	7/6	72...10.....0	0...14.....6	1.....1.....8
Susanna BIBB	248	8/1	100.....4.....8	1.....0.....6	1...10.....9
John BLACKWELL	98 1/2	do.	39...16.....3	0.....8.....0	0...12.....0
Elijah BRUMFIELD	200	10/3	102...10.....0	1.....0.....6	1...10.....9
John BRUMFIELD	125	8/1	50...10.....5	0...10.....2	0...15.....2
John BRADSHAW	450	6/9	151...17.....6	1...10.....5	2.....5.....8
Callam BAILEY	150	4/1	30...12.....6	0.....6.....2	0.....9.....4
John BOWDRY	10	do.	2.....0...10	0.....0.....6	0.....0.....8
William BURGESS	100	do.	20.....8.....4	0.....4.....2	0.....6.....2
John BOLLING, SENR.	1440		677.....7.....6	6...15.....6	10.....3.....4
John BOLLING, JUNR.	600	9/8	290.....0.....0	2...10.....0	4.....7.....0
Thomas BOLLING (Chesterfield)	3599 1/3		4029...13...10	40.....6.....0	60.....8...10
Claibourne BRADSHAW	138	8/1	55...15.....6	0...11.....2	0...16...10
Sarah BRADSHAW	69	7/2	24...14.....6	0.....5.....0	0.....7.....6
Thomas F. BATES	500	13/10	345...16.....8	3.....9.....2	5.....3...10
William BLUNKALL	3 1/2	16/2	2...16.....7	0.....0.....8	0.....1.....0
William BRITT	850	4/9	201...17.....6	2.....0.....5	3.....0.....8
Capt. John BRITT	245	7/4	89...16.....8	0...18.....0	1.....7.....0
William BOWMAN	100	4/1	20.....8.....4	0.....4.....2	0.....6.....2
Gideon BOWLES	350	6/8	116...13.....4	1.....3.....4	1...15.....0
Charles BOWLES (of Jesse LACY)	133 1/2	4/1	32...16.....5	0.....6.....8	0.....9...10
William BUSBY	150		27...14.....2	0.....5.....8	0.....8.....6
John BARNETT	200	7/5	74.....3.....4	0...15.....0	1.....2.....6
James CURD	568		238...12.....0	2.....7.....9	3...11.....5
Richard CROUCH	257	8/1	103...17.....5	1.....0...10	1...10...11
Philip CHILDERS	276	4/1	56.....7.....0	0...11.....5	0...17.....0
Thomas CHANCELLOR	125	6/6	40...12.....6	0.....8.....3	0...12.....4
Judith CHEADLE	299	13/6	201...16.....6	2.....0.....6	3.....0.....8
Daniel CLARKE	100	6/1	30.....8.....4	0.....6.....2	0.....9.....2
Richard COCKE	580 1/2	14/10	430....3.....4	4.....6.....1	6.....9.....1
Estate of Allen COCKE, deced.	1195	14/11	891.....5.....5	8...18.....4	13.....7.....6
John CLARKE	44	6/2	13...11.....4	0.....2...10	0.....4.....3

(page 44. Goochland County Land Tax Return for 1786)

Proprietors	Quantity of Land	Price	Amt. of Land	Certificate Tax	Specie Tax
Turner CLARKE	90	6/1	27.....7.....6	0.....5.....6	0.....8.....4
Joseph CLARKE	160		45...15.....0	0.....9.....2	0...13...10
Susanna CROUCH	100	8/1	40.....8.....4	0.....8.....2	0...12.....2
James COCKE	300	do.	121.....5.....0	1.....4.....4	1...16.....6
Edward CARTER	34	do.	13...10.....4	0.....2...10	0.....4.....2
William CLARKSON	50	9/9	24.....7.....6	0.....5.....0	0.....7.....4
Colo. John CURD	609	10/9	327.....6.....9	3.....5.....8	4...18.....4
Capt. Edmund CURD	340		181.....0...10	1...16.....3	2...14.....4
Sarah CURD	211	8/1	56...11.....8	0...11.....3	0...16...10
Benjamin COCKE	122	do.	49.....6.....2	0...10.....0	0...14...10
James COCKE, (P.tan)	54	do.	21...16.....6	0.....2.....3	0.....3.....4
Thomas COCKE	140	do.	56...11.....8	0...11.....4	0...17.....0
Martha CARR	499	do.	201...13.....7	2.....0.....6	3.....0.....8

(page 44 contd. Goochland County Land Tax Return for 1786)

Proprietors	Quantity of Land	Price	Amt. of Land	Certificate Tax	Specie Tax
Benjamin CRENSHAW	440	5/11	130.....3....4	1.....6.....2	1...19.....2
Nathaniel CAWLEY	60	8/1	24.....5....0	0.....5.....0	0.....7....4
Mary COLEY	100	do.	40.....8....4	0.....8.....2	0...12.....2
Susanna COLEY	100	4/1	20.....8....4	0.....4.....2	0.....6....2
Ann COLEY	100	8/1	40.....8....4	0.....8.....2	0...12.....2
Sally COLEY	100	6/1	30.....8....4	0.....6.....2	0.....9.....2
Francis COLEY	106 1/2	6/3	33.....2....6	0.....6.....8	0...10.....2
Francis CLARKE for Mr. DOUGLAS	150	4/1	30...12....6	0.....6.....4	0.....8...10
Estate of Robert CARDIN, deced.	200	5/1	50...16....8	0...10.....3	0...15.....4
John CLEMENTS	116	5/10	33...16....8	0.....6.....8	0...10.....2
Stephen CROUCH	200	5/1	50...16....8	0...10.....3	0...15.....4
Bryant CONLEY	150	5/5`	40...12....6	0.....8.....2	0...12.....4
Bowler COCKE, Esqr.	1509		1165...12.....0	11...13.....2	17.....9....6
Samuel COSBY	225	4/5	50...12....6	0...10.....2	0...15.....4
Walter CLOPTON	220	8/1	88...18....4	0...17...10	1.....6...10
James CLEMENTS	179	6/4	56...13....8	0...11.....5	0...17.....2
Roger CARRELL	83	4/1	16...18...11	0.....3.....6	0.....5.....2
Gideon CAWTHON	220	6/8	73.....6....8	0...15.....4	1.....3.....0
Edward COX	200		66...13....4	0...13.....6	0...19.....3
David CRENSHAW	238	6/2	73.....7....8	0...14.....9	1.....2.....2
Judith CARTER	100	4/10	24.....3....4	0.....4...10	0.....7....4
Turner CHRISTIAN	235	6/2	72.....7....0	0...14.....6	1.....1.....8
George CROWDAS	50	7/	17...10....0	0.....3.....6	0.....5.....3
Benjamin CLOPTON	400		150...16....8	1...10.....3	2.....5.....4
John CHILTON	100	4/	20.....0....0	0.....4.....0	0.....6.....0
Edward CARRINGTON	500	14/6	362...10.....0	3...12.....6	5.....8.....9
John DOWDY	122	7/5	45.....4...10	0.....9.....1	0...13.....8

(page 45. Goochland County Land Tax Return for 1786)

Proprietors	Quantity of Land	Price	Amt. of Land	Certificate Tax	Specie Tax
Thomas DRUMWRIGHT	1030	6/2	317...11.....8	3.....3.....8	4...15.....4
John DAVIS, (Hanover)	200		72.....1....8	0...14.....6	1.....1.....8
Ichabod DANIEL	200	5/8	56...13....4	0...11.....4	0...17.....0
Reverend William DOUGLAS	500	6/1	152.....1....8	1...10.....6	2.....5.....8
David DAVIS	100	7/	35.....0.....0	0.....7.....0	0...10.....6
Noton DICKINSON	400	3/6	70.....0.....0	0...14.....0	1.....1.....0
Susanna DAVIS	200	do.	35.....0.....0	0.....7.....0	0...10.....6
John ELLIS (Henrico)	392	12/1	236...16....8	2.....7.....4	3...11.....0
Stephen ELLIS	97	16/2	78.....8.....2	0...15.....9	1.....3.....8
David ELLIS	372	8/1	151...7.....3	1...10.....4	2.....5.....6
William EDWARDS	80	4/1	16.....6....8	0.....3.....4	0.....5.....0
Joseph EVANS	134	6/1	40...15.....2	0.....8.....2	0...12.....4
Francis EVANS	133 1/2	5/5	36.....3.....2	0.....7.....4	0...11.....0
Thomas ELDRIDGE	203	8/1	82.....0...11	0...16.....2	1.....4.....4
David ENGLAND	80	6/1	24.....6.....8	0.....4...11	0.....7.....4
Benjamin EAST	121 1/2	8/1	49.....2.....2	0...10.....0	0...14...10
Thomas EDWARDS	50	6/6	16.....5....0	0.....3.....4	0.....5.....0
Thomas EMMERSON	200		42...10.....0	0.....8.....6	0...12.....9
Henry EMMERSON	240	6/6	78.....0.....0	0...15.....8	1.....3.....5

(page 45 contd. Goochland County Land Tax Return for 1786)

Proprietors	Quantity of Land	Price	Amt of. Land	Certificate Tax	Specie Tax
Thomas EMMERSON, JUNR.	100	6/6	32...10.....0	0.....6.....6	0.....9.....9
Joseph ELAM	50	10/	25.....0.....0	0.....5.....0	0.....7.....6
William FARRAR	886	10/5	461.....9.....2	4...12.....4	6...18.....6
John FARRAR	298	10/9	160.....3.....6	1...12.....1	2.....8.....2
William FORD	200	8/1	80...16.....8	0...16.....2	1.....4.....4
Elizabeth FORD	233	do.	94.....3.....5	0...18...11	1.....8.....4
Joseph FARRAR	56	12/1	33...16.....8	0.....6...11	0...10.....4
Mary FRAYSER	205	8/1	82...17.....1	0...16.....8	1.....5.....0
Reuben FORD	147	do.	59.....8.....3	0...12.....0	0...18.....0
John FARISH	100	6/1	30.....8.....4	0.....6.....2	0.....9.....2
Estate of Colo. Tarlton FLEMING, deced.	1900	20/2	1915...16.....8	19.....3.....2	28...14...10
Honble. William FLEMING, Esqr.	390	20/4	396...10.....0	3...19.....4	5...19.....0
Colo. Charles FLEMING	390	do.	396...10.....0	3...19.....4	5...19.....0
John FURLONG	100	3/6	17...10.....0	0.....3.....6	0.....5.....4
Hugh FRENCH	250	3/4	77...10.....4	0...15.....6	1.....3.....4
Daniel FORD	90	8/	36.....0.....0	0.....7.....2	0...10...10
John GLASS	62		21...19.....0	0.....4.....2	0.....6.....2
John Tayloe GRIFFIN	3311		3902.....6.....5	39.....6.....5	58...10...10
John GORDEN	186		77...18.....3	0...15.....8	1.....3.....5

(page 46. Goochland County Land Tax Return for 1786).

Proprietors	Quantity of Land	Price	Amt of. Land	Certificate Tax	Specie Tax
Henry GRAY	100	8/1	40.....8.....4	0.....8.....2	0...12.....2
John GUERRANT, Gent.	636		334.....2.....6	3.....6...11	5.....0.....6
John GILLAM (Pr. George)	500	9/9	243...15.....0	2.....8.....9	3...13.....2
Capt. William GEORGE	325		90...14.....7	0...18.....2	1.....7.....4
John GRAY	85	10/3	44.....8.....4	0.....8...11	0...13.....6
Major John GUERRANT	442		184.....5.....3	1...16...11	2...15.....6
James GEORGE	100	8/1	40.....8.....4	0.....8.....2	0...12.....2
John GILLAM, SENR.	546	7/9	211...11.....6	2.....2.....4	3.....3.....6
David GRANTHAM	35	7/6	13.....2.....6	0.....2.....8	0.....4.....0
Robert GILLAM (Pr. George)	1021	3/4	2699.....2.....6	26...19...11	40.....9...10
Stephen GRANGE	80	7/2	28...13.....4	0.....5...10	0.....8.....8
Robert GEORGE	150	6/	45.....0.....0	0.....9.....0	0...13.....6
Anselm GEORGE	175	4/	35.....0.....0	0.....7.....0	0...10.....6
John GILBERT	150	3/6	26.....5.....0	0.....5.....4	0.....8.....0
Daniel GRUBBS	150	do.	26.....5.....0	0.....5.....4	0.....8.....0
William GAY	600	2/3	957.....7...10	9...11.....6	14.....7.....3
David HUDSON	443	1/4	200...15.....4	2.....0.....2	3.....0.....2
John HYLTON	411	10/9	220...18.....3	2.....4.....3	3.....6.....4
John HUSON	47	5/	11...15.....0	0.....2.....5	0.....3.....8
Francis Eppes HARRIS	440	1/2	391.....3.....3	3...18.....5	5...17.....6
John HINES	330	9/4	154.....0.....0	1...10...11	2.....6.....4
Thomas HARDING	543		289.....0.....6	2...17...10	4.....6.....9
Strangeman HUTCHINS	55	8/1	22.....4.....7	0.....4.....5	0.....6.....8
Capt. Thomas HATCHER	510	9/9	248...12.....6	2.....9...10	3...14.....8
James HUNNICUTT	287	8/1	115...19...11	1.....3.....3	1...14...10
Benjamin HUGHES	627	do.	253.....8.....3	2...10.....9	3...16.....2

(page 46 contd. Goochland County Land Tax Return for 1786)

Proprietors	Quantity of Land	Price	Amt. of Land	Certificate Tax	Specie Tax
Capt. Gideon HATCHER	360	9/7	172...10.....0	1...14.....6	2...11...10
William HUGHES (Hanover)	115	9/2	52...14.....2	0...10...7	0...15...10
Giles HARDING	316	8/6	134.....6.....0	1.....7.....0	2.....0.....4
William HAY	521		293.....0.....5	2...18.....8	4.....7...11
John HENDERSON	200	4/1	40...16.....8	0.....8.....2	0...12.....4
John HUMBER	561	8/1	226...14.....9	2.....5.....5	3.....8.....2
Zachariah HADEN	660	5/1	167...15.....0	1...13.....8	2...10.....6
Drury HATCHER	5 1/2	4/6	1.....4.....9	0.....0.....4	0.....0.....6
Jesse HODGES	160	5/7	44...13.....4	0.....9.....0	0...13.....6
John HILL (Amherst)	150	6/1	91.....5.....0	0...18.....3	1.....7.....4
Mesheck HICKS	450	6/4	142...10.....0	1.....8.....6	2.....2...10
Harrison HARRIS	530	7/4	194.....6.....8	1...18...11	2...18.....4
Mary HICKS	300	6/1	91.....5.....0	0...18.....2	1.....7.....4
Francis HOUCHINS	117	5/10	34.....2.....6	0.....6...11	0...10.....4

(page 47. Goochland county Land Tax Return for 1786)

Proprietors	Quantity of Land	Price	Amt. of Land	Certificate Tax	Specie Tax
Charles HOUCHINS, JR.	117	5/10	34.....2.....6	0.....6...11	0...10.....4
James HOLMAN	275	5/11	81.....7.....1	0...16.....3	1.....4.....6
William HODGES	100	4/10	24.....3.....4	0.....4...11	0.....7.....4
Capt. William HOLMAN	590	4/1	120.....9.....2	1.....4.....2	1...16.....2
Colo. John HOPKINS	1650	6/7	534.....2.....6	5.....6...11	8.....0.....5
Lewis HERNDON	300	6/9	101.....5.....0	1.....0.....4	1...10.....6
John HERNDON	199	7/4	72...19.....4	0...14.....8	1.....2.....0
John HOPPER	210	7/2	75.....5.....0	0...15.....2	1.....2.....8
Lucy HODGES	50	5/1	12...14.....2	0.....2.....7	0.....3...10
John HOLLAND	272 1/4	7/3	98...13...10	0...19...10	1.....9.....8
William HICKS	125	do.	45.....6.....3	0.....9.....7	0...13...10
James HOWARD	136	do.	54.....6.....0	0...10...11	0...16.....4
John HOWARD	166	6/	49...10.....0	0...10.....0	0...15.....0
Anthony HADEN (Fluvanna)	400	4/	80.....0.....0	0...16.....0	1.....4.....0
Nathaniel HOLLAND	200	7/3	72...10.....0	0...14.....6	1.....1...10
John HANES (Hanover)	100	8/	40.....0.....0	0.....8.....0	0...12.....0
John JOHNSON (Henrico)	611 1/2		244.....5.....8	2.....9.....0	3...13.....5
Charles JOHNSON	124	6/6	40.....6.....0	0.....8.....2	0...12.....2
Charles JOHNSON, JR.	220	11/5	125...11.....8	1.....5.....2	1...17...10
David JOHNSON (Geneto)	115	8/1	46.....9.....7	0.....9.....4	0...14.....0
John JOHNSON (do.)	271	9/4	126.....9.....4	1.....5.....4	1...18.....0
Isham JOHNSON (do.)	115	9/2	52...14.....2	0...10.....8	0...16.....0
Richard JOHNSON	150	do.	68...15.....0	0...13...10	1.....0.....8
William ISBELL	792	5/7	221.....2.....0	2.....4.....2	3.....6.....4
Estate of Joseph JOHNSON for Mr. DOUGLAS	500	4/1	102.....1.....8	1.....0.....5	1...10.....8
Estate of Benjamin JOHNSON (Byrd)	140	7/	49.....0.....0	0.....9...11	0...14...10
William JOHNSON (do.)	250	6/1	76.....0...10	0...15.....3	1.....2...10
Honble. Thomas JEFFESON, Esqr.	612	8/1	247.....7.....0	2.....9.....6	3...14.....2
Archibald JARRETT	353	4/9	83...16.....9	0...16.....9	1.....5.....2
do. for JENNINGS	201	4/1	41.....0.....9	0.....8.....2	0...12.....4
Devereux JARRETT	290	do.	59.....4.....9	0...11...11	0...17...10
David JARRETT	250	do.	51.....0...10	0...10.....2	0...15.....4

(page 47 contd. Goochland County Land Tax Return for 1786)

Proprietors	Quantity of Land	Price	Amt. of Land	Certificate Tax	Specie Tax
Charles JOHNSON	200	7/2	71...13.....4	0...14.....3	1.....1.....6

(page 48. Goochland County Land Tax Return for 1786)

Proprietors	Quantity of Land	Price	Amt. of Land	Certificate Tax	Specie Tax
Sarah JORDAN	75	16/2	60...12.....6	0...12.....2	0...18.....4
David JOHNSON (of Charles)	150	4/	30.....0.....0	0.....6.....0	0.....9.....0
William JAMES (of Thomas RIDDLE)	100	5/11	29...11.....8	0.....6.....0	0.....9.....0
Susanna LAPRADE	300	10/8	160.....0.....0	1...12.....0	2.....8.....0
John LAPRADE	128	do.	68.....5.....6	0...13.....8	1.....0.....6
Capt. Elisha LEAKE	818	9/7	391...19.....2	3...18.....3	5...17.....8
John LAYNE	50	4/1	10.....4.....2	0.....2.....1	0.....3.....2
John LEWIS (C. Maker)	200	8/1	80...16.....8	0...16.....2	1.....4.....4
Ayres LAYNE	155	6/8	51...13.....4	0...10.....4	0...15.....6
Henry LAYNE	100	4/1	20.....8.....4	0.....4.....2	0.....6.....2
Matthew LACY	97	4/10	23.....8...10	0.....4.....9	0.....7.....2
Mary LAYNE	50	4/1	10.....4.....2	0.....2.....1	0.....3.....2
Benjamin LACY	88	do.	21...12.....8	0.....4.....4	0.....6.....6
Sarah LACY	138	5/	34...10.....0	0.....6...11	0...10.....6
Samuel LAMAY	81	4/1	16...10.....9	0.....3.....6	0.....5.....2
Armiger LILLY (Fluvanna)	400	do.	81...13.....4	0...16.....3	1.....4.....6
Howel LEWIS	490	7/	171...10.....0	1...14.....4	2...11.....6
Colo. Robert LEWIS	1105	13/6	745...17.....6	7.....9.....2	11.....3.....9
Estate of John LEE, deced.	350	4/8	81...13.....4	0...16.....3	1.....4.....4
William LEWIS (R.C.)	100	4/1	20.....8.....4	0.....4.....2	0.....6.....2
Capt. Josiah LEAKE	800	8/1	323.....6.....8	3.....4.....8	4...17.....0
Joseph LEWIS	860 1/3		309.....1.....2	3.....1...11	4...12.....9
John LAURENCE	50	4/6	11.....5.....0	0.....2.....4	0.....3.....6
Joseph LOWRY	200	3/6	35.....0.....0	0.....7.....0	0...10.....6
Matthew LOWRY	400	4/	80.....0.....0	0...16.....0	1.....4.....0
Stephen G. LETCHER	49	8/1	19...16.....4	0.....4.....0	0.....6.....0
Yancy LIPSCOMB	350 1/2	8/6	148...19.....3	1.....9...10	2.....4...10
Colo. Nathaniel G. MORRIS	400	9/1	181...13.....4	1...16.....4	2...14.....6
John MADDOX	150	6/9	50...12.....6	0...10.....2	0...15.....4
Martin MIMS	194	8/1	78.....8.....2	0...15...10	1.....3.....8
Thomas MITCHELL (Mercht.)	473 1/4		110.....4.....1	1.....2.....1	1...13.....2
Estate of Edward MATTHEWS, deced.	323		118...14.....9	1.....3.....6	1...15.....3
William MATTHEWS	200	7/5	74.....3.....4	0...14...11	1.....2.....6
Edward MATTHEWS	200	do.	74.....3.....4	0...14...11	1.....2.....6
Capt. William MILLER	440 1/2		174.....9.....6	1...15.....0	2.....12.....6
Thomas MILLER	553 1/2		259...10.....8	2...12.....0	3...18.....0
Estate of David MIMS, deced.	315	7/5	116...16.....3	1.....3.....9	1...15.....2

(page 49. Goochland County Land Tax Return for 1786)

Proprietors	Quantity of Land	Price	Amt. of Land	Certificate Tax	Specie Tax
Thomas MASSIE (Overseer)	347	7/	121.....9.....0	1.....4.....4	1...16.....6
Colo. Thomas MERIWETHER, Richmond	300 1/2	8/1	121.....9.....1	1.....4.....4	1...16.....6
Thoms MARTIN (taken from FluvannA)	100	do.	40.....8.....4	0.....8.....2	0...12.....3
William McCAUL	81	14/1	57.....0.....7	0...11.....4	0...17.....2
Amos L. MOORE	260	10/	130.....0.....0	1.....6.....0	1...19.....0

(page 49 contd. Goochland County Land Tax Return for 1786)

Proprietors	Quantity of Land	Price	Amt. of of Land	Certificate Tax	Specie Tax
Stokes McCAUL	295	8/1	119.....4.....7	1.....3...11	1...16.....0
Mary MILLER	426	8/10	188.....3.....0	1...17.....9	2...16.....6
Edward McBRIDE	200	6/1	60...16.....8	0...12.....2	0...18.....4
Revd. Daniel McCALLA	200	do.	60...16.....8	0...12.....2	0...18.....4
Charles MASSIE	300	8/1	121.....5.....0	1.....4.....4	1...16.....6
Ann MITCHELL	291	6/5	93.....7.....3	0...18.....8	1.....8.....0
David MARTIN	235	do.	75.....7...11	0...15.....2	1.....2.....8
Paul MEACHUM	295	5/6	81.....2.....6	0...16.....4	1.....4.....6
Benjamin MOSBY	200	5/1	50...16.....8	0...10.....2	0...15.....4
William MITCHELL, Gent.	865 1/2	8/1	349...12.....1	3...10.....0	5.....5.....0
Gideon MIMS	360	7/5	133...10.....0	1.....7.....3	2.....0...10
Elizabeth MIMS	250	7/3	90...12.....6	0...18.....3	1.....7.....4
Sarah MIMS	50	6/1	15.....4.....2	0.....3.....2	0.....4.....8
John MARTIN	700	6/2	215...16.....8	2.....3.....2	3.....4...10
Ann MERRIAN	400	4/1	81...13.....4	0...16.....4	1.....4.....6
Wright MOURLAND	100	6/11	34...11.....8	0.....7.....0	0...10.....6
Capt. David MULLINS	197	8/1	79...12.....5	0...16.....0	1.....4.....0
Capt. Henry MULLINS	400	7/2	143.....6.....8	1.....8.....9	2.....3.....0
Conally MULLINS of the Estate	350	6/5	112.....5...10	1.....2.....6	1...13.....9
Samuel MOSS	200	4/	40.....0.....0	0.....8.....0	0...12.....0
William MARTIN	400	6/	120.....0.....0	1.....4.....0	1...16.....0
Major Thomas MASSIE	2285	do.	685...10.....0	6...17.....2	10.....5...10
John MOSS	75	8/	30.....0.....0	0.....6.....0	0.....9.....0
William MASSIE	223	7/3	80...16.....9	0...16.....2	1.....4.....4
Capt. Nathaniel MASSIE	955 3/4	8/	382.....6.....0	3...16.....6	5...14.....8
Matthew NIGHTINGALE	59 3/4	9/10	29.....6.....9	0.....6.....0	0.....9.....0
Thomas NOWELL	100	6/	30.....0.....0	0.....6.....0	0.....9.....0
James NOWELL	300	do.	90.....0.....0	0...18.....0	1.....7.....0
Samuel NUCHOLDS	115	7/2	41.....4.....2	0.....8.....3	0...12.....6
John NEAVES	290	7/5	107...10...10	1.....1.....8	1...12.....4
Stephen NOWLIN	150	6/9	50...12.....6	0...10.....2	0...15.....4
Henry NASH (Fluvanna)	100	6/6	32...10.....0	0.....6.....6	0.....9.....9
William NUCHOLDS, JR.	121	8/1	48...18.....1	0.....9...10	0...14...10
Pouncy NUCHOLDS	110	do.	44.....9.....2	0.....9.....0	0...13.....5

(page 50. Goochland County Land Tax Return for 1786)

Proprietors	Quantity of Land	Price	Amt. of of Land	Certificate Tax	Specie Tax
Charles NUCHOLDS	104	7/2	37.....5.....4	0.....7.....6	0...11.....4
Thomas NUCHOLDS	115	do.	41.....4.....2	0.....8.....4	0...12.....6
Thomas OLIVER	273	8/1	110.....6...10	1.....2.....2	1...13.....2
Estate of Barnet OWEN, deced.	100	3/3	16.....5.....0	0.....3.....4	0.....5.....0
Colo. Josiah PARKER					
(of Ann COCKE)	986 1/2	14/10	731...13.....1	7.....6.....4	10...19.....8
Sherard PARISH	291		63.....4.....0	0...12...10	0...19.....3
William PURKINS (of John)	254	5/10	74.....1.....8	0...15.....0	1.....2.....6
John PURKINS	263 1/2		94...10.....8	0...19.....0	1.....8.....6
Archer PURKINS	263 1/2		94...10.....8	0...19.....0	1.....8.....6
Capt. Humphry PARISH	606		203...10...11	2.....0...10	3.....1.....2

(page 50 contd. Goochland County Land Tax Return for 1786)

Proprietors	Quantity of Land	Price	Amt. of of Land	Certificate Tax	Specie Tax
William PAYNE	92	10/9	49....9.....0	0...10.....0	0...15.....0
John PAGE	50	6/	15.....0.....0	0.....3.....0	0.....4.....6
Charles N. PURKINS	160	8/	64.....0.....0	0...12...11	0...19.....4
Hezekiah PURYEAR	654	8/1]			
do. of John JONES	100	4/]	310.....6.....7	3...2.....2	4...13.....2
Richard PLEASANTS	728		356.....1.....4	3...11.....3	5.....6...10
Capt. Joseph PAYNE	734		296.....4...10	2...19.....3	4.....8...11
Estate of Colo. John PAYNE, deced.	1953	8/	781.....4.....0	7...16.....3	11...14.....6
Abram PREWIT (Jno. MILLER's)	150	5/5	40...12.....6	0.....8.....2	0...12.....3
Thomas PLEASANTS (Mercht.)	1833		1456.....9...11	14...11.....4	21...17.....0
Isaac PLEASANTS	539	21/6	579.....8.....6	5...16.....0	8...14.....0
Matthew PLEASANTS	250	8/1	101.....0...10	1.....0.....3	1...10.....4
Meredith PARISH	100	4/6	22...10.....0	0.....4.....6	0.....6.....9
William PROFIT	30		10.....7.....6	0.....2.....2	0.....3.....3
Archer PAYNE, Gent.	950		381.....0...10	3...16.....3	5...14.....4
Samuel PARSONS	523 1/3	15/	392...10.....0	3...18.....6	5...17.....9
John PRICE (Henrico)	268	13/6	180...18.....0	1...16.....2	2...14.....4
William POWELL	266	7/2	95.....6.....4	0...19.....1	1.....8.....8
Major POWERS	180	8/1	72...15.....0	0...14.....8	1.....2.....0
Anderson PEERS	559	do.	225...18.....7	2.....5.....3	3.....7...10
James PLEASANTS, Gent.	500	16/7	414...11.....8	4.....3.....0	6.....4.....6
Joseph PLEASANTS	200	8/1	80...16.....8	0...16.....2	1.....4.....4
Robert PLEASANTS (Buff)	140	7/	49.....0.....0	0.....9...11	0...14...10
Philip PLEASANTS	151		58...13.....0	0...11...10	0...17...10
William POWERS	368	6/6	148...14.....8	1.....9...11	2.....4.....8
Doctor William PASTEUR	700	13/4	466...13.....4	4...13.....4	7.....0.....0
Estate of Francis PLEDGE, deced.	50	8/1	20.....4.....2	0.....4.....1	0.....6.....2
Estate of William PLEDGE, deded	50	9/9	24.....7.....6	0.....4...11	0.....7.....4

(page 51. Goochland County Land Tax Return for 1786)

Proprietors	Quantity of Land	Price	Amt. of of Land	Certificate Tax	Specie Tax
Archer PLEDGE	50	11/5	28...10...10	0.....5...10	0.....8.....8
John PAYNE	439	14/5	316.....8...11	3.....3.....4	4...15.....0
Robin POOR	350	10/5	182.....5...10	1...16.....6	2...14...10
Joseph POLLARD, Gent.	447	9/11	221...12.....9	2.....4.....3	3.....6.....6
Mary PURKINS	250	do.	101.....0...10	1.....0.....2	1...10.....4
William PURKINS	200	6/1	60...16.....8	0...12.....2	0...18.....4
William PURKINS, JR.	265	6/	79...10.....0	0...16.....0	1.....4.....0
Estate of Walker PURKINS, deced.	111 3/4	9/10	54...18...11	0...11.....0	0...16.....6
Benjamin PURKINS	250	3/3	40...12.....6	0.....9.....2	0...12.....4
Colo. George PAYNE	456		208...16.....8	2.....1...10	3.....2.....8
Robert PLEASANTS, JR.	1300	10/7	687...18.....4	6...17.....9	10.....6.....6
Joel PARISH	121	4/10	29.....4...10	0.....5...11	0.....8...10
Aaron PARISH	71 1/4	4/1	14...11.....0	0.....3.....0	0.....4.....6
Mary PARISH	121 1/4	do.	24...15.....2	0.....5.....0	0.....7.....6
Booker PARISH	180 1/4	do.	36.....6.....1	0.....7.....5	0...11.....2
Samuel PRYOR, Gent.	475		187.....3.....9	1...17.....5	2...16.....2
William PRYOR	200	12/1	120...16.....8	1.....4.....2	1...16.....4
Moses PARISH	168	4/1	34.....6.....0	0.....6...11	0...10.....4
Daniel POWERS	33 1/2	5/11	9...18.....3	0.....2.....0	0.....3.....0
Samuel POWELL	350	4/1	71.....9.....2	0...14.....4	1.....1.....6

(page 51 contd. Goochland County Land Tax Return for 1786)

Proprietors	Quantity of Land		Price	Amt. of of Land	Certificate Tax	Specie Tax
Thomas POLLOCK	617 3/4	7/3		223...18.....9	2.....4...10	3.....7.....3
Estate of George PAYNE, O.K., deced	200	5/7		55...16.....8	0...11.....2	0...16...10
Robert PAYNE	800	8/1		323.....6.....8	3.....4.....8	4...17.....0
Robert PAGE	133	8/1		47...13.....2	0.....9.....7	0...14.....4
William PAGE	133	8/1		53...15.....1	0...10.....9	0...16.....2
Estate of Jesse PAYNE, deced.	697 1/2			291...17.....4	2...18.....5	4.....7.....8
Thomas POOR	525	5/1		133.....8.....9	1.....6.....9	2.....0.....2
Abram POOR	200	6/1		60...16.....8	0...12.....2	0...18.....4
Joseph PACE	150	6/3		46...17.....6	0.....9.....5	0...14.....2
John PACE	130	5/		32...10.....0	0.....6.....6	0.....9.....9
William PACE	200	6/1		60...16.....8	0...12.....2	0...18.....4
John PHILPOTT	100	4/1		20.....8.....4	0.....4.....2	0.....6.....2
Benjamin PAGE	100	6/1		30.....8.....4	0.....6.....2	0.....9.....2
John PREWIT	91	7/2		32.....2.....2	0.....6.....6	0.....9.....9
Archibald PLEASANTS	299	13/6		201...13.....6	2.....0.....5	3.....0.....8

(page 52. Goochland County Land Tax Return for 1786)

Proprietors	Quantity of Land		Price	Amt. of of Land	Certificate Tax	Specie Tax
Alexander PARISH	250	5/		62...10.....0	0...12.....6	0...18.....9
George PRIDDY	49 1/4	6/		14...15.....6	0.....3.....0	0.....4.....6
Anderson PARISH	170	3/3		27...12.....6	0.....5.....9	0.....8.....5
William PARISH	250	7/		87...10.....0	0...17.....6	1.....6.....4
Josias PAYNE	335	5/8		111...13.....4	1.....2.....4	1...13.....6
David ROSS, Esqr.	9949			4284.....0.....0	42...16.....5	64.....5.....0
Jesse REDD	397	8/1		160.....9.....1	1...12.....2	2.....8.....3
Capt. John ROYSTER	400	12/1		241...13.....4	2.....8.....4	3...12.....6
John REDD	252			88.....4.....8	0...17.....4	1.....6.....7
William RICHARDS	49	8/1		18...16.....1	0.....3...10	0.....5.....8
Edward RADFORD	295			221...15...10	2.....4.....4	3.....6.....6
William RADFORD, Mercht.	195	4/1		39...16.....3	0.....8.....0	0...12.....0
Estate of William ROUNTREE, deced	108	10/5		56.....5.....0	0...11.....4	0...17.....0
Samuel ROUNTREE	121	do.		63.....0.....5	0...12.....8	0...19.....0
William ROUNTREE	121	do.		63.....0.....5	0...12.....8	0...19.....0
Randal ROUNTREE	247	11/5		140...19...11	1.....8.....3	2.....2.....5
Matthew RIDDLE	70	7/		24...10.....0	0.....5.....0	0.....7.....6
Isaac RAGLAND	150	6/9		50...12.....6	0...10.....2	0...15.....4
William ROYSTER, Gent.	543	11/1		300...18.....3	3.....0.....2	4...10.....4
Thomas ROYSTER	166 2/3			84.....1.....6	0...16.....7	1.....4...10
Milner RADFORD	539	9/8		260...10.....4	2...12.....2	3...18.....2
Colo. Thomas M. RANDOLPH	3052			2764.....3.....8	27...13.....0	41.....9.....6
Mary ROGERS	17	8/1		6...17.....5	0.....1.....4	0.....2.....0
William RONALD, Esqr.	1370			738.....9.....2	7.....7.....6	11.....1.....8
William RUTHERFORD	433	5/4		115.....9.....4	1.....3.....2	1...14.....8
William RIGSBY	50	3/3		8.....2.....6	0.....1.....8	0.....2.....6
Thomas RIDDLE	335	5/11		99.....2.....1	1.....0.....0	1...10.....0
Doctor John K. READ	408	8/1		164...18.....0	1...13.....0	2.....9.....6
Estate of Charles RICE, deced.	175	5/10		51.....0...10	0...10.....3	0...15.....4
Capt. Samuel RICHARDSON	536	7/2		192.....1.....4	1...18.....5	2...17.....8
Thomas RANDOLPH, Esqr.	3000	9/9		1462...10.....0	14...12.....6	21...18.....9
George RICHARDSON	1612	6/10		550...15.....4	5...10.....2	8.....5.....4

(page 52 contd. Goochland County Land Tax Return for 1786)

Proprietors	Quantity of Land	Price	Amt. of of Land	Certificate Tax	Specie Tax
James ROBARDS	343	3/4	57.....3.....4	0...11.....6	0...17.....4
Robert SMITH	175	7/3	63.....8.....9	0...12.....8	0...19.....0
William SADLER	130	11/9	76.....7.....6	0...15.....4	1.....3.....0
James SCRUGGS	230	8/	92.....0.....0	0...18.....5	1.....7.....8
Josiah SEAY	145		49...17...11	0...10.....0	0...15.....0
William SAUNDERS	20	8/1	8.....1.....8	0.....1...10	0.....2.....9

(page 53. Goochland County Land Tax Return for 1786)

Proprietors	Quantity of Land	Price	Amt. of of Land	Certificate Tax	Specie Tax
Major Stephen SOUTHALL	644		252.....3.....0	2...10.....6	3...15.....9
William SMITH, JR. (P.tan)	40	10/	20.....0.....0	0.....4.....0	0.....6.....0
Elizabeth STODGHILL	28	12/1	16...18.....4	0.....3.....6	0.....5.....2
Thomas SHOEMAKER	200	10/1	100...16.....8	1.....0.....2	1...10.....4
Colo. John SYME	318	8/1	128...10.....6	1.....5...10	1...18.....8
John SAUNDERS	30	8/1	12.....2.....6	0.....2.....5	0.....3.....8
Capt. Stephen SAMPSON	566	do.	266...10.....0	2...13.....2	3...19.....4
Estate of Charles SAMPSON, deced.	234	do	94...11.....6	0...19.....0	1.....8.....6
John SHELTON, Gent.	462		191.....2.....0	1...18.....2	2...17.....6
David SHELTON	840		440.....0.....0	4.....8.....0	6...12.....0
Joseph SHELTON	529		314...10.....0	3.....2...11	4...14.....6
Benjamin SADLER	100	4/1	20.....8.....4	0.....4.....2	0.....6.....2
Arthur SLAYDEN	182	do.	37.....3.....2	0.....7.....5	0...11.....2
John SLAYDEN	100	do.	20.....8.....4	0.....4.....2	0.....6.....2
William S. SMITH	211	7/2	75...12.....2	0...15.....2	1.....2.....9
John STRONG	137 1/2	8/1	55...11.....6	0...11.....2	0...16...10
Nathan STRONG	137 1/2	do.	55...11.....6	0...11.....2	0...16...10
Edward SCRUGGS	100	6/1	30.....8.....4	0.....6.....2	0.....9.....2
Richard SAMPSON	250	7/3	90...12.....6	0...18.....2	1.....7.....4
James SALMONS	230	4/7	52...14.....2	0...10.....7	0...16.....0
Major Robert H. SAUNDERS	330	13/6	222...15.....0	2.....4.....8	3.....7.....0
Philip TINSLEY	50	12/1	30.....4.....2	0.....6.....2	0.....9.....2
Thomas TOWLES, Esqr.	348 1/2	9/4	162...12.....8	1...12.....8	2.....8...10
Bartholomew TURNER	200	8/1	80...16.....8	0...16.....2	1.....4.....4
Sarah THOMAS	160	4/1	32...13.....4	0.....6.....7	0.....9...10
Mary TOWLER	200	do.	40...16.....8	0.....8.....2	0...12.....4
Cornelius TOWLER	190	do.	38...15...10	0.....7...10	0...11.....8
William THURSTON	122	7/5	45.....4...10	0.....9.....2	0...13.....8
John THURSTON	110	7/1	38...19.....2	0.....7...11	0...11...10
Esther THURSTON	53	4/5	11...14.....1	0.....2.....6	0.....3.....8
Horatio TURPIN	1200	5/9	345.....0.....0	3.....9.....0	5.....3.....6
James THOMAS	110	4/1	24...10.....0	0.....6.....0	0.....7.....6
John TOWLER	62 1/2	do.	12...15.....3	0.....2.....7	0.....3...10
Reuben THURSTON	53	5/	13.....5.....0	0.....2.....9	0.....4.....2

(page 54. Goochland County Land Tax Return for 1786)

Proprietors	Quantity of Land	Price	Amt. of of Land	Certificate Tax	Specie Tax
Benjamin THACKER	100	3/3	16.....5.....0	0.....3.....4	0.....5.....0
William UTLEY	125	8/1	50...10.....5	0...10.....2	0...15.....4

(page 54 contd. Goochland County Land Tax Return for 1786)

Proprietors	Quantity of Land	Price	Amt. of of Land	Certificate Tax	Specie Tax
Obadiah UTLEY	8	8/1	3.....4.....8	0.....0.....8	0.....1.....0
Ann UTLEY	116	6/4	36...14.....8	0.....7.....5	0...11.....2
John UTLEY	125	8/1	50...10.....5	0...10.....2	0...15.....4
Hezekiah UTLEY	58	6/1	17...12...10	0.....3.....7	0.....5.....4
Elizabeth UNDERWOOD	100	11/5	57.....1.....8	0...11.....5	0...17.....2
George UNDERWOOD	526	7/4	192...17.....4	1...18.....8	2...18.....0
Thomas UNDERWOOD, Esqr.	600	8/9	262...10.....0	2...12.....6	3...18...10
Estate of James UNDERWOOD, deced.	215	6/8	71...13.....4	0...14.....4	1.....1.....6
Matthew VAUGHAN, Gent.	753 1/2	9/1	342.....4.....4	3.....8.....6	5.....2.....9
James VAUGHAN	362	7/7	137.....5.....2	1.....7.....5	2.....1.....4
Shadrach VAUGHAN	913	8/1	369.....0.....1	3...14.....0	5...10...10
Colo. John WOODSON	611		996...19.....4	9...19.....5	14...19.....2
Matthew WOODSON	1526		1080...11.....8	10...16.....2	16.....4.....4
William WALKER	169		36...17.....6	0.....7.....8	0...11.....6
John WILLIAMS, D. C.	863		219...18.....4	2.....4.....0	3.....6.....0
Daniel WADE	(?)36 1/2		142.....7.....5	1.....8.....6	2.....2.....2
Joseph WATKINS	597		278.....8.....6	2...15.....8	4.....3.....6
Peter WALKER (Geneto)	155	8/1	62...12...11	0...12.....7	0...18...10
Shadrach WALKER	75	do.	30.....6.....3	0.....6.....2	0.....9.....2
Richard WADE	197	9/7	94.....8.....0	0...19.....0	1.....8.....6
Robert WADE	97	8/1	39.....4.....1	0.....8.....0	0...12.....0
Reuben WEATHERSPOON	50	6/11	17.....5...10	0.....3.....6	0.....5.....3
Thomas WAFFORD	208		54.....6.....0	0...11.....0	0...16.....6
Henry WOOD	300	7/3	108...15.....0	1.....1.....9	1...12.....8
Solomon WILLIAMS	206		72...19.....2	0...14.....8	1.....2.....0
Major Joseph WOODSON	578	8/1	233.....2.....0	2.....6.....8	3...10.....0
Susanna WOODWARD	500	12/1	302.....1.....8	3.....0.....5	4...10.....8
John WADE	73	8/1	29...10.....1	0.....6.....0	0.....9.....0
Pleasant WILLIS	458	do.	185.....2.....2	1...17.....2	2...15.....8
Eleonar WILLIS	100	6/1	30.....8.....4	0.....6.....2	0.....9.....2
William WOODALL	63	6/6	20.....9.....6	0.....4.....2	0.....6.....2
William WEBBER, Preacher	177	6/4	56.....1.....0	0...11.....3	0...16...10
Edward WILLIS	160	8/1	64...13.....4	0...13.....0	0...19.....6
Thomas WOODSON	200	12/1	120...16.....8	1.....4.....2	1...16.....4

(page 55. Goochland County Land Tax Return for 1786)

Proprietors	Quantity of Land	Price	Amt. of of Land	Certificate Tax	Specie Tax
Nathaniel WEBSTER	140	6/6	45...10.....0	0.....9.....0	0...13.....6
Robert WINGFIELD	90	8/1	36.....7.....6	0.....7.....4	0...11.....0
David WEBSTER	75	10/6	39...17.....6	0.....8.....0	0...12.....0
Joseph WOODSON, (Geneto)	225	9/	101.....5.....0	1.....0.....4	1...10.....6
Estate of Joseph WOODSON, deced.	222	10/	111.....0.....0	1.....2.....2	1...13.....4
Joseph WOODSON (of Tucker)	400		150...17.....6	1...10.....2	2.....5.....3
Dorothy WATKINS	170	8/1	68...14.....2	0...13.....2	1.....0.....8
Thomas WATKINS	583	do.	235...12.....7	2.....7.....2	3...10...10
Benjamin WATKINS	238	9/5	112.....1.....2	1.....2.....5	1...13.....8
John WATKINS	519	8/11	231.....7.....9	2.....6.....3	3.....9.....6
William WEBBER, SENR.	340	10/6	178...10.....0	1...15...10	2...13.....8
Benjamin WOODSON (Fluvanna)	205	9/1	93.....2.....1	0...18.....8	1....( ).....( )

(page 55 contd. Goochland County Land Tax Return for 1786)

Proprietors	Quantity of Land	Price	Amt. of of Land	Certificate Tax	Specie Tax
Benjamin WATKINS, JR.	156	9/5	73.....9.....0	0...14.....9	1.....2.....2
Henry WHITLOW, JR.	50	8/1	20.....4.....2	0.....4.....2	0.....6.....2
Henry WHITLOW, SENR.	99	do.	40.....0.....3	0.....8.....1	0...12.....2
John WITT	17	do.	6...17.....5	0.....1.....4	0.....2.....0
Tucker WOODSON	600	17/8	530.....0.....0	5.....6.....0	7...19.....0
John WOODSON (C. Ferry)	1265		647...15.....5	6.....9.....6	9...14.....4
Henry WALMACK	100	8/1	40.....8.....4	0.....8.....2	0...12.....2
Isaac WINSTON (Hanover)	735	do.	297.....1.....3	2...19.....6	4.....9.....2
Drury WILLIAMS	600		232...10.....0	2.....6.....6	3...10.....0
John WALKER	100	3/3	16.....5.....0	0.....3.....4	0.....5.....0
Estate of Colo. Valentine WOOD, deced.	2762		1076.....2.....2	10...15.....4	16.....3.....0
William WILLIAMS	50	4/1	10.....4.....2	0.....2.....2	0.....3.....2
John WILLIAMSON	200	do.	40...16.....8	0.....8.....2	0...12.....4
Lewis WILBOURNE	100	do.	20.....8.....4	0.....4.....2	0.....6.....4
Dabney WADE	300	6/3	93...15.....0	0...18.....6	1.....8.....2
Estate of William WADE, deced.	215	7/3	77...18.....9	0...15.....8	1.....3.....6
John WOODSON (Meadow)	300	8/1	121.....5.....0	1.....4.....4	1...16.....6
William WILBOURNE	200	3/3	32...10.....0	0.....6.....6	0.....9.....9
John WILLIAMS, JR.	250	6/6	81.....5.....0	0...16.....4	1.....4.....6
James WILLIAMS	10	7/	3...10.....0	0.....0.....8	0.....1.....0
Philip WILLIAMS	200	6/	60.....0.....0	0...12.....0	0...18.....0
Capt. John WARE	925	6/6	300...12.....6	3.....0.....2	4...10.....2
William WOODALL	63	do.	20.....9.....6	0.....4.....2	0.....6.....2
Ann YOUNGER	100	3/3	16.....5.....0	0.....3.....4	0.....5.....0

        Certificate Tax   843...18.....7
        Specie Tax   1265...15.....1

(page 56.)

I do hereby certify that the within State of the Land Tax is a true copy of the Original

THOMAS F. BATES, Commr.

Witness JOHN HUMBER

(page 57)

List of the Land Tax within the District of THOMAS F. BATES, Commr. of the County of Goochland, April 1787.

Proprietors Names	Quantity of Land	Rate p Acre	Amount of Value	Certificate Tax	Amt. Tax at 1 1/2 p cent
James ALLEN	175	4/7	34...16.....3	0.....7.....0	0...10.....6
David ALVIS	125	4/1	25...10.....5	0.....5.....2	0.....7.....9
William ANDERSON, Esqr.	1500	8/	600.....0.....0]		
do. of Majr. Thomas MASSIE	2285	6/	685...10.....0]	12...17.....3	19.....5...10
Jesse BOWLES	151 1/4		37.....5.....0	0.....7.....6	0...11.....3
Thomas BRYANT (Albemarle)	50	3/6	8...15.....0	0.....2.....0	0.....2...11
Elijah BRUMFIELD	149	10/3	76.....7.....3	0...15.....4	1.....3.....0
Callam BAILEY	150	4/1	30...12.....6	0.....6.....3	0.....9.....4
John BOWDRY	10]				
Entry	50]	do.	12.....5.....0	0.....2.....6	0.....3.....9
William BURGESS	100	d0.	20.....8.....4	0.....4.....2	0.....6.....2
John BOLLING, SENR.	1440		677.....7.....6	6...15.....8	10.....3.....4
John BOLLING, JR.	600	9/8	290.....0.....0	2...18.....0	4.....7.....0
Thomas BOLLING	3599 2/3		4029...13...10	40.....6.....0	60.....8...10
Claibourne BRADSHAW	128	8/1	51...14.....8	0...10.....5	0...15.....7
Thomas F. BATES	500	13/10	345...16.....8	3.....9.....3	5.....3...10
Capt. John BRITT	245	7/4]			
do. of the Estate	125	4/9]	119...10.....5	1.....4.....0	1...16.....0
Gideon BOWLES	350	6/8	116...13.....4	1.....3.....4	1...15.....0
Charles BOWLES	133 1/2	4/1	32...16.....5]		
do. of Sarah LACY	91	5/	22...15.....0]	0...11.....2	0...16.....8
William BUSBY	150		27...14.....2	0.....5.....8	0.....8.....6
John BARNETT	200	7/5	74.....3.....4	0...15.....0	1.....2.....6
Obadiah BRITT	400	4/9	95.....0.....0	0...19.....0	1.....8.....6
William BRITT	225	do.	53.....8.....9	0...10.....8	0...16.....0
John BANKS	50	5/11	14...15...10	0.....3.....0	0.....4.....6
Thomas BERNARD	700	10/7	370.....8.....4	3...14.....2	5...11.....2
John BELLAMY	50	6/1	15.....4.....2	0.....3.....1	0.....4.....7
Larner BRADSHAW	79		28...15.....4	0.....5...10	0.....8.....9
Benjamin CRENSHAW	440	5/11	130.....3.....4	1.....6.....2	1...19.....2
Martha CARR	449	8/1	201...13.....7	2.....0.....6	3.....0.....8
Nathaniel CAWLEY	66	do.	24.....5.....0	0.....4...11	0.....7.....4
Mary COLEY	100	do.	40.....8.....4	0.....8.....2	0...12.....2
Susanna COLEY	100	4/1	20.....8.....4	0.....4.....2	0.....6.....2
Ann COLEY	100	8/1	40.....8.....4	0.....8.....2	0...12.....2
Sally COLEY	100	6/1	30.....8.....4	0.....6.....2	0.....9.....2
Francis COLEY	106 1/2	6/3	33.....2.....6	0.....6.....8	0...10.....0
Estate of Robert CARDIN	200	5/1	50...15.....8	0...10.....3	0...15.....4
John CLEMENTS	116	5/10	33...16.....8	0.....6...10	0...10.....2
Bowler COCKE, Esqr.	1509		1165...12.....0	11...13.....0	17.....9.....6
Samuel COSBY	196	4/5	44.....2.....0	0.....8...10	0...13.....2
Walter CLOPTON	220	8/1	88...18.....4	0...17...11	1.....6...10
James CLEMENTS	179	6/4	56...13.....8	0...11.....6	0...17.....2
Roger CARRELL	83	4/1	16...13...11	0.....3.....6	0.....5.....2
Gideon CAWTHON	220	6/8	73.....6.....8	0...15.....4	1.....3.....0
Edward COX	200		66...13.....4	0...13.....2	0...19.....9

(page 57 contd. Goochland County Land Tax Return of Thomas F. Bates for 1787)

Proprietors Names	Quantity of Land	Rate p Acre	Amount of Land	Certificate Tax	Amt. of Tax at 1 1/2 p cent
David CRENSHAW	238	6/2	73.....7.....8	0...14...10	1.....2.....2
Judith CARTER	100	4/10	24.....3.....4	0.....5.....0	0.....7.....4

(page 58. Goochland County Land Tax Return of Thomas F. Bates for 1787)

Proprietors Names	Quantity of Land	Rate p Acre	Amount of Land	Certificate Tax	Amt. of Tax at 1 1/2 p cent
Turner CHRISTIAN	235	6/2	72.....7.....0	0...14....6	1.....1.....8
George CROWDAS	50	7/	17...10.....0	0.....3....6	0.....5.....3
Benjamin CLOPTON	400		150...16.....8	1...10....3	2.....5.....4
John CHEATHAM	100	4/	20.....0.....0	0.....4....0	0.....6.....0
Charles CARR (MILLER's)	150	5/5	40...12.....6	0.....8....2	0...12.....3
Lewis CHAUDOIN	50	4/1	10.....4.....2	0.....2....2	0.....3.....2
John DOWDY	122	7/5	45.....4...10	0.....9....2	0...13.....8
Thomas DRUMWRIGHT	1030	6/2	317...11.....8	3.....3....8	4...15.....4
John DAVIS (Hanover)	200		72.....1.....8	0...14....6	1.....1.....8
Ichabod DANIEL	50	5/8	14.....3.....4	0.....2...10	0.....4.....3
Ezekiel DANIEL	50	do.	14.....3.....4	0.....2...10	0.....4.....3
Mouley DANIEL	50	do.	14.....3.....4	0.....2...10	0.....4.....3
John DANIEL	50	do.	14.....3.....4	0.....2...10	0.....4.....3
Reverend William DOUGLAS	500	6/1	152.....1.....8]		
do. of Joseph JOHNSON's Estate	500	4/1	102.....1.....8]		
do. of Francis CLARKE	150	do.	30...12.....6]	2...17.....0	4.....5.....6
David DAVIS	100	7/	35.....0.....0	0.....7....0	0...10.....6
Noton DICKINSON	400	3/6	70.....0.....0	0...14....0	1.....1.....0
Gwathney DABNEY	418	7/3	151...10.....6	1...10....3	2.....5.....4
Thomas ELDRIDGE	203	8/1	82.....0...11	0...16....6	1.....4.....9
David ENGLAND	80	6/1	24.....6.....8	0.....4...11	0.....7.....4
Benjamin EAST	121 1/2	8/1	49.....2.....2	0.....9...11	0...14...10
Henry EMMERSON	240	6/6	78.....0.....0	0...15....8	1.....3.....5
Thomas EMMERSON, JR.	100	do.	32...10.....0]		
do. of Thomas EMMERSON, SENR.	200		42...10.....0]	0...15.....0	1.....2.....6
Joseph ELAM	50	10/	25.....0.....0	0.....5.....0	0.....7.....6
Estate of Colo. Tarlton FLEMING	1900	20/2	1915...16.....8	19.....3....3	28...14...10
Honble. William FLEMING	390	20/4	396...10.....0	3...19....4	5...19.....0
Colo. Charles FLEMING	390	do.	396...10.....0	3...19....4	5...19.....0
John FURLONG	100	3/6	17...10.....0	0.....3....8	0.....5.....4
Hugh FRENCH	250 3/4		77...10.....4]		
do. of Estate of Charles RICE	40	5/10	11...13.....4]	0...17...10	1.....6.....8
Daniel FORD	90	8/	36.....0.....0	0.....7....4	0...10...10
John GLASS	62		21...19.....0	0.....4....4	0.....6.....6
Capt. William GEORGE	75		15...14.....7	0.....3....2	0.....4.....9
John GRAY	85	10/3	44.....8.....4]		
do. of William SADLER	15	11/9	8...16.....3]	0...10...11	0...16.....4
John GILLAM, SENR.	546	7/9	211...11.....6	2.....2....4	3.....3.....6
David GRANTHAM	35	7/8	13.....2.....6	0.....2....8	0.....4.....0
Robert GILLAM (Pr. Geo.)	1021 3/4		2699.....2.....6	26...19...11	40.....9...10
Stephen GRANGE	80	7/2	28...13.....4	0.....5...10	0.....8.....8
John GILBERT	150	3/6	26.....5.....0	0.....5....4	0.....8.....0

(page 58 contd. Goochland County Land Tax Return of Thomas F. Bates for 1787)

Proprietors Names	Quantity of Land	Rate p Acre	Amount of Land	Certificate Tax	Amt. of Tax at 1 1/2 p cent
Daniel GRUBBS	150	3/6	26.....5.....0	0.....5.....4	0.....8.....0
Robert GEORGE	80	6/5	25...13.....4	0.....5.....2	0.....7...8
Estate of David HUDSON	443 1/4		172...10.....2	1...14...11	2...12.....4
John HUSON	47	5/	11...15.....0	0.....2...6	0.....3.....8
John HENDERSON	200	4/1	40...16.....8	0.....8...3	0...12.....4
John HUMBER	561	8/1	226...14.....9	2.....5...6	3.....8.....2
Zachariah HADEN	660	5/1	167...15.....0]		
do. of Archer PAYNE	260	3/3	42.....5.....0]	2.....2.....0	3.....3.....0

(page 59. Goochland County Land Tax Return of Thomas F. Bates for 177)

Proprietors Names	Quantity of Land	Rate p Acre	Amount of Land	Certificate Tax	Amt. of Tax at 1 1/2 p cent
Drury HATCHER	5 1/2	4/6	1.....4.....9	0.....0.....4	0.....0.....6
Jesse HODGES	160	5/7	44...13.....4	0.....9.....0	0...13.....6
John HILL (Amherst)	150	6/1	45...12.....6	0.....9...3	0...13...10
Harrison HARRIS	530	7/4	194.....6.....8	1...18...11	2...18.....4
Mary HICKS	150	6/1	45...12.....6	0.....9...2	0...13.....8
Moses HICKS	150	do.	45...12.....6	0.....9...2	0...13.....8
Mesheck HICKS	450	6/4	142...10.....0	1.....8...7	2.....2...10
Francis HOUCHINS	117	5/10	34.....2.....6	0.....7.....0	0...10.....4
Lucy HOUCHINS	117	do.	34.....2.....6	0.....7.....0	0...10.....4
James HOLMAN	220	5/11	65.....1.....8	0...13...2	0...19.....8
William HODGES	100	4/10	24.....3.....4	0.....4...11	0.....7.....4
Capt. William HOLMAN	590	4/1	120...9.....2	1.....4...2	1...16.....3
Colo. John HOPKINS	1650	6/7	534.....2.....6	5.....7.....0	8.....0.....5
Lewis HERNDON	300	6/9	101.....5.....0	1.....0...4	1...10.....6
John HERNDON	199	7/4	72...19.....4	0...14...8	1.....2.....0
John HOPPER	210	7/2	75.....5.....0	0...15...2	1.....2.....8
Lucy HODGES	50	4/10	12.....1.....8	0.....2...6	0.....3.....8
Major HANCOCKE	80	6/7	26.....6.....8	0.....5...4	0.....8.....0
John HOLLAND	272 1/4	7/3	98...13...10	0...19...10	1.....9.....8
William HICKS (D.C.)	125	do.	45.....6.....3	0.....9...3	0...13...10
James HOWARD	136	do.	54.....6.....0	0...10...11	0...16.....4
John HOWARD	166	6/	49...10.....0	0...10.....0	0...15.....0
Anthony HADEN (Fluvanna)	400	4/	80.....0.....0	0...16.....0	1.....4.....0
Nathaniel HOLLAND	200	7/3	72...10.....0	0...14...7	1.....1...10
John HANES	100	8/	40.....0.....0	0.....8.....0	0...12.....0
John HUGHES	200	3/6	35.....0.....0	0.....7.....0	0...10.....6
Estate of George HOLLAND	280	7/3	101...10.....0	1.....0...4	1...10.....6
Richard JOHNSON of Cornelius TOWLER	190	4/1	38...15...10	0.....7...10	0...11.....8
William ISBELL	792	5/7	221.....2.....0	2.....4...3	3.....6.....4
Benjamin JOHNSON (Byrd)	140	7/	49.....0.....0	0...10.....0	0...14...10
William JOHNSON (do.)	250	6/1	76.....0...10	0...15...3	1.....2...10
Thomas JEFFERSON Esqr.	612	8/1	247.....7.....0	2.....9...6	3...14.....2
Archibald JARRETT	253	4/9	83...16.....9]		
do. of JENNINGS	201	4/1	41.....0.....9]	1.....5.....0	1...17.....6
Devereux JARRETT	290	do.	59.....4.....9	0...12.....0	0...17...10
David JARRETT	250	do.	51.....0...10	0...10...3	0...15.....4
Charles JOHNSON	200	7/2	71...13.....4	0...14...4	1.....1.....6

(page 59 contd. Goochland County Land Tax Return of Thomas F. Bates for 1787)

Proprietors Names	Quantity of Land	Rate p Acre	Amount of Land	Certificate Tax	Amt. of Tax at 1 1/2 p cent
William JAMES	100	5/11	29...11.....8]		
do. of James HOLMAN	5	do.	1.....9.....7]	0.....6.....6	0.....9.....9
Thomas JENNETT of HUNTER	100	4/1	20.....8.....4	0.....4.....2	0.....6.....3
Ayres LAYNE	155	6/8	51...13.....4	0...10.....4	0...15.....6
Henry LAYNE	100	4/1	20.....8.....4	0.....4.....2	0.....6.....2
Matthew LACY	97	4/10	23.....8...10	0.....4...10	0.....7.....2
Mary LAYNE	50	4/1	10.....4.....2	0.....2.....2	0.....3.....2
Sarah LACY	46	5/	11...10.....0	0.....2.....4	0.....3.....6
Samuel LAMAY	81	4/1	16...10.....9]		
do. of Estate of Valentine WOOD	34 1/4		13.....8.....4]	0.....6.....3	0.....9.....4
Armiger LILLY	400	4/1	81...13.....4	0...16.....3	1.....4.....4
Howel LEWIS	490	7/	171...10.....0	1...14.....4	2...11.....6
Colo. Robert LEWIS	1105	13/6	745...17.....6]		
do. of William BOWMAN	100	4/1	20.....8.....4]	7...13.....4	11.....9...11

(page 60. Goochland County Land Tax Return of Thomas F. Bates for 1787)

Proprietors Names	Quantity of Land	Rate p Acre	Amount of Land	Certificate Tax	Amt. of Tax at 1 1/2 p cent
Betty LEE	350	4/8	81...13.....4	0...16.....3	1.....4.....4
William LEWIS, R. C.	100	4/1	20.....8.....4	0.....4.....2	0.....6.....2
Capt. Josiah LEAKE	800	8/1	323.....6.....8	3.....4.....8	4...17.....0
Henry LAURENCE	50	4/5	11.....5.....0	0.....2.....4	0.....3.....6
Joseph LOWRY	150	3/6	26.....5.....0	0.....5.....3	0.....7...10
Joel LOWRY	50	do.	8...15.....0	0.....1...10	0.....2.....8
Matthew LOWRY	400	4/	80.....0.....0	0...16.....0	1.....4.....0
Robert LEWIS, JR.	250	6/6	81.....5.....0	0...16.....4	1.....4.....6
Charles LOGAN, Esqr.	40	8/1	16.....3.....4	0.....3.....4	0.....5.....0
Thomas LAURENCE	100	4/1	20.....8.....4]		
do. of John GREEN	8 1/2	do.	1...14.....9]	0.....4.....7	0.....6...10
Martin MIMS	194	8/1	78.....8.....2	0...15...10	1.....3.....8
Thomas MITCHELL, Mercht.	373 1/4	4/10	90.....4.....1	0...18.....2	1.....7.....2
Estate of Edward MATTHEWS, deced.	123		45.....1.....5	0.....9.....2	0...13.....8
William MATTHEWS	200	7/5	74.....3.....4	0...15.....0	1.....2.....6
Edward MATTHEWS	184	do.	68.....4.....8	0...13...10	1.....0.....8
Capt. William MILLER	440 1/2		174.....9...6	1...15.....0	2...12.....6
Thomas MILLER	400		190.....9.....2	1...18.....2	2...17.....2
Estate of David MIMS, deced.	315	7/5	116...16.....3	1.....3.....6	1...15.....2
Colo. Thomas MERIWETHER	300 1/2	8/1	121.....9.....1	1.....4.....4	1...16.....6
Thomas MARTIN	100	do.	40.....8.....4	0.....8.....2	0...12.....3
Charles MASSIE	300	do.	121.....5.....0]		
do. of Shadrach VAUGHAN	38	d0.	15.....7.....2]	1.....7.....6	2.....1.....2
Ann MITCHELL	211	6/5	67...13...11	0...13.....8	1.....0.....4
David MARTIN	235	do.	75.....7...11	0...15.....2	1.....2.....8
Paul MEACHUM	295	5/6	81.....2.....6	0...16.....4	1.....4.....6
Benjamin MOSBY	200	5/1	50...16.....8	0...10.....3	0...15.....4
Archibald BRYCE &					
William MITCHELL	865 1/2	8/1	349...12.....1	3...10.....0	5.....5.....0
Gideon MIMS	360	7/5	133...10.....0	1.....7.....3	2.....0...10
Elizabeth MIMS	125	7/3	45.....6.....3	0.....9.....2	0...13.....8
Robert MIMS (of Elizabeth)	125	do.	45.....6.....3	0.....9.....2	0...13.....8

(page 60 contd. Goochland County Land Tax Return of Thomas F. Bates for 1787)

Proprietors Names	Quantity of Land	Rate p Acre	Amount of Land	Certificate Tax	Amount of Tax at 1 1/2 p cen
Sarah MIMS	50	6/1	15.....4.....2	0.....3.....2	0.....4.....8
Colo. John MARTIN	700	6/2	215...16.....8	2.....3.....3	3.....4...10
John MERRIAN	80	4/1	16.....6.....8	0.....3.....4	0.....4...11
Samuel MERRIAN	80	do.	16.....6.....8	0.....3.....4	0.....4...11
Matthew MERRIAN	80	do.	16.....6.....8	0.....3.....4	0.....4...11
Bartholomew MERRIAN	80	do.	16.....6.....8	0.....3.....4	0.....4...11
Jesse MERRIAN	80	do.	16.....6.....8	0.....3.....4	0.....4...11
Thomas MASSIE, Gent.	232 1/2	8/	93.....0.....0	0...18.....8	1.....8.....0
Wright MOURLAND	100	6/11	34...11.....8	0.....7.....0	0...10.....6
Capt. David MULLINS	197	8/1	79...12.....5	0...16.....0	1.....4.....0
Capt. Henry MULLINS	400	7/2	143.....6.....8	1.....8.....8	2.....3.....0
Conally MULLINS	234	6/5	75.....1.....6	0...15.....0	1.....2.....6
Elizabeth MULLINS	116	do.	37.....4.....4	0.....7.....6	0...11.....3
Samuel MOSS	200	4/	40.....0.....0	0.....8.....0	0...12.....0
William MARTIN	400	6/	120.....0.....0	1.....4.....0	1...16.....0
John MOSS	75	8/	30.....0.....0	0.....6.....0	0.....9.....0
William MASSIE	223	7/3	80...16.....9	0...16.....3	1.....4.....4
Nathaniel MASSIE, Gent.	723 1/2	8/	289.....6.....0	2...17...10	4.....6.....8
William MITCHELL, JR.	100	4/9	23...15.....0	0.....4...10	0.....7.....2
Angus McDONALD	100	7/10	39.....3.....4	0.....8.....0	0...12.....0

(page 61. Goochland County Land Tax Return of Thomas F. Bates for 1787)

Proprietors Names	Quantity of Land	Rate p Acre	Amount of Land	Certificate Tax	Amount of Tax at 1 1/2 p cen
John MICHIE, Esqr.	577 1/2	8/1	233.....8.....2]		
do. of Estate of Valentine WOOD	43	7/10	16...16...10]	2...10.....2	3...15.....2
Thomas NOWELL	100	6/	30.....0.....0	0.....6.....0	0.....9.....0
James NOWELL	300	do.	90.....0.....0	0...18.....0	1.....7.....0
David NOWLIN	347	7/	121.....9.....0	1.....4.....4	1...16.....6
Barnett OWEN	50	3/3	8.....2.....6	0.....1.....8	0.....2.....6
Mary OWEN	50	3/3	8.....2.....6	0.....1.....8	0.....2.....6
Colo. Josiah PARKER	986 1/2	14/10	731...13.....1	Lower District	
Sherard PARISH	291		63.....4.....0	0...12...10	0...19.....3
John PERKINS	263 1/2		94...10.....8	0...19.....0	1.....8.....6
Archelaus PERKINS	263 1/2		94...10.....8	0...19.....0	1.....8.....6
William PERKINS (of John)	254	5/10	74.....1.....8	0...15.....0	1.....2.....6
Capt. Humphry PARISH	423		150.....3.....5	1...10.....2	2.....5.....2
William PAYNE	92	10/9	49.....9.....0	0...10.....0	0...15.....0
John PAGE	50	6/	15.....0.....0	0.....3.....0	0.....4.....6
Capt. Joseph PAYNE	734		296.....4...10	2...19.....4	4.....8...11
Estate of Colo. John PAYNE, deced.	1673	8/	715.....4.....0	7.....3.....2	10...14.....8
Meredith PARISH	100	4/6	22...10.....0	0.....4.....6	0.....6.....9
Thomas POOR (of Abraham)	30		10.....7.....6	0.....2.....2	0.....3.....3
Robert PLEASANTS, JR.	600	10/7	317...10.....0	3.....3.....8	4...15.....4
Joel PARISH	121	4/10	29.....4...10	0.....6.....0	0.....8...10
Aaron PARISH	71 1/4	4/1	14...11.....0	0.....3.....0	0.....4.....6
Mary PARISH	121 1/4	do.	24...15.....2	0.....5.....0	0.....7.....6
Booker PARISH	180 1/4	do.	36.....6.....1]		
do. of Robert GEORGE resurveyed	115	6/	34...10.....0]	0...15.....6	1.....1.....8

(page 61 contd. Goochland County Land Tax Return of Thomas F. BATES for 1787)

Proprietors Names	Quantity of Land	Rate p Acre	Amount of Land	Certificate Tax	Amt. of Tax at 1 1/2 p cent
Samuel PRYOR Gent_	75		29...11.....2	0.....6.....0	0.....9.....0
William PRYOR	200	12/1	120...16.....8	1.....4.....3	1...16.....4
Moses PARISH	168	4/1	34.....6.....0	0.....6...11	0...10.....4
Daniel POWERS	33 1/2	5/11	9...18.....3	0.....2.....0	0.....3.....0
Samuel H. POWEL	250	4/1	50.....0...10	0...10.....2	0...15.....3
Estate of George PAYNE, deced. (O.K.)	200	5/7	55...16.....8	0...11.....3	0...16...10
William PROPHET (resurveyed)	87 3/4	6/6	28...10.....5	0.....5.....8	0.....8.....6
Winnifred PAGE	133	7/2	47...13.....2	0.....9.....7	0...14.....4
Robert PAYNE	800	8/1	323.....6.....8	3.....4.....8	4...17.....0
William PAGE (of Robert)	133	do	53...15.....1	0...10...10	0...16.....2
Estate of Jesse PAYNE, deced.	697 1/2		291...17.....4	2...18.....6	4.....7.....8
Thomas POOR	525	5/1	133.....8.....9	1.....6...10	2.....0.....2
Abram POOR	200	6/1	60...16.....8	0...12.....3	0...18.....4
Joseph PACE	150	6/3	46...17.....6	0.....9.....6	0...14.....2
John PACE	130	5/	32...10.....0	0.....6.....6	0.....9.....9
William PACE	200	6/1	60...16.....8	0...12.....3	0...18.....4
John PHILPOTT	100	4/1	20.....8.....4	0.....4.....2	0.....6.....3
Benjamin PAGE	100	6/1	30.....8.....4	0.....6.....2	0.....9.....3
John PREWIT	16 1/2	7/2	5.....8.....2	0.....1.....2	0.....1.....9
Obadiah PREWIT	74 1/2	do.	26...14.....0	0.....5.....4	0.....8.....0

(page 62. Goochland County Land Tax Return of Thomas F. BATES for 1787)

Proprietors Names	Quantity of Land	Rate p Acre	Amount of Land	Certificate Tax	Amt. of Tax at 1 1/2 p cent
Alexander PARISH	250	5/	62...10.....0	0...12.....6	0...18.....9
George PRIDDY	49 1/4	6/	14...15.....6	0.....3.....0	0.....4.....6
Anderson PARISH	170	3/3	27...12.....6	0.....5.....8	0.....8.....5
William PARISH	250	7/	87...10.....0	0...17.....7	1.....6.....4
John PURKINS of A.G.	175	4/	35.....0.....0	0.....7.....0	0...10.....6
William PURKINS of T. M.	100	do.	20.....0.....0	0.....4.....0	0.....6.....0
Ann PARISH	75	4/1	15.....0.....6	0.....3.....1	0.....4.....7
Philip PAYNE	194 1/2	7/10	76.....3.....7	0...15.....3	1.....2...10
Thomas POLLOCK of Estate of E.M.	200	7/5	74.....3.....4	0...14...10	1.....2.....3
Humphry PARISH, JR.	183	5/10	53.....7.....6	0...10.....8	0...16.....0
David ROSS, Esqr.	9949		4284.....0.....0]		
do. of Horatio TURPIN	1200	5/9	345.....0.....0]	46.....5.....8	69.....8.....6
William RICHARDS	49	8/1	18.....6.....1]		
do. of John PARISH	165	6/	49...10.....0]	0...13.....8	1.....0.....6
William RUTHERFORD	433	5/4	115.....9.....4	1.....3.....2	1...14.....8
William RIGSBY	50	3/3	8.....2.....6	0.....1.....8	0.....2.....6
Thomas RIDDLE	335	5/11	99.....2.....1	1.....0.....0	1...10.....0
Doctor John K. READ	408	8/1	164...18.....0	1...13.....0	2.....9.....6
Estate of Charles RICE, deced.	135	5/10	39.....7.....6	0.....8.....0	0...12.....0
Capt. Samuel RICHARDSON	536	7/2	192.....1.....4	1...18.....6	2...17.....8
Thomas RANDOLPH, Esquire D.	3000	9/9	1462...10.....0]		
do. of William GAY	400 2/3		876...11.....2]	23.....7...10	35.....1.....9
George RICHARDSON	1612	6/10	550...15.....4	5...10.....3	8.....5.....4
James ROBARDS	343	3/4	57.....3.....4]		
do. of Estate of Colo. Jno. PAYNE	120	8/	48.....0.....0]	1.....1.....4	1...11...10
John RICHARDS of J. P.	165	6/	49...10.....0]		
do. of Shadrach VAUGHAN	53	8/1	21.....8.....5]	0...14.....3	1.....1.....5

(page 62 contd. Goochland County Land Tax Return of Thomas F. Bates for 1787)

Proprietors Names	Quantity of Land	Rate p Acre	Amount of Land	Certificate Tax	Amt. of Tax at 1 1/2 p cent
Nathaniel RAINE of J. P.	100	4/1	20.....8.....4	0.....4.....2	0.....6.....2
Capt. Holman RICE of J. FARISH	100	6/1	30.....8.....4	0.....6.....2	0.....9.....2
Robert SMITH	175	7/3	63.....8.....9	0...12.....8	0...19.....0
William SADLER	115	11/9	67...11.....3	0...13.....6	1.....0.....2
James SCRUGGS	230	8/	92.....0.....0	0...19.....2	1.....7.....8
Capt. Stephen SAMPSON	566	8/1	266...10.....0]		
do. of Thomas MILLER	153 1/2	9/	69.....1.....6]	3.....6...11	5.....0.....4
David SHELTON	840		440.....0.....0	4.....8.....0	6...12.....0
Joseph SHELTON	529		314...10.....0	3.....3.....0	4...14.....6
Arthur SLAYDEN	182	4/1	37.....3.....2	0.....7.....6	0...11.....2
John SLAYDEN	100	do.	20.....8.....4	0.....4.....2	0.....6.....2
William S. SMITH	211	7/2	75...12.....2	0...15.....2	1.....2.....9
John STRONG	137 1/2	8/1	55...11.....6]		
do. of Samuel COSBY	29	4/5	6...10.....6]	0...12.....8	0...19.....0
Nathan STRONG	137 1/2	8/1	55...11.....6	0...11.....3	0...16...10
Richard SCRUGGS	50	6/11	15.....4.....2	0.....3.....1	0.....4.....7
James SALMONS	230	4/7	52...14.....2	0...10.....8	0...16.....0
John SCOTT of William GAY	200	8/1	80...16.....8	0...16.....3	1.....4.....4
Benjamin SALMONS of W. G.	250	6/	75.....0.....0	0...15.....0	1.....2.....6

(page 63. Goochland County Land Tax Return of Thomas F. Bates for 1787)

Proprietors Names	Quantity of Land	Rate p Acre	Amount of Land	Certificate Tax	Amt. of Tax at 1 1/2 p cent
Robert SHELTON, Glebe	200	8/1	80...16.....8	0...16.....3	1.....4.....4
Capt. William SAMPSON	175	7/3	63.....8.....9	0...12...10	0...19.....2
William SHELTON of B. LACY	88	4/1	21...12.....8	0.....4.....4	0.....6.....6
Sarah THOMAS	160	4/1	32...13.....4	0.....6.....7	0.....9...10
Mary TOWLER	200	do.	40...16.....8	0.....8.....3	0...12.....4
William THURSTON	72	7/5	26...14.....0	0.....5.....4	0.....8.....0
John THURSTON	110	7/1	38...19.....2	0.....7...11	0...11...10
Esther THURSTON	53	4/5	11...14.....1	0.....2.....6	0.....3.....8
James THOMAS	110	4/1	24...10.....0	0.....5.....0	0.....7.....6
William TURNER	62 1/2	do.	12...15.....3	0.....2.....7	0.....3...10
Mary THURSTON of Reuben	53	5/	13.....5.....0	0.....2...10	0.....4.....2
Benjamin THACKER	100	3/3	16.....5.....0	0.....3.....4	0.....5.....0
Thomas TERRY (of J. W., D. C.)	432	4/5	97.....4.....0	0...19.....6	1.....9.....2
Shadrach VAUGHAN	672	8/1	271...12.....0]		
do. of Estate of Valentine WOOD	100	7/10	39.....3.....4 '	3.....2.....3	4...13.....4
Lucy WOOD	600	do.	235.....0.....0	2.....7.....0	3...10.....6
William WALKER	169		36...17.....6	0.....7.....8	0...11.....6
John WILLIAMS, D.C.	127		30.....5.....0	0.....6.....2	0.....9.....3
Reuben WEATHERSPOON	50	6/11	17.....5...10	0.....3.....6	0.....5.....3
Thomas WAFFORD	208		54.....6.....0	0...11.....0	0...16.....6
Henry WOOD, Esqr.	300	7/3	108...15.....0]		
do. of the Estate	1325 1/4	7/10	518...19.....2]		
do. of S. VAUGHAN	150	8/1	60...12.....6]	6...17.....8	10.....6.....6

(page 63 contd. Goochland County Land Tax Return of Thomas F. Bates for 1787)

Proprietors Names	Quantity of Land	Rate p Acre	Amount of Land	Certificate Tax	Amt. of Tax at 1 1/2 p cent
Solomon WILLIAMS	206		72...19.....2]		
do. of William THURSTON	50	7/5	18...10...10]		
do. of William PROPHET	10	7/	3...10.....0]	0...19....0	1.....8.....6
Joseph WOODSON of Tucker	400		150...17.....6	1...10....2	2.....5.....3
John WOODSON of T.	1265		647...15.....5	6.....9.....7	9...14.....4
Henry WALMACK	100	8/1	40.....8.....4	0.....8.....2	0...12.....2
Isaac WINSTON	735	do.	297.....1.....3	2...19.....6	4.....9.....2
Drury WILLIAMS	600		232...10.....0	2.....6.....8	3...10.....0
John WALKER	100	3/3	16.....5.....0	0.....3.....4	0.....5.....0
John WILLIAMSON	200	4/1	40...16.....8	0.....8.....3	0...12.....4
Lewis WILBOURNE	100	do.	20.....8.....4	0.....4.....3	0.....6.....4
Dabney WADE	257 1/2	6/3	81.....9.....4	0...16.....6	1.....4.....8
Estate of William WADE, deced.	257 1/2	7/3	94.....7.....0	0...19.....0	1.....8.....6
John WOODSON, Meadow	300	8/1	121.....5.....0	1.....4.....4	1...16.....6
William WILBOURNE	200	3/3	32...10.....0	0.....6.....6	0.....9.....9
Philip WILLIAMS	200	6/	60.....0.....0	0...12.....0	0...18.....0
Capt. John WARE	925	6/6	300...12.....6]		
do. of Bryant CONLEY	150	5/5	40...12.....6]		
do. of Edward MATTHEWS	16	7/5	5...18.....8]	3...9.....6	5.....4.....3
Peter WALKER, Constable	265	7/10	103...15...10	1.....0...10	1...11.....2
William WILLIAMS	100	do.	39.....3.....4	0.....7...10	0...11.....9
Ann YOUNGER	100	3/3	16.....5.....0	0.....3.....4	0.....5.....0

105,392 1/2 acres   459.....8.....8   688...14.....3

A Copy of the List of Land Tax taken by THOMAS F. BATES, Gent. Commr. in Goochland and examined according to Law

Teste WM. MILLER D. C.

(page 64.)

A List of the Land Tax within the District of ARCHIBALD PLEASANTS, Commissioenr of the County of Goochland, April 1787.

Proprietors Names	Quantity of Land	Rate p Acre	Amount of Land	Certificate Tax	Amount of Tax at 1 1/2 p cent
Colo. Richard ADAMS	1982	8/9	867.....2.....6	8...13.....6	13.....0.....2
Mary ATKINSON	310	8/1	125.....5...10	1.....5.....2	1...17.....8
William ANDERSON	97	6/2	30.....1.....3	0.....6.....1	0.....9.....2
Charles BATES	350	12/	211.....9.....2	2.....2.....4	3.....3.....6
William BARNETT	200	7/6	72...10.....0	0...14.....6	1.....1.....9
Jesse BLACKWELL	98 1/2	8/1	39...16.....3	0.....8.....0	0...12.....0
John BRUMFIELD	125	do.	50...10.....5	0...10.....2	0...15.....2
John BRADSHAW	401	6/9	135.....6.....9	1.....7.....2	2.....0.....9

(page 64 contd. Goochland County Land Tax Return of Archibald Pleasants for 1787)

Proprietors Names		Quantity of Land	Rate p Acre	Amount of Land	Certificate Tax	Amount of Tax at 1 1/2 p cent
Burwell BAUGH		500	14/6	362...10.....0	3...12.....6	5.....8.....9
James CURD		568		238.....2.....0	2.....7.....9	3...11.....5
Richard CROUCH		257	8/1	103...17.....5	1.....0...10	1...10...11
Philip CHILDERS		276	4/1	56.....7.....0	0...11.....5	0...17.....0
Thomas CHANCELOR		125	6/6	40...12.....6	0.....8.....3	0...12.....4
Judith CHEADLE		299	13/6	201...16.....6	2.....0.....6	3.....0.....8
Daniel CLARKE		100	6/1	30.....8.....4	0.....6.....2	0.....9.....2
Richard COCKE		580 1/2	14/10	430.....3.....4	4.....6.....1	6.....9.....1
Estate of Allen COCKE		1195	14/11	891.....5.....5	8...18.....4	13.....7.....6
John CLARKE		44	6/2	13...11.....4	0.....2...10	0.....4.....3
Turner CLARKE		90	6/1	27.....7.....6	0.....5.....6	0.....8.....4
Joseph CLARKE		160		45...15.....0	0.....9.....2	0...13...11
Susanna CROUCH		100	8/1	40.....8.....4	0.....8.....2	0...12.....2
James COCKE		300	do.	121.....5.....0	1.....4.....4	1...16.....6
Edward CARTER		34	do.	13...10.....4	0.....2...10	0.....4.....2
William CLARKSON		50	9/9	24.....7.....6	0.....5.....0	0.....7.....4
Colo. John CURD		609	10/9	327.....6.....9	3.....5.....8	4...18.....4
Capt. Edmond CURD		340		181.....0...10	1...16.....3	2...14.....4
Sarah CURD		211	8/1	85.....5.....7	0...17.....1	1.....5.....7
Benjamin COCKE		122	do.	49.....6.....2	0...10.....0	0...14...10
James COCKE	(P.tan)	54	do.	21...16.....6	0.....4.....3	0.....6.....4
Thomas COCKE		140	do.	56...11.....8	0...11.....4	0...17.....0
Stephen CROUCH		425		212...10.....0	2.....2.....6	3.....3.....9
William CHRISTIAN	C.C.	304	6/1	92.....9.....4	0...18.....6	1.....7.....9
Estate of John DOWDY		122	7/5	45.....4...10	0.....9.....1	0...13.....9
John ELLIS	Henrico	392	12/1	236...16.....8	2.....7.....4	2...11.....0
Stephen ELLIS	Resurveyed	129 1/2	16/2	104...19.....6	1.....1.....0	1...10.....6
David ELLIS		372	8/1	151.....7.....3	1...10.....4	2.....5.....6
William EDWARDS, JUNR.		80	4/1	16.....6.....8	0.....3.....4	0.....5.....0
Francis EVANS		133 1/2	5/5	36.....3.....2	0.....7.....4	0...11.....0
Thomas EDWARDS		50	6/6	16.....5.....0	0.....3.....4	0.....5.....0
Mary EDWARDS		3 1/2	16/2	2...16.....7	0.....0.....8	0.....1.....0
Thomas EVANS		134	6/1	40...15.....2	0.....8.....3	0...12.....4

(page 65. Goochland County Land Tax Return of Archibald Pleasants for 1787)

Proprietors Names		Quantity of Land	Rate p Acre	Amount of Land	Certificate Tax	Amount of Tax at 1 1/2 p cent
William FARRAR		886	10/5	461.....9.....2	4...12.....4	6...18.....6
William FORD		200	8/1	80...16.....8	0...16.....2	1.....4.....4
Elizabeth FORD		233	do.	94.....3.....5	0...18...11	1.....8.....4
Joseph FARRAR		56	12/1	33...16.....8	0.....6...11	0...10.....4
Mary FRAZIER	Resurveyed	159 1/2	8/1	64.....9.....4	0...13.....0	0...19.....6
Reuben FORD		147	do.	59.....8.....3	0...12.....0	0...18.....0
John T. GRIFFIN, Esqr.		2671		2738.....0.....0	27.....7.....8	41.....1.....7
John GORDEN		186		77...18.....3	0...15.....8	1.....3.....5
Henry GRAY		100	8/1	40.....8.....4	0.....8.....2	0...12.....2
John GUERRANT, Gent.		636		334.....2.....6	3.....6...11	5.....0.....6
John GILLAM	(Pr. Geo.)	500	9/9	243...15.....0	2.....8.....9	3...13.....2

(page 65 contd. Goochland County Land Tax Return of Archibald Pleasants for 1787)

Proprietors Names	Quantity of Land	Rate p Acre	Amount of Land	Certificate Tax	Amt. of Tax at 1 1/2 p cent
Colo. John GUERRANT	442		184...15.....3	1...16...11	2...15.....6
James GEORGE	100	8/1	40.....8.....4	0.....8.....2	0...12.....2
William GARTHRIGHT	298	10/9	160.....3.....6	1...12.....2	2.....8.....2
Francis GRAVES	640		1164.....0.....0	11...12...10	17.....9.....3
John HYLTON	411	10/9	220...18.....9	2.....4.....3	3.....6.....4
Francis E. HARRIS	440 1/2		391.....3.....3	3...18.....5	5...17.....6
John HINES	330	9/4	154.....0.....0	1...10...11	2.....6.....4
Thomas HARDING	549		289.....0.....6	2...17...10	4.....6.....9
Strangeman HUTCHINS	55	8/1	22.....4.....7	0.....4.....5	0.....6.....8
Capt. Thomas HATCHER	510	9/9	248...12.....6	2.....9...10	3...14.....8
James HUNNICUTT	287	8/1	115.....9...11	1.....3.....3	1...14...10
Benjamin HUGHES	627	do.	253.....8.....3	2...10.....9	3...16.....2
Capt. Gideon HATCHER	360	9/7	172...10.....0	1...14.....6	2...11...10
William HUGHES (Hanover)	115	9/2	52...14.....2	0...10.....7	0...15...10
Giles HARDING	316	8/6	104.....6.....0	1.....7.....0	2.....0.....4
William HAY	521		293.....0.....5	2...18.....8	4.....7...11
Thomas HODGES	50	5/1	12...14.....2	0.....2.....7	0.....3...10
John JOHNSON (0)	611 1.2		244.....5.....8	2.....9.....0	3...13.....5
Charles JOHNSON	124	6/6	40.....0.....6]		
do. of William ROUNDTREE	121	10/5	63.....0.....5]	1.....0...10	1...11.....3
David JOHNSON (Geneto)	115	8/1	46.....9.....7	0.....9.....4	0...14.....0
John JOHNSON (do.)	271	9/4	126.....9.....4	1.....5.....4	1...18.....0
Isham JOHNSON (do.)	115	9/2	52...14.....2	0...10.....8	0...16.....0
Richard JOHNSON	150	do.	68...15.....0	0...13...10	1.....0.....8
Sarah JORDAN	75	16/2	60...12.....6	0...12.....2	0...18.....4
Daniel JOHNSON	150	4/	30.....0.....0	0.....6.....0	0.....9.....0
Susanna LAPRADE	300	10/8	160.....0.....0	1...12.....0	2.....8.....0
John LAPRADE	128	do.	68.....5.....6	0...13.....8	1.....0.....6
Capt. Elisha LEAKE	818	9/7	391...19.....2]		
do. of John ROYSTER	9 1/2	12/1	5...14...10]	3...19.....8	5...19.....6
John LAYNE	50	4/1	10.....4.....2	0.....2.....2	0.....3.....2
John LEWIS (C.M.)	200	8/1	80...16.....8	0...16.....2	1.....4.....4
Joseph LEWIS	860 1/3		309.....1.....2	3.....1...11	4...12.....9

(page 66. Goochland County Land Tax Return of Archibald Pleasants for 1787)

Proprietors Names	Quantity of Land	Rate p Acre	Amount of Land	Certificate Tax	Amt. of Tax at 1 1/2 p cent
Stephen G. LETCHER	49	8/1	19.....6.....1	0.....4.....0	0.....6.....0
Yancy LIPSCOMB	350 1/2	8/6	148...19.....3	1.....9...10	2.....4...10
Colo. Nathaniel G. MORRIS	400	9/1	181...13.....4	1...16.....4	2...14.....6
John MADDOX	150	6/9	50...12.....6	0...10.....2	0...15.....4
William McCAUL	81	14/1	57.....0.....7	0...11.....4	0...17.....2
Amos L. MORE	260	10/	130.....0.....0	1.....6.....0	1...19.....0
Stokes McCAUL	295	8/1	119.....4.....7	1.....3...11	1...16.....0
Mary MILLER	426	8/10	188.....3.....0	1...17.....9	2...16.....6
Edward McBRIDE	200	6/1	60...16.....8	0...12.....2	0...18.....4
Matthew NIGHTINGALE	59 2/3	9/10	29.....6.....9	0.....6.....0	0.....9.....0

(page 66 contd. Goochland County Land Tax Return of Archibald Pleasants for 1787)

Prorprietors Names	Quantity of Land	Rate p Acre	Amount of Land	Certificate Tax	Amt. of Tax at 1 1/2 p cent
Samuel NUCKOLDS	115	7/2	41.....4.....2	0.....8.....3	0...12...6
John NEAVES	290	7/5	107...10...10	1.....4.....8	1...12...4
Stephen NOWLIN	150	6/9	50...12.....6	0...10.....2	0...15...4
William NUCKOLDS, JUNR.	121	8/1	48...18.....1	0.....9...10	0...14...10
Pouncy NUCKOLDS	110	do.	44.....9.....3	0.....9.....0	0...13...6
Charles NUCKOLDS	104	7/2	37.....5.....4	0.....7.....6	0...11...4
Thomas NUCKOLDS	115	do.	41.....4.....2	0.....8.....4	0...12...6
Rene NAPIER	180	8/1	72...15.....0	0...14.....7	1...1...11
Colo. Josiah PARKER	986 1/2	14/10	731...13.....1	7.....6.....4	10...19.....8
Charles N. PURKINS	160	8/	64.....0.....0	0...12...11	0...19...11
Hezekiah PURYEAR	754		310.....6.....7]		
do. of Mary FRAZIER	6 1/2	8/1	2...12.....7]	3.....2...10	4...14.....3
Richard PLEASANTS	728		356.....1.....4	3...11.....3	5.....6...10
Thomas PLEASANTS	1833		1456.....9...11	14...11.....4	21...17.....0
Isaac W. PLEASANTS	539	21/6	579.....8.....6	5...16.....0	9...14.....0
Matthew PLEASANTS	250	8/1	101.....0...10	1.....0.....3	1...10....4
Archer PAYNE, Gent.	850	8/7	364...15...10]		
do. of Thomas OLIVER	273	8/1	110.....6...10]		
do. of John BRADSHAW	49	6/9	16...10.....9]	4...18.....4	7.....7...6
Samuel PARSONS	523 1/3	15/	392...10.....0	3...18.....6	5...17...9
John PRICE (Henrico)	268	13/6	180...18.....0	1...16.....2	2...14...4
William POWEL	266	7/2	95.....6.....4	0...19...1	1.....8...8
Major POWERS	180	8/1	72...15.....0	0...14.....8	1.....2.....0
Anderson PEERS	559	do.	225...18.....7]		
do. of Pleasant WILLIS	278	do.	112.....7.....2]		
do. of Charles JOHNSON, JUNR.	220	11/5	125...11.....8 [	4...12...10	6...19.....3
James PLEASANTS	500	16/7	414...11.....8	4.....3.....0	6.....4...6
Joseph PLEASANTS	200	8/1	80...16.....8	0...16.....2	1.....4...4
Robert PLEASANTS (Buff)	140	7/	49.....0.....0	0.....9...11	0...14...10
Philip PLEASANTS	151		58...19.....0	0...11...10	0...17...10

(page 67. Goochland County Land Tax Return of Archibald Pleasants for 1787)

William POWERS	368	6/6	119...12.....0	1.....3...11	1...16.....0
Doctor William PASTEUR	700	13/4	466...13.....4	4...13.....4	7.....0.....0
Estate of Francis PLEDGE, deced.	50	8/1	20.....4.....2	0.....4.....1	0.....6...2
Estate of William PLEDGE, deced.	50	9/9	24.....7.....6	0.....4...11	0.....7...4
Archer PLEDGE	50	11/5	28...10...10	0.....5...10	0.....8...8
John PAYNE	439	14/5	316.....8...11	3.....3.....4	4...15.....0
Robin POOR	350	10/5	182.....5...10	1...16.....6	2...14...10
Joseph POLLARD, Gent.	447	9/11	221...12.....9	2.....4.....3	3.....6...6
Mary PURKINS	161 1/2	8/1	65.....5.....6	0...13.....1	0...19...8
Molly PURKINS	250	do.	101.....0...10	1.....0.....2	1...10...4
William PURKINS	200	6/1	60...16.....8	0...12.....2	0...18...4
William PURKINS, JUNR.	265	6/	79...10.....0	0...16.....0	1.....4...0
Estate of Walker PERKINS, deced.	111 3/4	9/10	54...18...11	0...11.....0	0...16...6
Benjamin PERKINS	250	3/3	40...12.....6	0.....8.....2	0...12...4
Colo. George PAYNE	256	10/	128.....0.....0]		
do. of David WEBSTER	50	10/6	26.....5.....0]	1...10...11	2.....6...5
Isaac PERRIN	225	12/1	135...18.....9	1.....7.....3	2.....0...11

(page 67 contd. Goochland County Land Tax Return of Archibald Pleasants for 1787)

Proprietors Names	Quantity of Land	Rate p Acre	Amount of Land	Certificate Tax	Amt. of Tax at 1 1/2 p cent
Archibald PLEASANTS	299	13/6	201...16.....6	2......0.....5	3.....0.....8
Josias PAYNE	335	6/8	111...13.....4	1.....2.....4	1...13.....6
Jesse REDD	397	8/1	160.....9.....1	1...12.....2	2.....8.....3
Capt. John ROYSTER	175	12/1	105...14.....4	1.....1.....3	1...11...11
John REDD	252		88.....4.....8	0...17.....4	1...6.....7
Edward REDFORD	295		221...15...10	2.....4.....2	3.....6.....6
William RADFORD, Mercht.	195	4/1	39...16.....3	0.....8.....0	0...12.....0
Thomas ROUNDTREE	108	10/5	56.....5.....0	0...11.....4	0...17.....0
Samuel ROUNTREE	121	d0.	63.....5.....0	0...12.....8	0...19.....0
Randal ROUNDTREE	247	11/5	140...19...11	1.....8.....3	2.....2.....5
Matthew RIDDLE	70	7/	24...10.....0	0.....5.....0	0.....7.....6
Isaac RAGLAND	150	6/9	50...12.....6	0...10.....2	0...15.....4
William ROYSTER, Gent.	543	11/1	300...18.....3	3.....0.....2	4...10.....4
Capt. Thomas ROYSTER	166 2/3		84.....1.....6	0...16.....9	1.....4...10
Milner REDFORD	539	9/8	260...10.....4	2...12.....2	3...18.....2
Thomas M. RANDOLPH, Esqr.	3052		2764.....3.....8	27...13.....0	41.....9.....6
Mary ROGERS	17	8/1	6...17.....5	0.....1.....4	0.....2.....0
William RONALD, Esqr.	1370		738.....9.....2	7.....7.....6	11...1.....8
Josiah SEAY	145		49...17...11	0...10.....0	0...15.....0
William SAUNDERS	20	8/1	8.....1.....8	0.....1...10	0.....2.....9
Major Stephen SOUTHALL	644		252.....3.....0	2...10.....6	3...15.....9
Elizabeth STODGHILL	28	12/1	16...18.....4	0.....3.....6	0.....5.....2

(page 68. Goochland County Land Tax Return of Archibald Pleasants for 1787)

Proprietors Names	Quantity of Land	Rate p Acre	Amount of Land	Certificate Tax	Amt. of Tax at 1 1/2 p cent
Thomas SHOEMAKER	200	10/1	100...16.....8	1.....0.....2	1...10.....4
Colo. John SYME	318	8/1	128...10.....6]		
do. of Susanna BIBB	248	do.	100.....4.....8]	2...6...10	3.....9.....0
John SAUNDERS	30	do.	12.....2.....6	0.....2.....5	0.....3.....8
Estate of Charles SAMPSON	234	do.	94...11.....6	0...19.....0	1.....8.....6
John SHELTON, Gent.	462		191.....2.....0	1...18.....2	2...17.....6
Richard SAMPSON	250	7/3	90...12.....6	0...18.....2	1.....7.....4
Majro Robert H. SAUNDERS	330	13/6	222...15.....0	2.....4.....8	3.....7.....0
Philip TINSLEY	50	12/1	30.....4.....2	0.....6.....2	0.....9.....2
Thomas TOWLES, Esqr.	348 1/2	9/4	162...12.....8	1...12.....8	2.....8...10
Barthomomew TURNER	200	8/1	80...16.....8	0...16.....2	1.....4.....4
William UTTLEY	125	do.	50...10.....5	0...10.....2	0...15.....4
Obadiah UTTLEY	8	do.	3.....4.....8	0.....0.....8	0.....1.....0
Ann UTTLEY	116	6/4	36...14.....8	0.....7.....5	0...11.....2
John UTTLEY	125	8/1	50...10.....5	0...10.....2	0...15.....4
Hezekiah UTTLEY	58	6/1	17...12...10	0.....3.....7	0.....5.....4
Elizabeth UNDERWOOD	100	11/5	57.....1.....8	0...11.....5	0...17.....2
George UNDERWOOD	526	7/4	192...17.....4	1...18.....8	2...18.....0
Thomas UNDERWOOD, Esqr.	600	8/9	262...10.....0	2...12.....6	3...18...10
Estate of James UNDERWOOD	215	6/8	71...13.....4	0...14.....4	1.....1.....6
Matthew VAUGHAN	753 1/2	9/1	342.....4.....4	3.....8.....6	5.....2.....9

(page 68 contd. Goochland County Land Tax Return of Archibald Pleasants for 1787)

Proprietors Names	Quantity of Land	Rate p Acre	Amount of Land	Certificate Tax	Amt. of Tax at 1 1/2 p cent
James VAUGHAN	362	7/7	137.....5.....2	1.....7.....5	2.....1.....4
Colo. John WOODSON	611		996...19.....4	9...19.....5	14...19.....2
Matthew WOODSON	1101		868.....1.....8	8...13.....8	13.....0.....7
Daniel WADE	346 1/2		142.....7.....5	1.....8.....6	2.....2.....8
Joseph WATKINS	597		278.....8.....6	2...15.....8	4.....3.....6
Peter WALKER, (Geneto)	155	8/1	62...12...11	0...12.....7	0...18...10
Shadrach WALKER	75	do.	30.....6.....3	0.....6.....2	0.....9.....2
Richard WADE	197	9/7	94.....8.....0	0...19.....0	1.....8.....6
Robert WADE	97	8/1	39.....4.....1	0.....8.....0	0...12.....0
Major Joseph WOODSON	578	do.	233...12.....2	2.....6.....8	3...10.....0
John WADE	73	do	29...10...1	0.....6.....0	0.....9.....0
Eleanor WILLIS	100	6/1	30.....8.....4	0.....6.....2	0.....9.....2
William WOODALL	63	6/6	20.....9.....6	0.....4.....2	0.....6.....2
William WEBBER, Preacher	177	6/4	51.....1.....0	0...11.....3	0...16...10
Edward WILLIS	160	8/1	64...13.....4	0...13.....0	0...19.....6
Thomas WOODSON	200	12/1	120...16.....8	1.....4.....2	1...16.....4
Nathaniel WEBSTER	140	6/6	45...10.....0	0.....9.....0	0...13.....6

(page 69. Goochland County Land Tax Return of Archibald Pleasants for 1787)

Proprietors Names	Quantity of Land	Rate p Acre	Amount of Land	Certificate Tax	Amt. of Tax at 1 1/2 p cent
Robert WINGFIELD	90	8/1	36.....7.....6	0.....7.....4	0...11.....0
David WEBSTER	25	10/6	13.....2.....6	0.....2.....8	0.....4.....0
Joseph WOODSON (Geneto)	225	9/	101.....5.....0	1.....0.....4	1...10.....6
Estate of Joseph WOODSON, deced.	222	10/	111.....0.....0	1.....2.....2	1...13.....4
Dorothy WATKINS	170	8/1	68...14.....2	0...13...10	1.....0.....8
Thomas WATKINS	583	do.	235...12.....7	2.....7.....2	3...10...10
Benjamin WATKINS	238	9/5	112.....1.....2	1.....2.....5	1...13.....8
John WATKINS	519	8/11	231.....7.....9	2.....6.....3	3.....9.....6
William WEBBER, SENR.	340	10/6	178...10.....0	1...15...10	2...13.....8
Benjamin WOODSON, (Fluvanna)	205	9/1	93.....2.....1	0...18.....8	1.....8.....0
Benjamin WATKINS, JUNR.	156	9/5	73.....9.....0	0...14.....9	1.....2.....2
Henry WHITLOW, JUNR.	50	8/1	20.....4.....2	0.....4.....2	0.....6.....2
Henry WHITLOW, SENR.	99	do.	40.....0.....3	0.....8.....1	0...12.....2
John WITT	17	do.	6...17.....5	0.....1.....4	0.....2.....0
Tucker WOODSON	600	17/6	530.....0.....0	5.....6.....0	7...19.....0
Samuel WOODWARD	450	12/1	271...17.....6	2...14.....4	4.....1.....6
John WOODWARD	50	do.	30.....4.....2	0.....6.....1	0.....9.....2

69,082 1/2   L. 387...13...10   L. 580...19.....4

ARCHIBALD PLEASANT, Commr.

Examined and compared the 30th July 1787.

GEORGE PAYNE CL CT.

(page 70).

A List of Transferences, &c. in Goochland County in the year 1783.

Proprietors		Quantity Land	Price	Amount of Land	Tax
Athanasius BARNETT	By Jesse BLACKWELL				
	Whole Tract	87 1/2	8/1	39...16.....3	0...12.....0
John PREWIT	By John BOLLING				
	Part do.	149	7/2	53.....7....10	0...16.....0
Joseph WATKINS	By Elijah BRUMFIELD				
	Part do.	200	10/3	102...10.....0	1...10.....9
do.	By John GRAY				
	Part do.	85		44.....8.....4	0...13.....6
Aaron PARISH	By William BUSBY				
	Part do.	50	4/1	10.....4.....2	0.....3.....1
Charles CHRISTIAN, deced	By George CHRISTIAN				
	Whole Tract	217	10/	108...10.....0	1.....2.....7
William FLEMING, Esqr.	By Charles FLEMING				
	Half do.	390	20/4	396...10.....0	5...19.....0
Jane VADEN	By Joseph R. FARRAR				
	Whole Tract	400	12/1	241...13.....4	3...12.....6
Benjamin SALMONDS	By William GEORGE				
	Whole Tract	250	4/10	60.....8.....4	0...18.....2
Josias PAYNE, JR.	By John HYLTON				
	Part Tract	411	10/9	220...18.....3	3.....6.....3
Josias PAYNE, JR.	By William PAYNE				
	Balance	201	do.	108.....0.....9	1...12.....6
Samuel WOODSON	By David HUDSON				
	Whole Tract	368	8/1	148...14.....8	2.....4.....9
Charles HOUCHINS, deced.	By Charles HOUCHINS, JR.				
	Whole Tract	117	5/10	34.....2.....6	0...10.....3
Jennings PULLAM	By John HUSON				
	Whole Tract	47	5/	11...15.....0	0.....3.....7
Mary LEWIS	By Colo. Robert LEWIS				
	Whole Tract	1030	13/6	695.....5.....0	10.....8.....7
Joseph LEWIS, SENR. deced.	By Estate of Joseph LEWIS, SENR., deced.				
	Whole Tract	281	8/1	113...11.....5	1...14.....1
Isham RICHARDSON	By Thomas MILLER				
	Whole Tract	181	12/6	113.....2.....6	1...14.....0
John MULLINS, deced.	By Estate of John MULLINS, deced.				
	Whole Tract	350	6/5	112.....5...10	1...13.....4
James NOWALL	By Thomas NOWALL				
	Part Tract	100	6/	30.....0.....0	0.....9.....0
Barnett OWEN, deced.	By Estate of Barnett OWEN, deced.				
	Whole Tract	100	3/3	16.....5.....0	0.....4...11
Jane JUDE	By John PRICE				
	Whole Tract	268	13/6	180...18.....0	2...14.....4
Jolly PARISH, deced.	By Estate of Jolly PARISH, deced.				
	Whole Tract	735	4/5	165.....7.....6	2.....9.....8
William GEORGE	By Thomas POLLOCK,				
	Court House	100	12/1	60.....8.....4	0...18.....2
William ROBARDS, JR.	By Joseph PERKINS, JR.				
	Whole Tract	265	6/	79...10.....0	1.....3...11

(page 70 contd. Goochland County Transferences, &c. in the year 1783)

Proprietors		Quantity of Land	Price	Amount of Land	Tax
John HUTCHINS	By Hezekiah PURYEAR				
	Whole Tract	256 1/2	8/1	130...13.....5	1...11.....2
Martin MIMS	By John PERKINS				
	Whole Tract	50	5/8	14.....3.....4	0.....4.....3
William HOLMAN	By David ROSS				
	Part Tract	400	4/1	81...13.....4	1.....4.....6
Benjamin BRADSHAW	By William RONALD				
	Whole Tract	200	6/1	60...16.....8	0...18.....3
Elijah BRUMFIELD	By Thomas WATKINS				
	Whole Tract	130	8/1	52...10...10	0...16...10
Bowler COCKE	By Foster WEBB, SENR.				
	Part Tract	200	8/1	80...16.....8	1.....4....( )
Japheth TOWLER	By Foster WEBB, SENR.				
	Whole Tract	275	5/2	70.....0...10	(torn)

(page 71. Goochland County Transferences, &c. in the year 1783)

Proprietors		Quantity of Land	Price	Amount of Land	Tax
Benjamin JOHNSON, Geneto	By Joseph WATKINS				
	Whole Tract	115	8/1	46.....9.....7	0...14.....0
William ROBARDS	By Estate of Valentine WOOD, deced.				
	Whole Tract	536	6/7	176.....8.....8	2...13.....0
Joseph WOODSON, SENR., deced.	By Estate of Joseph WOODSON, SENR., deced				
	Whole Tract	222	10/	111.....0.....0	1...13.....4
William WILLIAMS, deced.	By Drury WILLIAMS				
	Whole Tract	500	8/1	202.....1.....8	3.....0.....8
David ALVIS	By William WILLIAMS				
	Whole Tract	50	4/1	10.....4.....2	0.....3.....1
Thomas B. EADES	By John WILLIAMS, D.C.				
	Whole Tract	136	do.	27...15.....4	0.....8.....4

ARCHD: PLEASANTS   ]
THO. F. BATES   ] Commrs.

(page 71. Goochland County Transferences, &c. in the year 1784)

Proprietors		Quantity of Land	Price	Amount of Land	Tax
Anderson PEERS	By David ELLIS				
	Part Tract	138 1/2	8/1	55...19.....7	0...16...11
Samuel DUVAL, JR.	By Joseph MAYO				
	Whole Tract	500	14/6	362...10.....0	5.....9.....9
George PAYNE, JR., deced.	By Estate of George PAYNE, JR., deced.				
	Whole Tract	200	5/7	55...16.....8	0...16.....9
George PAYNE, SENR., deced.	By Capt. Joseph PAYNE				
	Whole Tract	977	8/1	394...17.....5	5...18.....6
John T. GRIFFIN, Esqr.	By Samuel PARSONS				
	Part Tract	490	15/	367...10.....0	5...10.....3
James MADDOX	By John SHELTON				
	Part Tract	50	9/10	24...11.....8	0.....7.....5
James MADDOX	By Estate of James UNDERWOOD				
	Part Tract	215	6/8	71...13.....4	1.....1.....6
Francis HILL	By Charles WADDELL				
	Whole Tract	262	6/1	79...13...10	1.....3...11

(page 71 contd. Goochland County Transferences, &c. in the year 1784)

Proprietors		Quantity of Land	Price	Amount of Land	Tax
John SALMONDS	by Richard WALMACK				
	Whole Tract	150	5/5	40...12.....6	0...12.....3
	ARCHD. PLEASANTS	]			
	THO; F. BATES	]	Commrs.		

(page 71 contd. Goochland County Transferences, &c. in the year 1785

John BOLLING, SENR.	By John BOLLING, JR.				
	Part Tract	600	9/8	290.....0.....0	4.....7.....0
Allen COCKE, deced.	By Estate of Allen COCKE, deced.				
	Whole Tract	1195	14/11	891.....5.....5	13.....7.....5
Jeffry CLARKE, deced.	By Estate of Jeffry CLARKE, deced.				
	Whole Tract	98	6/7	32.....5.....2	0.....9.....9
Robert CARDIN, deced.	By Estate of Robert CARDIN, deced.				
	Whole Tract	200	5/1	50...16.....8	0...15.....3
Thomas ELDRIDGE	By Majr. John GUERRANT				
	Part Tract	103	8/1	41...12.....7	0...12.....4
William A. ENGLAND	By Majr. John GUERRANT				
	Part Tract	89	7/	31.....3.....0	0.....9.....4
Stephen SAMPSON, Gent.	By John GUERRANT, Gent.				
	Part Tract	186		111.....0.....0	1...13.....3
Charles WADDELL	By Francis HILL				
	Whole Tract	262	6/1	78...13...10	1.....3.....1

(page 72. Goochland County Transferences, &c. in the year 1785)

Benjamin JOHNSON (Bryd.) deced.	By Estate of Benjamin JOHNSON, deced.				
	Whole Tract	140	7/	49.....0.....0	0...14.....9
John LAPRADE, deced.	By Estate of John LAPRADE, deced.				
	Whole Tract	788	10/8	420.....5.....4	6.....6.....1
Colo. Robert LEWIS	By Howel LEWIS				
	Part Tract	600	7/	221.....7.....6	3.....6.....8
Estate of Joseph LEWIS, SENR., deced.	By Joseph LEWIS, JR.				
	Whole Tract	281	8/1	113...11.....5	1...14.....1
George CHRISTIAN	By Thomas MILLER				
	Whole Tract	217	10/	108...10.....0	1...12.....7
Drury MURRELL	By Daniel McCAWLEY				
	Whole Tract	200	6/1	60...16.....8	0...18.....3
Stephen G. LETCHER	By William MERIWETHER				
	Whole Tract	516	8/1	208...11.....0	3.....2.....6
Edward MATTHEWS, deced.	By Estate of Edward MATTHEWS, deced.				
	2/3 Tract	582	7/5	215.....1.....8	3.....4.....8
Edward MATTHEWS, deced.	By Jane MATTHEWS				
	1/3 Tract	291	do.	107...10...10	1...12.....4
Rene NAPIER	By Stephen G. LETCHER				
	Whole Tract	49	8/1	19...16.....1	0.....6.....0

(page 72 contd. Goochland County Transferences, &c. in the year 1785)

Proprietors		Quantity of Land	Price	Amount of Land	Tax
Pleasant ATKINS	By John PAYNE				
	Whole Tract	65	6/7	21.....7...11	0.....6.....6
James MADDOX	By Josias PAYNE, JR.				
	Whole Tract	335	6/8	111...13.....4	1...13.....6
Francis PLEDGE, deced.	By Estate of Francis PLEDGE, deced.				
	Whole Tract	50	8/1	20.....4.....3	0.....6.....1
David ROSS	By Colo. George PAYNE				
	Part Tract	256	10/	128.....0.....0	1...17.....2
Capt. Joseph PAYNE	By Estate of Jesse PAYNE, deced.				
	Part Tract	100	8/1	40.....8.....4	0...12.....1
Colo. John PAYNE, deced.	By Estate of Colo. John PAYNE, deced.				
	Part Tract	2053	8/	821.....4.....0	12.....6.....5
New Entry from Land Office	Alexander PARISH				
		200	5/	62...10.....0	0...18.....9
John LOVELL	By James ROBARDS				
	Whole Tract	343	3/4	57.....3.....4	0...17.....3
William ROUNDTREE, deced.	By Estate of William ROUNDTREE, deced.				
	Part Tract	108	10/5	56.....5.....0	0...17.....0
William ROUNTREE, deced.	By Samuel ROUNDTREE				
	Part Tract	121	do.	63.....0.....5	0...19.....0
William ROUNDTREE, deced.	By William ROUNDTREE				
	Part Tract	121	do.	63.....0.....5	0...19.....0
William WHITFIELD	By David ROSS				
	Whole Tract	105	4/1	21.....8.....9	0.....6.....6
Charles RICE, deced.	By Estate of Charles RICE, deced.				
	Whole Tract	175	5/10	51.....0...10	0...15.....4
Capt. Edmund DUKE	By James SALMONDS				
	Whole Tract	230	4/7	52...14.....2	0...15...10
Mary JUDE	By Majr. Robert H. SAUNDERS				
	Whole Tract	330	13/6	222...15.....0	3.....6.....9
Capt. Joseph SHELTON, deced.	By David SHELTON				
	Part Tract	840		440.....0.....0	6...12.....0
Capt. Joseph SHELTON, deced.	By Joseph SHELTON, JR.				
	Balance	529		314...10.....0	4...14.....6
John SHELTON (Hanover)	By Majr. Stephen SOUTHALL				
	Whole Tract	400	8/1	161...13.....4	2.....8.....6
Capt. Robert SMITH, deced. (P.tan)	By Estate of Capt. Robert SMITH, deced.				
	Whole Tract	40	do.	16.....3.....4	0.....4...11
William A. ENGLAND	By Sarah TEBBS				
	Balance Tract	50	7/	15...10.....0	0.....5.....4
Augustine EASTIN	By Pleasant WILLIS				
	Whole Tract	180	8/1	72...15.....0	1.....1...10
William WHITLOCK	By Drury WILLIAMS				
	Whole Tract	100	6/1	30.....8.....4	0.....9.....2

ARCHD. PLEASANTS   ]
THO: F. BATES   ]   Commrs.

(page 73. A List of Transferences of Land in Goochland County since last Settlement

Proprietors		Quantity of Land	Price	Amount of Land	Tax
Aaron PARISH	to William BUSBY				
		50	4/1	10.....4.....2	0.....3.....1
Athanasius BARNETT	to Jesse BLACKWELL				
		98 1/1	8/1	100.....4.....8	1...10.....2
John PREWIT	to John BOLLING				
		144	7/2	51...12.....0	0...15.....5
Joseph WATKINS	to Elijah BRUMFIELD				
		200	10/3	102...10.....0	1...10.....9
Charles CHRISTIAN	to George CHRISTIAN				
		217	10/	108...10.....0	1...12.....7
William FLEMING, Esqr.	to Charles FLEMING				
		390	2-/4	395.....0.....0	5...19.....0
Jane VADEN	to Joseph R. FARRAR				
		400	12/1	241...13.....4	3...12.....6
Benjamin SALMONS	to William GEORGE				
		250	4/10	60.....8.....4	0...18.....2
Joseph WATKINS	to Joh GRAY				
		85	10/3	44.....8.....4	0...13.....6
Charles HOUCHINS, deced.	to Charles HOUCHINS, JR.				
		117	5/10	34.....2.....6	0...10.....3
Jennings PULLAM	to John HUSON				
		47	5/	11...15.....0	0.....3.....7
William HOLMAN	to Tandy HOLMAN				
		400	4/1	81...13.....4	1.....4.....5
Josias PAYNE, JR.	to John HYLTON				
		411	10/9	220...18.....3	3.....6.....3
Samuel WOODSON	to David HUDSON				
		368	8/1	148...14.....8	2...14.....9
Mary LEWIS	to Robert LEWIS				
		1030	13/6	695.....5.....0	10.....8.....7
Joseph LEWIS, SENR., deced	to Estate of Joseph LEWIS, deced.				
		281	8/1	113...11.....5	1...14.....1
John MULLINS, deced.	to Estate of John MULLINS, deced.				
		350	6/5	112.....5...10	1...13.....4
Stephen G. LETCHER	to William MERIWETHER				
		516	8/1	208...11.....0	3.....2.....6
Isham RICHARDSON	to Thomas MILLER				
		181	12/6	113.....2.....6	1...14.....0
James NOWELL	to Thomas NOWELL				
		100	6/	30.....0.....0	0.....9.....0
Barnett OWEN, deced.	to Estate of Barnett OWEN, deced.				
		100	3/3	16.....5.....0	0.....4...11
John HUTCHINS	to Hezekiah PURYEAR				
		256 1/2	8/1	130...13.....5	1...11.....2
Martin MIMS	to John PURKINS				
		50	5/8	14.....3.....4	0.....4.....3
John T. GRIFFIN, Esqr.	to Samuel PARSONS				
			15/		
Jane JUDE	to John PRICE				
		268	13/6	180...18.....0	2...14.....4

(page 73 contd. Goochland County Transference of Land since last Settlement)

Proprietors		Quantity of Land	Price	Amount of Land	Tax
Josias PAYNE, JR.	to William PAYNE				
		201	10/9	108.....0.....9	1...12.....6
Jolly PARISH, deced.	to Estate of Jolly PARISH, deced.				
		735	4/5	165.....7.....6	2.....9....8
William GEORGE	to Thomas POLLOCK, Courthouse				
		100	12/1	60.....8.....4	0...18.....2
Benjamin BRADSHAW	to William RONALD, Esqr.				
		200	6/1	60...16.....8	0...18.....3
David ALVIS	to William WILLIAMS				
		50	4/1	10.....4.....2	0.....3.....1
Thomas B. EADES	to John WILLIAMS, D. C.				
		136	do.	27...15.....4	0.....8.....4
Elijah BRUMFIELD	to Thomas WATKINS				
		130	8/1	52...10...10	0...15...10
Jeffery CLARKE	to Joseph WATKINS				
		98	6/7	32.....5.....2	0.....9.....9
Bowler COCKE	to John WEBB				
		200	8/1	80...16.....8	1.....4.....3
Japheth TOWLER	to John WEBB				
		275	5/2	70.....0...10	1.....1.....4
Benjamin JOHNSON, Geneto	to Joseph WATKINS				
		115	8/1	46.....9.....7	0...13.....8
William ROBARDS, deced.	to Estate of Colo. Valentine WOOD				
		536	6/7	176.....8.....8	2...13.....0
Joseph WOODSON, deced., Geneto.	to Estate of Joseph WOODSON, deced.				
		222	10/	111.....0.....0	1...13.....4

(page 74. Goochland County Transferences of Land since last Settlement)

Proprietors		Quantity of Land	Price	Amount of Land	Tax
William WILLIAMS, deced.	to Drury WILLIAMS				
		500	8/1	202.....1.....8	3.....0.....8
William ROBARDS, JR.	to Joseph PURKINS, JR.				
		265	6/	79...10.....0	1.....3...11

Goochland February 10th 1784.

ARCHD. PLEASANTS   ]
THO: F. BATES   ] Commrs.

(page 75.)

A List of Transferences, Resurveys, &c., of Land in Goochland County to October 1st, 1786.

Former Proprietors / Present Proprietors	Quantity of Land	Tax	Alterations in Tax	Quantity of Land	Tax
Ann COCKE	1567	17.....8.....9			
Richard COCKE				580 1/2	6.....9.....1
Ann COCKE					
Colo. Josiah PARKER				886 1/2	10...19.....8
Henry TUGGLE	100	0.....7.....9			
David ROSS, Esqr.				100	0.....7.....8
Samuel LAMAY	106	0.....6.....6	0.....4....11		
David ROSS, Esqr.				25	0..... 1.....7
William WALKER	94	0.....6.....0	0.....4.....5		
David ROSS, Esqr.				25	0.....1.....7
Thomas POLLOCK	1192 3/4	6...17.....2	5...19.....0		
David ROSS, Esqr.				100	0...18.....2
Estate of Jolly PARISH	735	2.....9.....9]			
William WALKER		]		100	0.....6.....9
Sherard PARISH		] 1..6..8	85		0.....6....( )
Meredith PARISH		]		100	0.....6.....9
John LAWRENCE		]		50	0.....3.....6
(400 acres of the above lies in Louisa and assessed in that County					
Reverend Francis HILL	262	1.....4.....0			
John WILLIAMS, resurveyed				304	1.....7.....4
Thomas WAFFORD	540	4...16.....6	0.....7.....4		
John WILLIAMS, resurveyed				432	1...6.....2
Matthew VAUGHAN	800	5.....9.....0	5.....2.....9		
Daniel WADE				46 1/2	0.....6.....3
Capt. Stockley TOWLES	348 1/2	2.....4.....6			
Yancy LIPSCOMB, resurveyed				350 1/2	2.....4...10
Richard WADE	297	2.....2...10	1...10.....8		
David WADE				100	0...12.....2
Estate of Jeffry CLARKE	98	0.....9.....10			
Joseph WATKINS				53	0.....5.....3
Estate of Jeffry CLARKE					
Joseph CLARKE				45	0.....4.....7
Estate of Walker PURKINS	171 1/2	1.....5.....4	0...16.....4		
Matthew NIGHTINGALE				59 2/3	0.....9.....0
John MOSS, JR.	200	1.....4.....4			
Benjamin CLOPTON				200	1.....4.....4
Thomas MASSIE (0)	289	1...10....4	0.....9....4		
Benjamin CLOPTON				200	1.....1.....0
Thomas POLLOCK	1092 2/3				
Robert SMITH				175	0...19.....0
Thomas POLLOCK					
Henry WOOD				300	1...12.....8
William CHEEK	232	1.....0.....4	0.....2.....2		
William PURKINS, resurveyed				254	1.....2.....6
John PERKINS	527	2...16..10	1.....8.....4		
Archer PERKINS				263 1/2	1.....5.....6

(page 75 contd. Goochland County Transferences, Resurveys &c. to 1st October 1786)

Former Proprietor / Present Proprietors	Quantity of Land	Tax	Alterations in Tax	Quantity of Land	Tax
Capt. Joseph PAYNE	877	5.....6.....8			
Martin MIMS				194	1.....3.....8
Capt. Joseph PAYNE			3...17.....4		
William RICHARDS				49	0.....5.....8
Estate of Colo. John PAYNE	2053	12.....6.....6	11...14.....6		
Capt. Joseph PAYNE				100	0...12.....0
Matthew WOODSON	1883	18.....4...10	15.....7.....5		
John JOHNSON				76 1/2	0.....9.....2
Matthew WOODSON					
John REDD				397	2.....8.....3
William WILLIS (of D.)	63 1/2	0.....7.....0			
John JOHNSON				64	0.....7.....0
William PAYNE	200	1...12.....6	0...14...10		
Capt. Humphry PARISH				109	0...17.....8
William PAYNE					
John PAGE (new entry)				50	0.....4....( )
Joseph LEWIS	688	3...18.....6	3...14...10		
William HAY, Esqr.				36	0.....4....( )
Armsby CREW	100	0.....7.....4	0.....0.....2		
Thomas MITCHELL, resurveyed				103	0.....7....( )
John WILLIAMS	536	1...19.....0]	0.....8.....1		
Thomas MITCHELL				270 1/4	0...19...( )
John WILLIAMS					
Jesse BOWLES				151 1/4	0...11...( )
John JONES	100	0.....6.....0			
Thomas MITCHELL				100	0.....6.....0
George CROWDAS	100	0...10.....6	0.....5.....3		
Estate of Edward MATTHEWS				50	0.....5....( )
David PERKINS	160	0...19.....4			
Charles N. PERKINS				160	0...19.....4
Elizabeth MEANLEY	130	1.....3.....0			
William SADLER				130	1.....3.....0

(page 76. Goochland County Transferences, Resurveys, &c. to 1st October 1786)

Former Proprietor / Present Proprietors	Quantity of Land	Tax	Alterations in Tax	Quantity of Land	Tax
Joseph PERKINS	258	1...16.....6			
Thomas MASSIE (0)				258	1...16.....6
New Entry					
Daniel FORD (New Entry)				90	0...10...10
John JONES	100	0.....6.....0			
Hezekiah PURYEAR				100	0.....6.....0
Colo. John WOODSON	844	16.....7.....2]			
Matthew WOODSON			]14...18.....6	72 1/2	0.....9.....0
Josiah SEAY			]	50	0.....6.....2
Francis HARRIS			]	110 1/2	0...13.....6
James ROBARDS	230	1.....7.....8			
James SCRUGGS				230	1.....7.....8
Peter WALKER (not Constable)	230	1.....8.....0	0...18...10		
Shadrach WALKER				75	0.....9.....2

(page 76 contd. Goochland County Transference, Resurveys &c. to 1st October 1786)

Former Proprietors / Present Proprietors	Quantity of Land	Tax	Alterations of Tax	Present Proprietors Quantity of Land	Tax
Randal ROUNTREE	300	2...11.....6	2.....2.....4		
John GORDON				53	0.....9.....2
William WOODWARD	150	1.....1.....4			
James CURD, Resurveyed				128	0...18.....2
George PRIDDY	250	1.....2.....6	0.....4.....4		
Hugh FRENCH				200 3/4	0...18.....2
Daniel GRUBBS	250	0...13.....2	0.....7...11		
William BUSBY				100	0.....5.....3
John JOHNSON	100	0.....6.....0			
John CHILTON				100	0.....6.....0
William PROPHET	30	0.....3.....2	0.....1.....9		
John GLASS				12	0.....1.....5
New Entry					
Thomas EMMERSON (new entry)				100	0.....7.....6
William SAUNDERS	25	0.....3.....2			
John REDD, Resurveyed				80	0.....9...10
Thomas BOLLING, Esqr.	4000	73...12.....0	59.....4.....9		
William GAY, Esqr.				400 2/3	14.....7.....3
Benjamin DARST	100	0...12.....2]			
Richard CROUCH		]	0.....3.....5	57	0.....5.....0
Benjamin DARST					
Majr. Joseph WOODSON				43	0.....3.....9
Estate of John LAPRADE	788	6.....6.....2			
Susanna LAPRADE				300	2.....8.....0
John LAPRADE				128	1.....0.....6
Richard PLEASANTS				360	2...17.....8
Hugh FRENCH	100	0...10.....6	0.....5.....3		
Reuben WEATHERSPOON				50	0.....5.....3
Peter WALKER (Constable)	116	0.....7.....2			
William RADFORD, Resurveyed				195	0...12.....0
William HAY, Esqr.	600	5.....8.....2	4.....7.....2		
Capt. Edmund CURD				115	1.....1.....0
Nathaniel RAINE	244	1.....7.....2			
Majr. Stephen SOUTHALL				244	1.....7.....2
Thomas MILLER	694	4...17.....2	3...18.....2		
William MILLER, Gent.				140 1/2	0...19.....0
New Entry					
Joseph ELAM				50	0.....7.....6
James BENNETT	200	0...18.....0			
Joseph LEWIS, Resurveyed				208 1/3	0...18.....9
Capt. William MERIWETHER	516	3.....2.....6	(215 1/2 now assessed in Louisa)		
Colo. Thomas MERIWETHER				300 1/2	1...16.....6
Jesse LACY	88	0.....6.....6			
Charles BOWLES, Resurveyed				133 1/2	0.....9...10
Jesse PAYNE	65	0.....6.....6			
David HUDSON, Resurveyed				75 1/4	0.....7...10
Nathaniel WEBSTER	170	0....16.....8	0...13.....8		
Philip PLEASANTS				30	0.....3.....0
75 Acres New Entry	50	0.....3.....2			
David ALVIS				125	0.....7.....9

(page 76 contd. Goochland County Transferences, Resurveys &c. to 1st October 1786)

Former Proprietors	Quantity of Land	Tax	Alterations of Tax	Present Proprietors Quantity of Land	Tax
Richard WALMACK	150	0...12.....4			
Abram PREWIT				150	0...12.....4
New Entry					
Thomas WAFFORD				100	0.....9.....0
Thomas RIDDLE	435	1...18.....8	1.....9.....8		
William JAMES				100	0.....9.....0
Joseph FARRAR	100	0...18.....2	0...10.....2		
Matthew WOODSON				44	0.....8.....0

(page 77. Goochland County Transferences, Resurveys &c. to 1st October 1786)

Former Proprietors	Quantity of Land	Tax	Alterations of Tax	Present Proprietors Quantity of Land	Tax
Isaac PLEASANTS	676	10...18.....2]			
Edward REDFORD		]	8...13...11	87	1.....8.....1
Thomas PLEASANTS		]		50	0...16.....2
John CLARKE	62	0.....5...10	0.....4.....2		
Thomas PLEASANTS				18	0.....1.....8
Matthew PLEASANTS	425	2...11.....6	1...10.....4		
Thomas PLEASANTS, Resurveyed				187	1.....2.....8
New Entry					
John HANES				100	0...12.....0
Sarah LACY	181	0...13.....8	0...10.....4		
Sherard PARISH				44	0.....3.....4
Stephen DAVIS	265	1.....8.....6			
John GLASS				50	0.....4.....0
William PROPHET				12	0.....1.....5
John DAVIS, Hanover				100	0...10.....9
Solomon WILLIAMS				103	0...11.....7
New Entry from Fluvanna					
Thomas MARTIN				100	0...12.....3
Joseph R. FARRAR	400	3...12.....6			
Capt. John ROYSTER				400	3...12.....6
John COX	100	0.....9.....2			
Edward COX				100	0.....9.....2
Benjamin CLOPTON	200	1.....4.....4			
William GAY, Esqr.				200	1.....4.....4
Jane MATTHEWS	291	1...12.....4			
John BARNETT				200	1.....1.....9
Estate of Edward MATTHEWS				91	0...10.....7
Estate of Robert SMITH, deced	40	0.....5.....0			
William SMITH, JR.				40	0.....5.....0
William GROOM	100	0.....5.....0			
Archer PAYNE, Gent.				100	0.....5.....0
Estate of James GEORGE, deced.	150	0...13.....6			
Robert GEORGE				150	0...13.....6
Strangeman HUTCHINS	370	2...11.....6	0.....4.....9		
Thomas HARDING				315	2.....6....( )
Joseph MAYO, deced.	500	5.....9.....9			
Honble. Edward CARRINGTON				500	5.....9.....7

(page 77 contd. Goochland County Transferences, Resurveys &c. to 1st October 1786)

Former Proprietors	Quantity of Land	Tax	Alterations of Tax	Present Proprietors	Quantity of Land	Tax
Estate of Edward MATTHEWS, deced.	582	3.....4.....8	]			
William MATTHEWS			] 0...19.....8		200	1.....2.....6
Edward MATTHEWS					200	1.....2.....6
David MIMS	315	1...15.....2				
Estate of David MIMS, deced.					314	1...15.....2
Estate of John MULLINS, deced.	350		1...13.....4			
Conally MULLINS					350	1...13.....4
Major Josias PAYNE, deced.	800		4...17.....0			
Robert PAYNE					800	4...17.....0

```
              270.....4...11  166.....4.....9                    120.....3.....5
                                    add the Alterations          166.....4.....9
                                                                 286.....8.....2
                                    deduct                       270.....4....( )
                                    exceeds last year's tax       16.....3....( )
```

THO. F. BATES   ]
ARCHD. PLEASANTS   ]   Commrs.

October 1st. 1786.
      Rec'd of the Commrs. of the Tax for Goochland County, the Sheriff's Collecting List for the present year due the first day of November next and in Certificates to Eight hundred forty three pounds, eighteen shillings and seven pence; for Stephen SAMPSON, Esqr., Sheriff

```
      1265...15.....1    Specie
       843...18.....7    Certificates
```

WILLIAM SAMPSON, D. S.
for STEP: SAMPSON Shf.

(page 78.)

A List of Transferences and Resurveys of Land in Goochland County to April 1st 1787.

Former Proprietors	Quantity of Land	Tax	Alterations of Tax	Present Proprietors	Quantity of Land	Tax
Major Thomas MASSIE	2285	10.....5...10				
William ANDERSON, London					2285	10.....5...10
William BRITT, deced.	850	3.....0.....8				
Obadiah BRITT					400	1.....8.....6
Capt. John BRITT					125	0.....9.....0
William BRITT					225	0...16.....0
Claibourne BRADSHAW	138	0...16...10	0...15...10			
Larner BRADSHAW					10	0.....1.....0

(page 78 contd. Goochland County Transferences & Resurveys to 1st April 1787)

Former Proprietors	Quantity of Land	Tax	Alterations of Tax	Present Proprietors	Quantity of Land	Tax
Sarah BRADSHAW	69	0.....7.....6				
Larner BRADSHAW					69	0.....7.....6
Sarah LACY	137	0...10.....6	0.....3.....8			
Charles BOWLES					91	0.....6...10
O Entry						
Thomas BRYANT					50	0.....2...11
do. John BOWDRY					50	0.....3.....2
James HOLMAN	275	1.....4.....6	1.....0.....0			
John BANKS					50	0.....4.....6
Robert PLEASANTS, JR.	1300	10.....6.....6	4...15.....4			
Thomas BERNARD					700	5...11.....2
Edward SCRUGGS	100	0.....9.....2				
John BELLAMY					50	0.....4.....7
Abram PREWIT	150	0...12.....3				
Charles CARR					150	0...12.....3
William WILLIAMS	50	0.....3.....2				
Lewis CHAUDOIN					50	0.....3.....2
Thomas POLLOCK	607 3/4	3.....7.....3				
Gwathney DABNEY					418	2.....5.....4
Ichabod DANIEL	200	0...17.....0	]			
Ezekiel DANIEL			]		50	0.....4.....3
John DANIEL			] 0.....4.....3		50	0.....4.....3
Mouley DANIEL			]		50	0.....4.....3
Estate of Joseph JOHNSON	500	1...10.....4				
Reverend William DOUGLAS					500	1...10.....4
Francis CLARKE	150	0.....9.....3				
Reverend William DOUGLAS					150	0.....9.....3
Thomas EMMERSON, SENR.	200	0...12.....9				
Thomas EMMERSON, JUNR.					200	0...12.....9
Estate of Charles RICE, deced.	175	0...15.....4	0...12.....0			
Hugh FRENCH					40	0.....3.....4
Ann MITCHELL	291	1.....8.....0	1.....0.....4			
Robert GEORGE					80	0.....7.....8
William SADLER	130	1.....3.....0	1.....0.....2			
John GRAY					15	0.....2...10
David HUDSON, deced.	443 1/4	2...12.....4				
Estate of David HUDSON, deced.					443 1/4	2...12.....4
Archer PAYNE, Gent. (Lower District)						
Zachariah HADEN					100	0.....4...11
Estate of Colo. John PAYNE, deced.	1953	11...14.....6	11.....6.....8			
Zachariah HADEN					160	0.....7...10
Susanna DAVIS	200	0...10.....6				
John HUGHES					200	0...10.....6
Thomas POLLOCK (before)						
Estate of George HOLLAND, Resurveyed					280	1...10.....6
Charles HOUCHINS	117	0...10.....4				
Lucy HOUCHINS					117	0...10.....4
Mary HICKS	300	1.....7.....4	0...13.....8			
Moses HICKS					150	0...13.....8

(page 78 contd. Goochland County Transferences Resurveys &c. to 1st April 1787)

Former Proprietors	Quantity of Land	Tax	Alterations of Tax	Present Proprietors Quantity of Land	Tax
James HOLMAN (before)					
William JAMES				5	0.....0.....9
Samuel H. POWELL	350	1.....1.....6	0...15.....3		
Thomas JENNETT				100	0.....6.....3
Cornelius TOWLER	190	0...11.....8			
Richard JOHNSON				190	0...11.....8
Estate of Benjamin JOHNSON, deced.	140	0...14...10			
Benjamin JOHNSON				140	0...14...10
JENNINGS's Estate	201	0...12.....4			
Nichelaus JARRETT				201	0...12.....4
William BOWMAN	100	0.....6.....2			
Colo. Robert LEWIS				100	0.....6.....2
Estate of Colo. Valentine WOOD, deced.	2762	16.....3.....0			
Samuel LAMAY				34 1/4	0.....4.....2
Joseph LOWRY	200	0...10.....6	0.....7...10		
Joel LOWRY				50	0.....2.....8
John WILLIAMS	250	1.....4.....6			
Robert LEWIS, JR.				250	1.....4.....6
William SMITH, JR.	40	0.....5.....0			
Charles LOGAN, Esqr.				40	0.....5.....0
O Entry					
Thomas LAWRENCE				108 1/2	0.....6...10
Estate of John LEE, deced	350	1.....4.....4			
Betty LEE				350	1.....4.....4
William BRITT, deced. (before)					
William MITCHELL, JR.				100	0.....7.....2

(page 79. Goochland County Transferences & Resurveys &c. to 1st of April 1787)

Former Proprietors	Quantity of Land	Tax	Alterations of Tax	Present Proprietors Quantity of Land	Tax
Conally MULLINS	350	1...13.....9	1.....2.....6		
Elizabeth MULLINS				116	0...11.....3
Shadrach VAUGHAN	913	5...10...10	5.....6.....2		
Charles MASSIE				38	0.....4.....8
Estate of Colo. Valentine WOOD (before)					
Angus McDONALD				100	0...12.....0
John MICHIE, Esqr.				43]	
Samuel PRYOR, (sold 400)	475	2.....6.....2			
John MICHIE, Esqr. resurveyed to				577 1/2]	3...15.....2
Ann MERRIAN	400	1.....4.....6			
John MERRIAN				80	0.....4...11
Samuel MERRIAN				80	0.....4...11
Matthew MERRIAN				80	0.....4...11
Bartholomew MERRIAN				80	0.....4...11
Jesse MERRIAN				80	0.....4...11
Capt. Nathaniel MASSIE	955 3/4	5...14.....8	4.....6.....9		
Thomas MASSIE, Gent.				232 1/2	1.....8.....0
Elizabeth MIMS	250	1.....7.....4	0...13.....8		
Robert MIMS (of E.)				125	0...13.....8
Thomas MASSIE (O)	347	1...16.....6			
David NOWLIN				347	1...16.....6

(page 79 contd. Goochland County Transferences, Resurveys &c. to 1st April 1787)

Former Proprietors	Quantity of Land	Tax	Alterations of Tax	Present Proprietors	Quantity of Land	Tax
Estate of Barnett OWEN, deced.	100	0.....5.....0				
Barnett OWEN					50	.0.....2....6
Mary OWEN					50	0.....2.....6
John PREWIT	91	0.....9.....9	0.....1.....9			
Obadiah PREWIT					74 1/2	0.....8.....0
Robert GEORGE	150	0...13.....6				
Booker PARISH, resurveyed to					114	0...10.....6
Estate of Colo. Valentine WOOD, (before)						
Philip PAYNE					194 1/2	1.....2...10
Estate of Edward MATTHEWS	323	1...15.....3	0...13.....0			
Thomas POLLOCK					200	1.....2.....3
William PROPHET	30	0.....3.....3				
Thomas POOR of A.					30	0.....3.....3
Henry NASH	100	0.....9.....9				
William PROPHET, resurveyed to					87 3/4	0.....8.....6
Robert PAGE	133	0...14.....4				
Winnifred PAGE					133	0...14.....4
Thomas MITCHELL, (Louisa)	473 1/4	1...13.....2	1.....7.....2			
William PURKINS					100	0.....6.....0
Anselm GEORGE	175	0...10.....6				
John PURKINS					175	0...10.....6
Capt. Humphry PARISH	606	3.....1.....2	2.....5.....2			
Humphry PARISH, JR.					183	0...16.....0
O. Entry						
Ann PARISH					75	0.....4.....7
William GAY	600 2/3	14.....7.....3				
Thomas RANDOLPH, D.					400 2/3	13....3.....0
O. Entry						
John RICHARDS					165]	
Shadrach VAUGHAN (before)						
John RICHARDS					53]	1.....1.....5
O. Entry						
Nathaniel RAINE					100	0.....6.....2
Horatio TURPIN	1200	5.....3.....6				
David ROSS					1200	5.....3.....6
O. Entry						
William RICHARDS					165	0...14...10
John FARISH	100	0.....9.....2				
Capt. Holman RICE					100	0.....9.....2
Estate of Colo. John PAYNE (before)						
James ROBARDS					120	0...14.....6
William GAY (before)						
John SCOTT					200	1.....4.....4
Capt. William GEORGE	324	1.....7.....4	0.....4...10			
Benjamin SALMONS					250	1.....2.....6
Colo. George PAYNE, (Lower District)						
Robert SHELTON					200	1.....4.....4
O. Entry						
Capt. William SAMPSON					175	0...19.....2

(page 79 contd. Goochland County Transferences, Resurveys &c. to 1st April 1787)

Former Proprietors	Quantity of Land	Tax	Alterations of Tax	Present Proprietors Quantity of Land	Tax
Thomas MILLER	553 1/2	3...18.....0	2...17.....2		
Capt. Stephen SAMPSON				153 1/2	1.....0...10
William S. SMITH, deced.	211	1.....2.....9			
William S. SMITH				211	1.....2.....9
Edward SCRUGGS, deced (before)					
Richard SCRUGGS				50	0.....4.....7
Samuel COSBY	225	0...15.....4	0...13.....2		
John STRONG				29	0.....2.....2
Benjamin LACY	88	0.....6.....6			
William SHELTON				88	0.....6.....6
Reuben THURSTON	53	0.....4.....2			
Mary THURSTON				53	0.....4.....2
John WILLIAMS (D.C.)	863	3.....6.....0	2...16...10		
Thomas TERRY				482	1.....0.....2
William CHRISTIAN (L.D.)				304	(no figures)

(page 80. Goochland County Transferences, Resurveys &c. to 1st April 1787.

Former Proprietors	Quantity of Land	Tax	Alterations of Tax	Present Proprietors Quantity of Land	Tax
John TOWLER	62 1/2	0.....3...10			
William TURNER				62 1/2	0.....3...10
Estate of Colo. Valentine WOOD (before)					
Shadrach VAUGHAN				100	0...1.....9
Lucy WOOD				600	3...10.....6
Peter WALKER (Constable)				265	1...11.....2
William WILLIAMS				100	0...11.....9
Henry WOOD				1325 1/4]	
Shadrach VAUGHAN (before)					
Henry WOOD				150]	8...14.....0
Edward MATTHEWS	200	1.....2.....6	1.....0.....8		
Capt. John WARE				16	0.....1...10
Bryant CONLEY	150	0...12.....4			
Capt. John WARE				150	0...12.....4
William THURSTON	122	0...13.....8	0.....8.....0		
Solomon WILLIAMS				50	0.....5.....8
O. Entry					
Solomon WILLIAMS				10	0.....1.....1

THO: F. BATES, Commr.

(page 81.)

A List of Transferences & Resurveys of Land in the Lower District of Goochland County
April 1st 1787

Former Proprietors	Quantity of Land	Tax	Alterations in the Tax	Present Proprietors Quantity of Land	Tax
George HANDCOCK	97	0.....9.....2			
William ADAMS				97	0.....9.....2
Colo. Edward CARRINGTON	500	5.....8.....9			
Burwell BAUGH				500	5.....8.....9
Francis HILL	304	1.....7.....9			
William CHRISTIAN				304	1.....7.....9
Matthew WOODSON	1526	16.....4.....4	13.....0.....7		
John CROUCH				425	3.....3.....9
John DOWDY, deced.	122	0...13.....9			
Elizabeth DOWDY				122	0...13.....9
William BLUNKALL	3 1/2	0.....1.....0			
Mary EDWARDS				3 1/2	0.....1.....0
Joseph EVANS	134	0...12.....4			
Thomas EVANS				134	0...12.....4
Stephen ELLIS, resurveyed	97	1.....3.....8			
Stephen ELLIS				129 1/4	1...10.....6
Mary FRAZIER, resurveyed	205	1.....5.....0			
Mary FRAZIER				166	1.....0.....2
Mary FRAZIER					
Hezekiah PURYEAR				6 1/2	0.....0...10
John FARRAR	298	2.....8.....2			
William GARTHRIGHT				298	2.....8.....2
John T. GRIFFIN, Esqr.	3311	58...10.....9	41.....1.....7		
Francis GRAVES				640	17.....9.....3
William ROUNDTREE	121	0...19.....0			
Charles JOHNSON				121	0...19.....0
John ROYSTER	400	3...12.....6	1...11...11		
Elisha LEAKE				9 1/2	0.....1.....8
Isaac PERRIN				225	2.....0...11
Pleasant WILLIS	180	1.....1...10			
Rene NAPIER				180	1.....1...10
John BRADSHAW	450	2.....0.....9	1...15.....9		
Archer PAYNE				49	0.....5.....0
Thomas OLIVER	273	1...13.....2			
Archer PAYNE				273	1...13.....2
Charles JOHNSON, JUNR.	220	1...17.....9			
Anderson PEERS				220	1...17.....9
Pleasant WILLIS	278	1...13.....9			
Anderson PEERS				278	1....13.....9
Estate of William ROUNDTREE	108	0...17.....0			
Thomas ROUNDTREE				108	0...17...0
Susanna BIBB	248	1...10.....2			
Colo. John SYME				248	1...10.....2
Susanna WOODWARD	500	4...10.....8			
Samuel WOODWARD				450	4.....1.....6
John WOODWARD				50	0.....9.....2

ARCHD. PLEASANTS, Commr.

(page 82.)

A List of the Land Tax within the District of THOMAS F. BATES, Commissioner of the
County of Goochland, taken 1788.

Proprietors Names	Quantity of Land	Rate p Acre	Amount of Value	Amount of Tax at 1 1/2 p cent
James ALLEN	175	4/7	34...16.....3	0...10.....6
David ALVIS	125	4/1	25...10.....5	0.....7.....9
William ANDERSON, London	3785		1285...10.....0	19.....5...10
Callam BAILEY	150	4/1	30...12.....6	0.....9.....4
William BURGESS	100	do.	20.....8.....4	0.....6.....2
John BOLLING (Chesterfield)	1440		677.....7.....6	10.....3.....4
John BOLLING, JR.	600	9/8	290.....0.....0	4.....7.....0
Thomas BOLLING (Chesterfield)	3599 2/3		4029...13...10	60.....8...10
Claibourne BRADSHAW	128	8/1	51...14.....8	0...15.....7
Learner BRADSHAW	79		28...15.....4	0.....8.....9
Thomas F. BATES	500	13/10	345...16.....8	5.....3...10
Capt. John BRITT	370		119...10.....5	1...16.....0
Gideon BOWLES	350	6/8	116...13.....4	1...15.....0
Charles BOWLES	133 1/2	4/1	32...16.....5	0...10.....0
William BUSBY	150		27...14.....2	0.....8.....6
John BARNETT	200	7/5	74.....3.....4	1.....2.....6
Obadiah BRITT	400	4/9	95.....0.....0	1.....8.....6
William BRITT	225	do.	53.....8.....9	0...16.....0
John BANKS	50	5/11	14...15...10	0.....4.....6
John BELLAMY	50	6/1	15.....4.....2	0.....4.....7
Francis BUSH (of Henry WOOD)	100	8/1	40.....8.....4	0...12.....2
Benjamin CRENSHAW, SENR.	440	5/11	130.....3.....4	1...19.....2
Martha CARR	449	8/1	201...13.....7	3.....0.....8
Nathaniel CAWLEY	60	do.	24.....5.....0	0.....7.....4
Mary COLEY	100	do.	40.....8.....4	0...12.....2
Susanna COLEY	100	4/1	20.....8.....4	0.....6.....2
Ann COLEY	100	8/1	40.....8.....4	0...12.....2
Sally COLEY	100	6/1	30.....8.....4	0.....9.....2
Francis COLEY	106 1/2	6/3	33...16.....8	0...10.....2
Estate of Robert CARDIN, deced.	200	5/1	50...16.....8	0...15.....4
John CLEMENTS	116	5/10	33...16.....8	0...10.....2
Bowler COCKE, Esqr. (Henrico)	1509		1165...12.....0	17.....9.....6
Samuel COSBY	196	4/6	44.....2.....0	0...13.....2
Walter CLOPTON	220	8/1	88...18.....4	1.....6...10
James CLEMENTS	179	6/4	56...13.....8	0...17.....2
Roger CARRELL	83	4/1	16...13...11	0.....5.....2
Gideon CAWTHON	220	6/8	73.....6.....8	1.....3.....0
Edward COX	200		66...13.....4	0...19.....9
David CRENSHAW	238	6/2	73.....7.....8	1.....2.....2
Judith CARTER	100	4/10	24.....3.....4	0.....7.....4
George CROWDAS	50	7/	17...10.....0	0.....5.....3
Benjamin CLOPTON	400		150...16.....8	2.....5.....4
John CHITTAM	100	4/	20.....0.....0	0.....6.....0
Charles CARR (MILLER's Land)	150	5/5	40...12.....6	0...12.....3
Lewis CHAUDOIN (of Gideon MIMS)	50	7/5	18...10...10	0.....5.....8
Benjamin CRENSHAW (of H. R..?..)	150	6/1	45...12.....6	0...13.....9

(page 82 contd. Goochland County Land Tax Return of Thomas F. Bates for 1788)

Proprietors Names		Quantity of Land	Rate p Acre	Amount of Value	Amount of Tax at 1 1/2 p cent
Samuel COUCH	(of W. FLEMING, Esqr.)	390	20/4		
do.	(of Charles FLEMING)	390	do.	793.....0.....0	
do.	(of Obadiah PREWIT)	74 1/2	7/2	26...14.....0	12.....6.....0

(page 83. Goochland County Land Tax Return of Thomas F. Bates for 1788)

Proprietors Names		Quantity of Land	Rate p Acre	Amount of Value	Amount of Tax at 1 1/2 p cent
Susanna CROUCH	(of Elijah BRUMFIELD)	149	10/3	76.....7.....3	1.....3.....0
William CARRELL	(of J. WOODSON)	31 1/4		11.....5.....0	0.....3.....8
Reuben CARDIN	(of Henry WOOD)	19 1/2	7/10	7...12.....9	0.....2.....6
John DOWDY		122	7/5	45.....4...10	0...13.....8
Thomas DRUMWRIGHT		1030	6/2	317...11.....8	4...15.....4
John DAVIS,	(Hanover)	200		92.....1.....8	1.....1.....8
Ichabod DANIEL		50	5/8	14.....3.....4	0.....4.....3
Ezekiel DANIEL		50	do.	14.....3.....4	0.....4.....3
Mousley DANIEL		50	do.	14.....3.....4	0.....4.....3
John DANIEL		50	do.	14.....3.....4	0.....4.....3
David DAVIS		100	7/	35.....0.....0	0...10.....6
Noton DICKINSON		400	3/6	70.....0.....0	1.....1.....0
Gwathney DABNEY		418	7/3	151...10.....6	2.....5.....4
Thomas ELDRIDGE		203	8/1	82.....0...11	1.....4.....9
David ENGLAND		80	6/1	24.....6.....8	0.....7.....4
Benjamin EAST		121 1/2	8/1	49.....2.....2	0...14...10
Henry EMMERSON		240	6/6	78.....0.....0	1.....3.....6
Thomas EMMERSON, JR.		300		75.....0.....0	1.....2.....6
Joseph ELAM		50	10/	25.....0.....0	0.....7.....6
Estate of Colo. Tarlton FLEMING, deced.		1900	20/8	1915...16.....8	28...14...10
John FURLONG		100	3/6	17...10.....0	0.....5.....4
Hugh FRENCH		250 3/4	5/10	77...10.....4	1.....3.....6
Mason FRENCH	(of do.)	41 1/2	do.	12.....2.....1	0.....3.....9
Daniel FORD		90	8/	36.....0.....0	0...10...10
John GLASS		62		21...19.....0	0.....6.....6
Capt. William GEORGE		75		15...14.....7	0.....4.....9
John GRAY		100		53...13.....7	0...16.....4
John GILLAM, SENR.		546	7/9	211...11.....6	3.....3.....6
David GRANTHAM		35	7/6	13.....2.....6	0.....4.....0
Robert GILLAM	(Pr. George)	1021 3/4		2699.....2.....6	40.....9...10
Stephen GRANGE		80	7/2	28...13.....4	0.....8.....8
John GILBERT		150	3/6	26.....5.....0	0.....8.....0
Daniel GRUBBS, resurveyed		250	do.	43...15.....0	0...13.....3
Alexander GRANT (of John BOWDRY)		60	4/1	12.....5.....0	0.....3.....9
Estate of David HUDSON, deced.		443 1/4		172...10.....2	2...12.....4
John HENDERSON		200	4/1	40...16.....8	0...12.....4
John HUMBER		561	8/1	226...14.....9	3.....8.....2
Zachariah HADEN		920		210.....0.....0]	
do. (of Henry WOOD)		116 1/2	7/10	45...12.....7]	3...16.....8
Drury HATCHER		5 1/2	4/6	1.....4.....9	0.....0.....6

(page 83 contd. Goochland County Land Tax Return of Thomas F. Bates for 1788)

Proprietors Names		Quantity of Land	Rate p Acre	Amount of Value	Amount of Tax at 1 1/2 p cent
Jesse HODGES		160	5/7	44...13.....4	0...13.....6
John HILL	(Amherst)	150	6/1	45...12...6	0...13...10
Harrison HARRIS		530	7/4	194.....6...8	2...18.....4
Mary HICKS		150	6/1	45...12...6	0...13...10
Mesheck HICKS		450	6/4	142...10.....0	2.....2...10

(page 84. Goochland County Land Tax Return of Thomas F. Bates for 1788)

Proprietors Names		Quantity of Land	Rate p Acre	Amount of Value	Amount of Tax at 1 1/2 p cent
Francis HOUCHINS		117	5/10	34.....2.....6	0...10.....4
Lucy HOUCHINS		117	do.	34.....2.....6	0...10.....4
James HOLMAN		220	5/11	65.....1.....8	0...19.....8
William HODGES		100	4/10	24.....3.....4	0.....7.....4
Capt. William HOLMAN		590	4/1	120.....9.....2	1...16.....3
Colo. John HOPKINS		1650	6/7	534.....2.....6	8.....0.....5
Lewis HERNDON		200	6/9	67...10.....0	1.....0.....4
James HOUCHINS	(of L. H.)	100	do.	33...15.....0	0...10.....2
John HERNDON		199	7/4	72...19.....4	1.....2.....0
John HOPPER		210	7/2	75.....5.....0	1.....2.....8
Lucy HODGES		50	4/10	12.....1.....8	0.....3.....8
Major HANCOCKE		80	6/7	26.....6.....8	0.....8.....0
John HOLLAND		272 1/4	7/3	98...13...10	1.....9.....8
William HICKS	(D.C.)	140	do.	50...15.....0	0...15.....3
James HOWARD		136	do.	54.....6.....0	0...16.....4
John HOWARD		166	6/	49...10.....0	0...15.....0
Anthony HADEN	(Fluvanna)	400	4/	80.....0.....0	1.....4.....0
Nathaniel HOLLAND		200	7/2	72...10.....0	1.....1...10
John HANES		100	8/	40.....0.....0	0...12.....0
John HUGHES		200	3/6	35.....0.....0	0...10.....6
Susanna HOLLAND (of the Estate)		56	7/3	20.....6.....0	0.....6.....2
Richard JOHNSON	(Louisa)	190	4/1	38...15...10	0...11.....8
William ISBELL		792	5/7	221.....2.....0]	
do. of Arthur SLAYDEN		182	4/1	37.....3.....2]	3...17.....6
Benjamin JOHNSON	(Byrd)	140	7/	49.....0.....0	0...14...10
William JOHNSON	(do.)	250	6/1	76.....0.....0	1.....2...10
Thomas JEFFERSON, Esqr.		612	8/1	247.....7.....0	3...14.....2
Archibald JARRETT		454		124...17.....6	1...17.....6
Devereux JARRETT		290	4/1	59.....4.....9	0...17...10
David JARRETT		250	do.	51.....0...10	0...15.....4
Charles JOHNSON		200	7/2	71...13.....4	1.....1.....6
William JAMES		105	5/11	31.....1.....3	0.....9.....9
Thomas JENNETT		100	4/1	20.....8.....4	0.....6.....3
Daniel JOHNSON		150	4/	30.....0.....0	0.....9.....0
Ayres LAYNE		155	6/8	51...13.....4	0...15.....6
Henry LAYNE		100	4/1	20.....8.....4	0.....6.....2
Matthew LACY		97	4/10	23.....8...10	0.....7.....2
Mary LAYNE		50	4/1	10.....4.....2	0.....3.....2
Sarah LACY		137 1/4	5/	34.....5.....0	0...10.....5
Samuel LAMAY		115 1/4		29...19.....1	0.....9.....0
Armiger LILLY		400	4/1	81...13.....4	1.....4.....4

(page 84 contd. Goochland County Land Tax Return of Thomas F. Bates for 1788)

Proprietors Names	Quantity of Land p	Rate Acre	Amount of Value	Amount of Tax at 1 1/2 p cent
Howell LEWIS	490	7/	171...10.....0	2...11.....6
Colo. Robert LEWIS	1205		766.....5...10	11.....0...11
Betty LEE	350	4/8	81...13.....4	1.....4.....6
William LEWIS (R.C.)	100	4/1	20.....8.....4	0.....6.....2
Capt. Josiah LEAKE	800	8/1	323.....6.....8	4...17.....0
Henry LAURENCE	50	4/6	11.....5.....0	0.....3.....6
Joseph LOWRY	150	3/6	26.....5.....0	0.....7...10
Joel LOWRY	50	do.	8...15.....0	0.....2.....8

(page 85. Goochland County Land Tax Return of Thomas F. Bates for 1788)

Proprietors Names	Quantity of Land p	Rate Acre	Amount of Value	Amount of Tax at 1 1/2 p cent
Matthew LOWRY	200	4/	40.....0.....0	0...12.....0
Thornton LOWRY	100	do.	20.....0.....0	0.....6.....0
Matthew LOWRY, JR.	100	do.	20.....0.....0	0.....6.....0
Robert LEWIS, JR.	250	6/6	81.....5.....0	1.....4.....6
Charles LOGAN, Esqr.	40	8/1	16.....3.....4	0.....5.....0
Thomas LAURENCE	108 1/2	4/1	22.....3 1	0.....6...10
David LAYNE, SENR. (of John HUSON)	47	5/	11...15.....0	0.....3.....8
David LAYNE, JUNR. (O. Entry)	100	6/1	30.....8.....4	0.....9.....3
Elliot LACY (of Henry WOOD)	25	7/10	9...15...10	0.....3.....0
Martin MIMS	194	8/1	78.....8.....2]	
do. of Robert MIMMS of Elizabeth	26	7/3	9.....8.....6]	1.....6.....6
Thomas MITCHELL, Merchant	373 1/4	4/10	90.....4.....1]	
do. of William PERKINS	100	4/	20.....0.....0]	1...13.....2
Estate of Edward MATTHEWS, deced.	123		45.....1.....5	0...13.....8
William MATTHEWS	200	7/5	74.....3.....4	1.....2.....6
Edward MATTHEWS	177 1/2	do.	65...16.....6	0...19.....9
Capt. William MILLER	362 1/2		144.....0.....0	2.....3.....3
Thomas MILLER	400		190.....9.....2	2...17.....2
Estate of David MIMS, deced.	315	7/5	116...16.....3	1...15.....2
Colo. Thomas MERIWETHER	300 1/2	8/1	121.....9.....1]	
do. of Jesse BOWLES	151 1/4		37.....5.....0]	2.....7.....9
Thomas MARTIN (of J. WILLIAMS)	127	do.	30.....5.....0	0.....9.....3
Charles MASSIE	338	do.	136...12.....2]	
do. of Robert GEORGE	40	6/5	12...16.....8]	2.....5.....0
Ann MITCHELL	211	do.	67...13...11	1.....0.....4
David MARTIN	235	do.	75.....7...11	1.....2.....8
Paul MEACHUM	295	5/6	81.....2.....6	1.....4.....6
Benjamin MOSBY	200	5/1	50...16.....8	0...15.....4
Archibald BRYCE and William MITCHELL	865 1/2	8/1	349...12.....1	5.....5.....0
Gideon MIMS	310	7/5	114...19.....0	0...14.....6
Elizabeth MIMS	125	7/3	45.....6.....3	0...13.....8
Robert MIMS (of Elizabeth)	99	do.	35...17.....9	0...10...10
Sarah MIMS	50	6/1	15.....4.....2	0.....4.....8
Colo. John MARTIN	500	6/2	154.....3.....4	2.....6.....6
Edward MARTIN of do.	200	do.	61...13.....4	0...18.....8
John MERRIAN	80	4/1	16.....6.....8	0.....4...11
Samuel MERRIAN	80	do.	16.....6.....8	0.....4...11
Matthew MERRIAN	80	do.	16.....6.....8	0.....4...11
Bartholomew MERRIAN	80	do.	16.....6.....8	0.....4...11

(page 85 contd. Goochland County Land Tax Return of Thomas F. Bates for 1788)

Proprietors Names	Quantity of Land	Rate p Acre	Amount of Value	Amount of Tax at 1 1/2 p cent
Jesse MERRIAN	80	4/1	16.....6.....8	0...4...11
Thomas MASSIE, Gent.	232 1/2	8/	93.....0.....0	1...8.....0
Wright MOURLAND	100	6/11	34...11.....8	0...10...6
Capt. David MULLINS	197	8/1	79...12.....5	1...4.....0
Capt. Henry MULLINS	400	7/2	143.....6.....8	2...3.....0
Conally MULLINS	234	6/5	75.....1.....6	1.....2.....8
Elizabeth MULLINS	116	do.	37.....4.....4	0...11.....3
Samuel MOSS	200	4/	40.....0.....0	0...12.....0
William MARTIN	400	6/	120.....0.....0	1...16.....0
John MOSS	75	8/	30.....0.....0	0.....9.....0
William MASSIE	223	7/3	80...16.....9	1.....4.....4
Nathaniel MASSIE, Gent.	723 1/2	8/	289.....6.....0	4.....6.....8
William MITCHELL, JR.	100	4/9	23...15.....0	0.....7.....2
Angus McDONALD	100	7/10	39.....3.....4	0...12.....0

(page 86. Goochland County Land Tax Return of Thoams F. Bates for 1788)

Proprietors Names	Quantity of Land	Rate p Acre	Amount of Value	Amount of Tax at 1 1/2 p cent
John MICHIE, Esqr.	620 1/2		250.....5.....0]	
do. of Thomas WAFFORD	208		54.....6.....0]	4...13.....0
William McMEKING (of Thomas BRYANT)	50	3/6	8...15.....0	0.....2...11
William MURROW (of Henry WOOD)	100	7/10	39.....3.....4	0...12.....0
Thomas MERIWETHER (of the ? Parson)	1150		284...15...10	4.....5.....6
Thomas NOWELL	100	6/1	30.....0.....0	0.....9.....0
James NOWELL	300	do.	90.....0.....0	1.....7.....0
David NOWLIN	347	7/	121.....9.....0	1...16.....6
Barnett OWEN	50	3/3	8.....2.....6	0.....2.....6
Mary OWEN	50	do.	8.....2.....6	0.....2.....6
Capt. Sherard PARISH	291		63.....4.....0	0...19.....3
John PERKINS	263 1/2		94...10.....8	1.....8.....6
Capt. Archelaus PERKINS	263 1/2		94...10.....8	1.....8.....6
William PERKINS (of John)	254	5/1	74.....1.....8	1.....2.....6
Capt. Humphry PARISH	423		150.....3.....5	2.....5.....2
William PAYNE	92	10/9	49.....9.....0	0...15.....0
John PAGE	50	6/	15.....0.....0	0.....4.....6
Smith PAYNE, Esqr. (of John PAYNE)	734		296.....4...10]	
do. of the Estate of Colo. John PAYNE)	300	8/	120.....0.....0]	
do. of Philip PAYNE, Esqr.	194 1/2	7/10	76.....3.....7]	7.....7.....9
Estate of Colo. John PAYNE, deced.	1373	8/	549.....4.....0	8.....5.....0
Meredith PAYNE (of Colo.)	100	4/5	22...10.....0	0.....6.....9
Thomas POOR (of Abraham)	30		10.....7.....6]	
do. of William PROPHET	50	6/8	16.....5.....0]	0.....7.....9
William PROPHET	37 3/4	do.	12.....5.....6	0.....3.....9
Robert PLEASANTS, JR.	600	10/7	317...10.....0	4...15.....4
Joel PARISH	121	4/10	29.....4...10	0.....8...10
Aaron PARISH	71 1/4	4/1	14...11.....0	0.....4.....6
Mary PARISH	121 1/4	do.	24...15.....2	0.....7.....6
Booker PARISH	305 1/4		73...16.....1	1.....2.....8
Capt. Samuel PRYOR	75		29...11.....2	0.....9.....0

(page 86 contd. Goochland County Land Tax Return of Thomas F. Bates for 1788)

Proprietors Names	Quantity of Land	Rate p Acre	Amount of Value	Amount of Tax at 1 1/2 p cent
William PRYOR	200	12/1	120...16.....8	1...16.....4
Moses PARISH	168	4/1	34.....6.....0	0...10.....4
Daniel POWERS	33 1/2	5/11	9...18.....3	0.....3.....0
Estate of Samuel H. POWELL	250	4/1	51.....0...10	0...15.....6
Estate of George PAYNE, deced. (O.K.)	144	5/7	40.....4.....0	0...12.....3
Winnifred PAGE	133	7/2	47...13.....2	0...14.....4
Robert PAYNE	800	8/1	323.....6.....8	4...17.....0
William PAGE (of Robert)	133	do.	53...15.....1	0...16.....2
Estate of John PAYNE, deced.	697 1/2		291...17.....4	4.....7.....8
Estate of Thomas POOR, deced.	262 1.2	5/1	66...14.....5	1.....0.....2
William POOR, (of Thomas)	262 1/2	do.	66...14.....5	1.....0.....2
Abram POOR	200	6/1	60...16.....8	0...18.....4
Joseph PACE	150	6/3	46...17.....6	0...14.....2
John PACE	130	5/	32...10.....0	0.....9.....9
Jesse PACE	200	6/1	60...16.....8	0...18.....4
John PHILPOTT	100	4/1	20.....8.....4	0.....6.....3

(page 87. Goochland County Land Tax Return of Thomas F. Bates for 1788)

Proprietors Names	Quantity of Land	Rate p Acre	Amount of Value	Amount of Tax at 1 1/2 p cent
Benjamin PAGE	100	6/1	30.....8.....4	0.....9.....2
Estate of John PREWIT, deced.	101 1/2	7/2	36.....7.....6	0...11.....0
Robert PLEASANTS, SENR.	700	10/7	370.....8.....4	5...11.....2
Alexander PARISH	250	5/	62...10.....0	0...18.....9
George PRIDDY	49 1/4	6/	14...15.....6	0.....4.....6
Anderson PARISH	170	3/3	27...12.....6	0.....8.....6
William PARISH	250	7/	87...10.....0	1.....6.....4
Ann PARISH	75	4/1	15.....0.....6	0.....4.....7
John PERKINS (Louisa)	175	4/	35.....0.....0	0...10.....6
Humphry PARISH, JUNR.	183	5/10	53.....7.....6	0...16.....0
Capt. Joseph PARISH (of T.C.)	235	6/2	72.....7.....0	1.....1.....8
David ROSS, Esqr.	11149		4629.....0.....0	69.....8.....6
William RICHARDS	214		68.....6.....1	1.....0.....6
William RUTHERFORD	433	5/4	115.....9.....4	1...14.....8
William RIGSBY	50	3/3	8.....2.....6	0.....2.....6
Thomas RIDDLE	335	5/11	99.....2.....1	1...10.....0
Doctor John K. READ	408	8/1	164...18.....0	2.....9.....6
Capt. Samuel RICHARDSON	546 1/2	7/2	195...16.....7	2...19.....0
Thomas RANDOLPH, Esqr.	3400 2/3		2339.....4.....2	35.....1.....9
George RICHARDSON	1612	6/10	550...15.....4]	
do. of Capt. William MILLER	78		34.....9.....6]	8...15.....9
James ROBARDS	483		105.....3.....4]	
do. of Estate of George PAYNE, (O.K.)	56	5/7	15...12.....8]	
do. of Benjamin SALMONDS	250	6/	75.....0.....0]	2...18.....9
John RICHARDS	218		70...18.....5	1.....1.....5
Nathaniel RAINE	100	4/1	20.....8.....4	0.....6.....2
Philip PAYNE (of Lewis CHAUDOIN)	50	do.	10.....4.....2	0.....3.....2
Robert SMITH (P.tan)	175	7/3	63.....8.....9]	
do. of Robert GEORGE	40	6/5	12...16.....8]	1.....3.....0
William SADLER	115	11/9	67...11.....3	1.....0.....2

(page 87 contd. Goochland County Land Tax Return of Thomas F. Bates for 1788)

Proprietors Names		Quantity of Land	Rate p Acre	Amount of Value	Amount of Tax 1 1/2 p cent
James SCRUGGS		230	8/1	92.....0.....0	1.....7.....8
Capt. Stephen SAMPSON		719 1/2		335...11.....6	5.....0.....4
David SHELTON	(Louisa)	840		440.....0.....0	6...12.....0
Joseph SHELTON		529		314.....0.....0	4...14.....6
John SLAYDEN		100	4/1	20.....8.....4	0.....6.....2
William S. SMITH		211	7/2	75...12.....2	1.....2.....9
John STRONG		166 1/2		62.....2.....0	0...19.....0
Nathan STRONG		137 1/2	8/1	55...11.....6	0...16...10
Richard SCRUGGS		50	6/11	15.....4.....2	0.....4.....7
James SALMONDS		230	4/7	52...14.....2	0...16.....0
John SCOTT	(R.C.)	200	8/1	80...16.....8	1.....4.....4
Robert SHELTON	(Glebe)	200	do.	80...16.....8	1.....4.....4
Capt. William SAMPSON		175	7/3	63.....8.....9	0...19.....2
do. of Thomas POLLOCK, MATTHEWS's		200	7/5	74.....3.....4	1.....2.....3
William SHELTON		88	4/1	21...12.....8	0.....6.....6
George SAUNDERS (of C.R.'s Estate)		135	5/10	39.....7.....6	0...12.....0
Sarah THOMAS		160	4/1	32...14.....4	0.....9...10
Mary TOWLER		200	do.	40...16.....8	0...12.....4
William THURSTON		72	7/5	26...14.....0	0.....8.....0
John THURSTON		110	7/1	38...19.....2	0...11...10

(page 88. Goochland County Land Tax Return of Thomas F. Bates for 1788)

Proprietors Names		Quantity of Land	Rate p Acre	Amount of Value	Amount of Tax 1 1/2 p cent
Esther THURSTON		53	4/5	11...14.....1	0.....3.....8
James THOMAS		110	4/1	24...10.....0	0.....7.....6
William TURNER		62 1/2	do.	12...15.....3	0.....3...10
Mary THURSTON		53	5/	13.....5.....0	0.....4.....2
Benjamin THACKER		100	3/3	16.....5.....0	0.....5.....0
Thomas TERRY		432	4/5	97.....4.....0	1.....9.....2
Shadrach VAUGHAN		772		310...15.....4	4...13.....4
Lucy WOOD		600	7/10	235.....0.....0	3...10.....6
William WALKER		169		36...17.....6	0...11.....6
John WILLIAMS	(D.C.)	100	8/1	40.....8.....4	0...12.....3
Reuben WEATHERSPOON		50	6/11	17.....5...10	0.....5.....3
Henry WOOD, Esqr.		1640 3/4		630.....9.....9]	
do. of the Estate of George HOLLAND, deced.		224	7/3	81.....4.....0]	10...13.....9
Solomon WILLIAMS		266		95.....0.....0	1.....8.....6
Joseph WOODSON	(of Tucker)	368 3/4		138...10.....0	2.....1.....8
John WOODSON	(C.T.)	1265		647...15.....5	9...14.....4
Henry WALMACK		100	8/1	40.....8.....4	0...12.....2
Isaac WINSTON	(Hanover)	735	do.	297.....1.....3	4.....9.....2
John WALKER		100	3/3	16.....5.....0	0.....5.....0
John WILLIAMSON		200	4/1	40...16.....8	0...12.....4
Lewis WILBOURNE		100	do.	20.....8.....4	0.....6.....4
Dabney WADE		257 1/2	6/3	81.....9.....4	1.....4.....8
Estate of William WADE, deced.		257 1/2	7/3	94.....7.....0	1.....8.....6
John WOODSON,	(Meadow)	300	8/1	121.....5.....0	1...16.....6
William WILBOURNE		200	3/3	32...10.....0	0.....9.....9

(page 88 contd. Goochland County Land Tax Return of Thomas F. Bates for 1788)

Proprietors Names	Quantity of Land	Rate p Acre	Amount of Value	Amount of Tax at 1 1/2 p cent
Philip WILLIAMS	200	6/	60.....0.....0	0...18.....0
Capt. John WARE	1096 1/2		349.....4.....2	5.....5.....0
Peter WALKER, Constable	265	7/10	103...15...10	1...11.....2
Thomas WHITLOCK (of W. W.)	100	do.	39.....3.....4	0...11.....9
Ann YOUNGER	100	3/3	16.....5.....0	0.....5.....0

THO. F. BATES, Commr.

A Copy. Examined Teste WM. MILLER, D. C.
9th Augt. 88

(page 89)

List of the Land Tax within the District of ARCHIBALD PLEASANTS, Commissioner of the County of Goochland, April 1788.

Proprietors Names	Quantity of Land	Rate p Acre	Amount of Value	Amount of Tax at 1 1/2 p cent
Colo. Richard ADAMS	1982	8/9	867.....2.....6]	
do. of Elijah BRUMFIELD	51	10/3	25...12.....6]	18.....8.....0
Mary ATKISSON	310	8/1	125.....5...10	1...17.....8
William ANDERSON	97	6/2	30.....1.....3	0.....9.....2
Charles BATES	350	12/1	211.....9.....2	3.....3.....6
William BARNETT	200	7/6	72...10.....0	1.....1.....9
Jesse BLACKWELL	98 1/2	8/1	39...16.....3	0...12.....0
John BRUMFIELD	125	do.	50...10.....5	0...15.....2
John BRADSHAW	401	6/9	135.....6.....9	2.....0.....9
Burwell BAUGH	500	14/6	362...10.....0	5.....8.....9
John BROOKES (original entry)	100	7/2	35...16.....8	0...10.....9
Elijah BRUMFIELD	100	8/1	40.....8.....4	0...12.....2
James CURD	318		133.....6.....0	2.....0.....0
Jesse CURD	250		104...15.....0	1...11.....5
Richard CROUCH	257	8/1	103...17.....5	1...16...11
Philip CHILDERS	276	4/1	56.....7.....0	0...17.....0
Thomas CHANCELOR	125	6/6	40...12.....6	0...12.....4
Judith CHEADLE	299	13/6	201...16.....6	3.....0.....8
Daniel CLARKE	100	6/1	30.....8.....4	0.....9.....2
Richard COCKE	580 1/2	14/10	430.....3.....4	6.....9.....1
Estate of Allen COCKE, deced.	1195	14/11	891.....5.....5	13.....7.....6
John CLARKE	44	6/2	13...11.....4	0.....4.....3
Turner CLARKE	90	6/1	27.....7.....6	0.....8.....4
Joseph CLARKE	160		45...15.....0	0...13...11

(page 89 contd. Goochland County Land Tax Return of Archibald Pleasansts for 1788)

Proprietors Names	Quantity of Land	Rate p Acre	Amount of Value	Amount of Tax at 1 1/2 p cent
James COCKE	300	8/1	121.....5.....0	1...16....6
Edward CARTER	34	do.	13...10.....4	0.....4....2
William CLARKSON	50	9/9	24.....7...6	0.....7....4
Colo. John CURD	309	10/9	166.....1...9	2.....9...11
Capt. Edmond CURD	340		181...0...10	2...14....4
Sarah CURD	211	8/1	85.....5....7	1.....5.....7
Benjamin COCKE	122	do.	49.....6.....2]	
do. of Thomas COCKE	18	do.	7.....5.....6]	0...17.....1
James COCKE (P.tan)	54	do.	21...16.....6	0.....6....4
Thomas COCKE	62	do.	25.....1.....2	0.....7.....6
Stephen CROUCH	200	5/1	50...16.....8	0...15.....4
John CROUCH	425		212...10.....0	3.....3.....9

(page 90. Goochland County Land Tax Return of Archibald Pleasants for 1788)

Proprietors Names	Quantity of Land	Rate p Acre	Amount of Value	Amount of Tax at 1 1/2 p cent
Estate of John DOWDY, deced.	122	7/5	45.....4...10	0...13.....9
John ELLIS (Henrico)	392	12/1	236...16.....8	3...11.....0
Stephen ELLIS	129 1/4	16/2	104...19.....6	1...10....6
David ELLIS	372	8/1	151.....7....3	2.....5....6
Francis EVANS	133 1/2	5/5	36.....3.....2	0...11.....0
Thomas EDWARDS	50	6/6	16.....5.....0	0.....5.....0
Mary EDWARDS	3 1/2	16/2	2...16.....7	0.....1.....0
William FARRAR, resurveyed	600	10/5	312...10.....0	4...13.....9
William FORD	200	8/1	80...16.....8	1.....4.....4
Elizabeth FORD	233	do.	94.....3....5	1.....8....4
Joseph FARRAR	56	12/1	33...16.....8	0...10.....4
Reuben FORD	147	8/1	59.....8....3]	
do. of Richard PLEASANTS	82		40.....2....1]	1...10.....1
John T. GRIFFIN, Esqr.	2671		2738.....0.....0	41....1.....7
John GORDEN	133		55...14.....3	0...16.....8
John GORDEN, JUNR.	53		22.....4.....0	0.....6....9
Henry GRAY	100	8/1	40.....8....4	0...12.....2
John GUERRANT, Gent.	636		334.....2....6	5.....0....6
John GILLAM (Pr. George)	500	9/9	243...15.....0	3...13.....2
Colo. John GUERRANT	442		184...15....3	2...15.....6
James GEORGE	100	8/1	40.....8....4	0...12.....2
William GARTHRIGHT	98	10/9	52...13.....6	0...15...11
Francis GRAVES (Richmond)	640		1164.....0.....0]	
do. of William McCAUL	81	14/1	57.....7.....0]	18.....6.....5
James GRAY	134	6/1	40...15.....2	0...12.....4
John HYLTON	411	10/9	220...18.....3	3.....6....4
Francis E. HARRIS	440 1/2		391.....3....3	5...17.....6
John HINES	330	9/4	154.....0....0	2.....6....4
Thomas HARDING	543		289.....0.....6	4.....6....9
Strangeman HUTCHINS	55	8/1	22.....4.....7	0.....6....8
Capt. Thomas HATCHER	510	9/9	248...12.....6	3...14.....8
James HUNNICUTT	287	8/1	115...19...11	1...14...10
Benjamin HUGHES	627	do.	253.....8....3	3...16.....2
Capt. Gideon HATCHER	360	9/7	172...10.....0	2...11...10

(page 90 contd. Goochland County Land Tax Return of Archibald Pleasants for 1788)

Proprietors Names		Quantity of Land	Rate p Acre	Amount of Value	Amount of Tax at 1 1/2 p cent
William HUGHES	(Hanover)	115	9/2	52...14.....2	0...15...10
Giles HARDING		316	8/6	134...6....0	2.....0....4
William HAY	(Richmond)	521		293...0...5	4.....7...11
Thomas HODGES		50	5/1	12...14.....2	0.....3...10
John JOHNSON	(Overseer)	611 1/2		244.....5....8]	
do. of William EDWARDS		80	4/1	16...6....8]	
do of William WEBBER, SENR. resurveyed		435	10/6	228.....7.....6]	7.....6....( )
Charles JOHNSON, JUNR.		245		103.....0...11	1...11.....3

(page 91. Goochland County Land Tax Return of Archibald Pleasants for 1788)

Proprietors Names		Quantity of Land	Rate p Acre	Amount of Value	Amount of Tax at 1 1/2 p cent
David JOHNSON	(Geneto)	115	8/1	46.....9.....7	0...14.....0
John JOHNSON	(do.)	271	9/4	126.....9.....4	1...18....0
Isham JOHNSON		115	9/2	52...14.....2	0...16....0
Richard JOHNSON		150	do.	68...15...0	1...0.....8
Sarah JORDAN		75	16/2	60...12.....6	0...18.....4
Daniel JOHNSON		150	4/	30.....0....0	0.....9.....0
Thomas JOHNSON		304	6/1	92.....9.....4	1.....7....9
Susanna LAPRADE		300	10/8	160.....0.....0	2...8.....0
John LAPRADE		128	do.	68.....5....6	1.....0....6
Capt. Elisha LEAKE		827 1/2		397...14.....0]	
do. of Henry WHITLOW, JUNR.		50	8/1	20.....4.....2]	
do. of Henry WHITLOW, SENR.		99	do.	40.....0.....3]	6...17...10
John LEWIS	(C.M.)	200	do.	80...16.....8	1.....4.....4
Joseph LEWIS		860 1/3		309.....1.....2	4...12.....9
Stephen G. LETCHER		49	8/1	19...16.....1	0.....6.....0
Yancy LIPSCOMB		350 1/2	8/6	148...19.....3	2.....4...10
Joseph LEWIS		300	10/9	161.....5.....0	2...8.....5
Nathaniel G. MORRIS		400	9/1	181...13.....4	2...14.....6
John MADDOX		150	6/9	50...12.....6	0...15.....4
Amos L. MORE		260	10/	130.....0.....0	1...19....0
Stokes McCAUL		295	8/1	119.....4.....7	1...16.....0
Mary MILLER		426	8/10	188.....3.....0	2...16.....6
Edward McBRIDE		108	6/1	32...17.....0	0.....9...11
Revd. Daniel McCALLA		200	do.	60...16.....8	0...18.....4
Matthew NIGHTINGALE		59 2/3	9/10	29.....6.....9	0.....9.....0
Samuel NUCKOLS		115	7/2	41.....4.....2	0...12.....6
John NEAVES		290	7/5	107...10...10	1...12.....4
Stephen NOWLIN		150	6/9	50...12.....6	0...15.....4
William NUCKOLS, JUNR.		121	8/1	48...18.....1]	
do. of Charles NUCKOLS		11	7/2	3...18...10]	0...16.....0
Pouncy NUCKOLS		110	8/1	44.....9.....2]	
do. of William FARRAR		317 1/2	10/5	165.....7.....3]	3...3.....2
Charles NUCKOLS		93	7/2	33.....6.....6	0...10.....2
Thomas NUCKOLS		115	do.	41.....4.....2	0...12.....6
Rene NAPIER		180	8/1	72...15.....0	1.....1...11
William NEAVES		200	10/9	107...10.....0	1...12.....3

(page 91 contd. Goochland County Land Tax Return of Archibald Pleasants for 1788)

Proprietors Names		Quantity of Land	Rate p Acre	Amount of Value	Amount of Tax at 1 1/2 p cent
Colo. Josiah PARKER		986 1/2	14/10	731...13.....1	10...19.....8
Charles N. PERKINS		150	8/1	64......0.....0	0...19.....4
Hezekiah PURYEAR		560 1/2		230...12.....1	3.....9.....6
Ellis PURYEAR		200		82.....7.....1	1.....4.....9
Richard PLEASANTS		646		315...19.....3	4...14.....9

(page 92. Goochland County Land Tax Return of Archibald Pleasants for 1788)

Proprietors Names		Quantity of Land	Rate p Acre	Amount of Value	Amount of Tax at 1 1/2 p cent
Thomas PLEASANTS		1833		1456.....9...11	21...17.....0
Isaac W. PLEASANTS		539	21/6	579.....8.....6	8...14.....0
Matthew PLEASANTS		250	8/1	101.....0...10	1...10.....4
Archer PAYNE, Gent.		1172		491...12.....9	7.....7.....6
Samuel PARSONS		523 1/3	15/	392...10.....0	5...17.....9
John PRICE	(Henrico)	268	13/6	180...18.....0	2...14.....4
William POWEL		266	7/2	95.....6.....4	1.....8.....8
Major POWERS		180	8/1	72...15.....0	1.....2.....0
Anderson PEERS		1057		463...17.....5	6...19.....3
James PLEASANTS		500	16/7	414...11.....8	6.....4.....6
Joseph PLEASANTS		200	8/1	80...16.....8	1.....4.....4
Robert PLEASANTS	(Buff)	140	7/	49.....0.....0	0...14...10
Philip PLEASANTS		151		58...13.....0	0...17...10
William POWERS		368	6/6	119...12.....0	1...16.....0
Doctor William PASTEUR		700	13/4	466...13.....4	7.....0.....0
Estate of Francis PLEDGE, deced.		50	8/1	20.....4.....2	0.....6.....2
Archer PLEDGE		50	11/5	28...10...10	0.....8.....8
Estate of William PLEDGE, deced.		50	9/9	24.....7.....6	0.....7.....4
John PAYNE		439	14/5	316.....8...11	4...15.....0
Robin POOR		350	10/5	182.....5...10	2...14...10
Joseph POLLARD		447	9/11	221...12.....9	3.....6.....6
Mary PERKINS		161 1/2	8/1	65.....5.....6	0...19.....8
Molly PERKINS		250	do.	101.....0...10	1...10.....4
William PERKINS		150	6/1	45...12.....6	0...13.....8
William PERKINS, JUNR.		265	6/	79...10.....0	1.....4.....0
Estate of Walker PERKINS, deced.		111 3/4	9/10	54...18...11	0...16.....6
Benjamin PERKINS		250	3/3	40...12.....6	0...12.....4
Colo. George PAYNE		306		154.....5.....0	2.....6.....5
Isaac PERRIN		225	12/1	135...18.....9	2.....0...11
Archibald PLEASANTS		299	13/6	201...16.....6	3.....0.....8
Josias PAYNE		335	6/8	111...13.....4	1...13.....6
Lewis POWERS		60	8/1	24.....5.....0	0.....7.....3
Jesse REDD		397	8/1	160.....9.....1	2.....8.....3
John ROYSTER		175	12/1	105...14.....4	1...11...11
John REDD		252		88.....4.....8	1.....6.....7
Edward REDFORD		295		221...15...10	3.....6.....6
William REDFORD	(Mercht.)	195	4/1	39...16.....3	0...12.....0
Thomas ROUNDTREE		108	10/5	56.....5.....0	0...17.....0
Samuel ROUNDTREE		121	do.	63.....0.....5	0...19.....0
Randal ROUNDTREE		247	11/5	140...19...11	2.....2.....5
Matthew RIDDLE		70	7/	24...10.....0	0.....7.....6

(page 93. Goochland County Land Tax Return of Archibald Pleasansts for 1788)

Proprietors Names	Quantity of Land	Rate p Acre	Amount of Value	Amount of Tax at 1 1/2 p cent
Isaac RAGLAND	150	6/9	50...12.....6	0...15.....4
William ROYSTER, Gent.	543	11/1	300...18.....3	4...10.....4
Thomas ROYSTER, Capt.	166 2/3		84.....1.....6	1.....4...10
Milner REDFORD	539	9/8	260...10.....4	3...18.....2
Thomas M. RANDOLPH, Esqr.	3052		2764.....3.....8	41.....9.....6
Mary ROGERS	17	8/1	6...17.....5	0.....2.....0
William RONALD, Esqr.	1370		738.....9.....2	11.....1.....8
Josiah SEAY	145		49...17...11	0...15.....0
William SAUNDERS	20	8/1	8.....1.....8	0.....2.....9
Stephen SOUTHALL	644		252.....3.....0	3...15.....9
Elizabeth STODGELL	28	12/1	16...18.....4	0.....5.....2
Thomas SHOEMAKER	200	10/1	100...16.....8	1...10.....4
Colo. John SYME	566	8/1	228...15.....2	3.....9.....0
John SAUNDERS	30	do.	12.....2.....6	0.....3.....8
Estate of Charles SAMPSON	234	do.	94...11.....6	1.....8.....6
John SHELTON, Gent.	462		191.....2.....0]	
do. of William PERKINS	50	6/1	15.....4.....2]	3.....2.....2
Richard SAMPSON	250	7/3	90...12.....6	1.....7.....4
Majr. Robert H. SAUNDERS	330	13/6	222...15.....0	3.....7.....0
William SANDRIDGE	159 1/2	8/1	64.....9.....4	0...19.....6
Philip TINSLEY	50	12/1	30.....4.....2	0.....9.....2
Thomas TOWLES	348 1/2	9/4	162...12.....8	2.....8...10
Bartholomew TURNER	200	8/1	80...16.....8	1.....4.....4
Thomas TOURMAN (Original Entry)	63 1/2	7/6	23...12.....0	0.....7.....0
William UTTLEY	125	8/1	50...10.....5	0...15.....4
Obadiah UTTLEY	8	do.	3.....4.....8	0.....1.....0
Ann UTTLEY	116	6/4	36...14.....8	0...11.....2
John UTTLEY	125	8/1	50...10.....5	0...15.....4
Hezekiah UTTLEY	58	6/1	17...12...10	0.....5.....4
Elizabeth UNDERWOOD	100	11/5	57.....1.....8	0...17.....2
George UNDERWOOD	657	7/4	240...18.....0]	
do. of Edward McBRIDE, resurveyed	92	6/1	27...19.....8]	4.....0.....9
Thomas UNDERWOOD	600	8/9	262...10.....0]	
do. of George UNDERWOOD	120	7/4	44.....0.....0]	
do. of Drury WILLIAMS (other District)	600		232...10.....0]	8.....1.....9
Estate of James UNDERWOOD	215	6/8	71...13.....4	1.....1.....6
Matthew VAUGHAN, Gent.	753 1/2	9/1	342.....4.....4	5.....2.....9

(page 94. Goochland County Land Tax Return of Archibald Pleasants for 1788)

Proprietors Names	Quantity of Land	Rate p Acre	Amount of Value	Amount of Tax at 1 1/2 p cent
James VAUGHAN	362	7/7	137.....5.....2	2.....1.....4
Colo. John WOODSON	611		996..19.....4	14...19.....2
Matthew WOODSON	1101		868.....1.....8	13.....0.....7
Daniel WADE	346 1/2		142.....7.....5	2.....2.....2
Joseph WATKINS	597		278.....8.....6	4.....3.....6
Peter WALKER (Geneto)	155	8/1	62...12...11	0...18...10

(page 94 contd. Goochland County Land Tax Return of Archibald Pleasants for 1788)

Proprietors Names	Quantity of Land	Rate p Acre	Amount of Value	Amount of Tax at 1 1/2 p cent
Shadrack WALKER	75	8/1	30.....6.....3	0.....9.....2
Richard WADE	197	9/7	94.....8.....0	1.....8.....6
Robert WADE	97	8/1	39.....4.....1	0...12.....0
Majr. Joseph WOODSON	578	do.	233...12.....2	3...10.....0
John WADE	73	do.	29...10.....1	0.....9.....0
Eleonar WILLIS	100	6/1	30.....8.....4	0.....9.....2
William WOODALL	63	6/6	20.....9.....6	0.....6.....2
William WEBBER (Preacher)	177	6/4	56.....1.....0	0...16...10
Edward WILLIS	160	8/1	64...13.....4	0...19.....6
Thomas WOODSON	200	12/1	120...16.....8	1...16.....4
Nathaniel WEBSTER	140	6/6	45...10.....0	0...13.....6
Robert WINGFIELD	90	8/1	36.....7.....6	0...11.....0
David WEBSTER	25	10/6	13.....2.....6	0.....4.....0
Joseph WOODSON (Geneto)	225	9/	101.....5.....0	1...10.....6
Estate of Joseph WOODSON, deced.	222	10/	111.....0.....0	1...13.....4
Dorothy WATKINS	170	8/1	68...14.....2	1.....0.....8
Thomas WATKINS	583	do.	235...12.....7	3...10...10
Benjamin WATKINS	238	9/5	112.....1.....2	1...13.....8
John WATKINS	519	8/11	231.....7.....9	3.....9.....6
Benjamin WOODSON, (Fluvanna)	205	9/1	93.....2.....1	1.....8.....0
Benjamin WATKINS, JUNR.	156	9/5	73.....9.....0	1.....2.....2
John WITT	17	8/1	6...17.....5	0.....2.....0
Tucker WOODSON	600	17/8	530.....0.....0	7...19.....0
Samuel WOODWARD	450	12/1	271...17.....6	4.....1.....6
John WOODWARD	50	do.	30.....4.....2	0.....9.....2
William WOODSON	50	4/1	10.....4.....2	0.....3.....2
Total amount	70304			L 588...13.....7

ARCHD: PLEASANTS, Commissoner

A Copy.   Examined.
                Teste   WM. MILLER, D. C.
                                11th Augt. 88

(page 95).

Sarah CURD	Overcharged	43 1/3	8/1		0.....5.....3
Total Amount		70261			L. 588.....8.....4

DARST
    Benjamin 1, 11, 23, 33, 75
DAVIS
    David 11, 84
    John 8, 11, 84
    Stephen 8
    Susanna 11, 20
DICKESON
    Noton 11
DICKERSON
    Noton 20
DICKINSON
    Noton 23, 34, 44, 55, 84
DOUGLAS
    Mr. 22, 25, 34, 46
    William 11, 23, 33, 44, 55, 78
DOWDY
    Elizabeth 82
    John 4, 11, 23, 33, 44, 55, 62, 84
    John (deceased) 82, 91
DRUMWRIGHT
    Thomas 5, 11, 23, 33, 44, 55, 84
DUKE
    Edmund 8, 11, 23, 70
DUVAL
    Samuel 1, 11
    Samuel Jr. 68
EADES 31
    Thomas B. 68, 72
EADS
    Thomas B. 6, 12
EAST
    Benjamin 9, 12, 23, 34, 44, 55, 84
EASTIN
    Augustine 1, 11, 23, 70
EDWARDS
    Mary 62, 82, 91
    Thomas 2, 12, 23, 34, 44, 62, 91
    William 2, 11, 23, 34, 44, 92
    William Jr. 62

ELAM
    Joseph 45, 55, 75, 84
ELDRIDGE

    Thomas 9, 12, 23, 34, 44, 55, 69, 84
ELLIS
    David 2, 11, 23, 34, 44, 62, 68, 91
    John 1, 11, 23, 34, 44, 62, 91
    Stephen 1, 11, 23, 34, 44, 62, 82, 91
EMMERSON
    Henry 12, 20, 23, 34, 44, 55, 84
    Thomas 12, 20. 34, 44, 55, 75
    Thomas Junr. 12, 20, 23, 34, 45, 55, 78, 85
    Thomas Senr. 78
ENGLAND
    David 9, 12, 23, 34, 44, 55, 84
    William A. 9, 12, 23, 34, 69, 70
EVANS
    Francis 2, 11, 23, 34, 44, 62, 91
    Joseph 2, 11, 23, 34, 44, 82
    Thomas 62, 82
FARISH
    John 6, 12, 24, 34, 45, 80
FARRAR
    John 12, 23, 34, 45, 82
    Joseph 12, 24, 34, 45, 62, 76, 91
    Joseph R. 24, 34, 67, 71, 76
    William 12, 23, 34, 45, 62, 91, 92
FARRER
    John 2
    Joseph 2
    William 1
FLEMING
    Charles 24, 34, 45, 55, 67, 71, 84
    Tarlton (estate) 8, 12, 24, 34, 45, 55, 84
    W. 84
    William 5, 12, 24, 34, 45, 55, 67, 71
FORD
    Daniel 45, 55, 74, 84
    Elizabeth 2, 24, 34, 45, 62, 91
    Reuben 12, 34, 45, 62, 91
    Reubin 4, 24

    William 2, 12, 23, 34, 45, 62, 91
FRAIZER
    Mary 3
FRAYSER
    Mary 12, 24, 34, 45
FRAZIER
    Mary 62, 82
FRENCH
    Hugh 8, 24, 34, 45, 55, 75, 78, 84
    Mason 84
FURLONG
    John 12, 20, 24, 34, 45, 55
GARTHRIGHT
    William 63, 82, 91
GAY
    William 45, 75, 76, 80
GEORGE
    Andrew 20
    Anselm 12, 24, 35, 45, 80
    James 5, 12, 24, 34, 45, 63, 91
    James (estate) 20, 24, 35, 76
    Robert 45, 55, 76, 78, 80, 86, 88
    William 4, 12, 24, 34, 45, 55, 67, 71, 72, 80, 84
GILBERT
    John 12, 20, 24, 35, 45, 55, 84
GILLAM
    John 12, 24, 34,45, 62, 91
    John Sr. 34, 45, 55, 84
    Robert 8, 24, 35, 45, 55, 84
GILLIAM
    John 4, 5
GLASS
    John 55, 75, 76

HUDSON
David 24, 35, 45, 67, 71, 75, 78
David (estate) 56, 78, 84
HUGHES
Benjamin 3, 24, 35, 45, 63, 91
John 56, 78, 85
William 4, 13, 24, 35, 46, 63, 92
HUMBER
John 5, 13, 24, 35, 46, 53, 56, 84
HUNNICUTT
James 13, 24, 35, 45, 63, 91
HUNNYCUT
James 3
HUSON
John 24, 35, 45, 56, 67, 71, 86
HUTCHINS
John 12, 68, 71
Strangeman 12, 35, 45, 63, 76, 91
HUTCHINGS
John 1
Strangeman 1
HYLTON
John 24, 35, 45, 63, 67, 71, 91
ISBELL
William 5, 13, 36, 46, 56, 85
JAMES
William 47, 57, 76, 79, 85
JARRETT
Archibald 8, 14, 25, 36, 46, 56, 85
David 14, 25, 36, 46, 56, 85
Devereux 14, 25, 36, 46, 56, 85
Nichelaus 79
JEFFERSON
Thomas 8, 14, 25, 36, 46, 56, 85
JENNETT
Thomas 57, 79, 85

JENNINGS 8, 14, 25, 36, 46, 56, 79
JOHNSON
Benjamin 3, 8, 13, 25, 56, 68, 69, 72, 79, 85
Benjamin (estate) 36, 46, 69, 79
Charles 2, 9, 14, 25, 36, 46, 47, 56, 63, 82, 85
Charles Junr. 2, 13, 25, 36, 46, 64, 82, 92
Daniel 14, 20, 25, 36, 63, 85, 92
David 3, 13, 25, 36, 46, 47, 63, 92
Isham 3, 13, 25, 36, 46, 63, 92
John 2, 3, 13, 14, 20, 25, 36, 46, 63, 74, 75, 92
Joseph 14, 25, 36, 78
Joseph (estate) 6, 13, 36, 46, 55
Richard 4, 13, 24, 36, 46, 56, 63, 79, 85, 92
Thomas 92
William 8, 14, 25, 36, 46, 56, 85
JONES
John 14, 20, 25, 74
JORDAN
Sarah 1, 14, 25, 36, 47, 63, 92
JUDE
Jane 1, 13, 67, 71
Mary 1, 13, 25, 70
LACY
Benjamin 6, 14, 26, 36, 47, 81
Elliot 86
Jesse 6, 14, 26, 36, 75
Matthew 6, 14, 26, 36, 47, 57, 85
Sarah 6, 14, 26, 36, 47, 54, 57, 76, 78, 85
LAMAY
Samuel 14, 26, 47, 57, 73, 79, 85

LAPRADE
John 14, 25, 36, 47, 63, 69, 75, 92
Susanna 47, 63, 75, 92
LAURENCE
Henry 57, 86
John 47
Thomas 57, 86
LAWRENCE
John 73
Thomas 79
LAYNE
Ayres 5, 14, 25, 36, 47, 47, 57, 85
David Junr. 86
David Senr. 86
Henry 5, 14, 26, 36, 57, 85
John 3, 14, 25, 36, 47, 63
Mary 6, 14, 26, 36, 47, 57, 85
LEAK
Josiah 14
LEAKE
Elisha 2, 14, 25, 36, 47, 63, 82, 92
Josiah 26, 36, 47, 57, 86
Josias 9
LEE
Betty 57, 79, 86
John (estate) 8, 14, 26, 36, 47, 79
LEMAY
Samuel 6, 36
LETCHER
Stephen G. 6, 14, 36, 47, 63, 69, 71, 92
LEWIS
Howel 47, 57, 69
Howell 36, 86
John 4, 14, 25, 36, 47, 63
John Junr. 4
Joseph 36, 47, 71, 75
Joseph Jr. 69

LEWIS (contd.)
Joseph Senr. (deced) 14, 26, 67, 69, 71,
Mary 8, 67, 71,
Mary (deced) 14,
Mr. 2, 12,
Robert (Colo.) 8, 14, 26, 36, 47, 57, 67, 69,
    71, 79, 86,
Robert Junr. 57, 79, 86,
William 9,
William (R.C.) 14, 26, 36, 47, 57, 86,
LILLY.
Armiger 8, 26, 57, 85,
Armiger (Fluvanna) 14, 36, 47,
LIPSCOMB.
Yancy 47, 63, 73, 92.
LOGAN.
Charles Esqr. 57, 79, 86,
LOVELL.
40,
John 7, 14, 26, 70,
LOWRY / LOURY
Joel 57, 79, 86,
Joseph 14, 20, 26, 36, 47, 57, 79, 86,
Matthew 14, 20, 26, 36, 47, 57, 86,
Matthew Junr. 86,
Thornton 86,

McBRIDE.
Edward 4, 14, 26, 37, 48, 63, 92. 94.
McCAUL
Stokes 3, 14, 26, 48, 63, 92.
William 3, 14, 26, 37, 47, 63, 91,
McCAULEY / McCALLA / McCAWLEY
Daniel (Revd.) 37, 48, 69, 92.
McDONALD
Angus 58, 79, 87,
McMEKING
William 87,

MADDOX.
39,
James 5, 14, 26, 29, 68, 70,
John 2, 14, 26, 36, 47, 63, 92.
MARTIN.
David 7, 15, 26, 37, 48, 57, 86,
Edward 86,
John 15, 26, 37, 48,
John (Colo.) 58, 86,
Thomas 47, 57, 76, 86,
William 15, 20,. 27, 37, 48, 58, 87,
MASSIE.
Charles 7, 14, 26, 37, 48, 57, 79, 86,
Nathaniel (Capt.) 15, 21, 27, 37, 48, 79,
Nathaniel (Gent.) 58, 87,
Thomas (Major, Frederick) 15, 27, 37, 48, 54,
    77,   (Massie, contd.)

MASSIE (contd._
Thomas 37, (Gent.-57), 79, 87,
Thomas (Overseer) 15, 20, 27, 47, 73, 74, 79,
William 15, 21, 27, 48, 58, 87,
MASTERS.
John (Colo.) 8,
MATTHEWS.
Edward 8, 15, 26, 47, 57, 61, 77, 80, 81, 86,
Edward's Estate 37, 47, 57, 69, 74, 76, 77,
    86,
Jane 37, 69, 76,
William 47, 57, 77, 86,
MAYO
Joseph Esqr. (Henrico) 26, 36, 76,
MEACHUM.
Paul 7, 15, 26, 37, 48, 57, 86,
MEANLY.
Elizabeth 5, 14, 26, 37, 74,
MEMINS.
Elizabeth 7,
MERIWETHER.
Thomas 87,
Thomas (Colo., Richmond) 47, 57, 75, 86,
William 69, 71,
William (Capt., Louisa) 26, 37, 75,
MERRIAN.
Ann 8, 15, 26, 37, 48, 79,
Bartholomew 58, 79, 86,
Jesse 58, 79, 87,
John 58, 79, 86,
Matthew 58, 79, 86,
Samuel 58, 79, 86,
MICHEL.
Ann 7,
William (Gent.) 7,
MICHIE.
John Esqr. 58, 79, 87,
MILLER.
30,
John 49,
Mary 3, 14, 26, 37, 48, 63, 92.
Pleasant 1,
Thomas 7, 15, 26, 37, 47, 57, 60, 67, 69, 71,
    75, 81, 86,
William 7, (Gent.-75),
William (Capt.) 15, 26, 37, 47, 57, 86, 88,
William (D.C.) 90, 95.
MIMS.
28,
David 7, 15, 26, 37, 77,
David's Estate 47, 57, 77, 86,
Elizabeth 15, 26, 37, 48, 57, 79, 86,
Gideon 7, 15, 26, 37, 48, 57, 83, 86,
Martin 7, 15, 47, 57, 68, 71, 74, 86,
Robert 57, 79, 86,
Sarah 15, 26, 37, 48, 58, 86,

PURYEAR.
Ellis 93.
Hezekiah 2, 15, 27, 38, 49, 64, 71, 74, 82, 93.

RADFORD.
Edward 50,
Milner 50,
William (Mercht.) 50, 65. 75,
RAGLAND.
Isaac 2, 17, 29, 39, 50, 65, 94.
RAINE
Nathaniel 5, 17, 29, 39, 60, 75, 80, 88,
RANDOLPH.
Thomas Esqr. 8, 17, 29, 39, 50, 59, 80, 88,
Thomas Mann Esqr. (Dor.), (Tuckahoe) 3, 65, 94.
Thomas M. (Colo., Tuckahoe) 17, 29, 39, 50,
READ.
John K. 7, (Doctor -17), 29, 39, 50, 59, 88,
REDD.
Jesse 50, 65, 93.
John 1, 17, 29, 39, 50, 65, 74, 75, 93.
REDFORD.
Edward 3, 17, 29, 39, 65, 76, 93,
Milner 3, 17, 29, 39, 65, 94.
William (Mercht.) 93,
RICE.
Charles 8, 17, 29,
Charles's Estate 39, 50, 55, 59, 70, 78,
Holman (Capt.) 60, 80,
RICHARDS.
John 59, 80, 88,
William 50, 59, 74, 80, 88,
RICHARDSON.
26,
George 17, 29, 40, 50, 59, 88,
Isham 5, 17, 67, 71,
Samuel 8,
Samuel (Capt.) 17, 29, 39, 50, 59, 88,
RIDDLE.
Matthew 2, 17, 29, 39, 50, 65, 93.
Thomas 7, 17, 29, 39, 47, 50, 59, 76, 88,
RIGSBY.
William 6, 17, 27, 39, 50, 59, 88,
ROBARDS.
28, 31,
James 40, 51, 59, 70, 74, 80, 88,
William 6, 17, 68,
William (deced) 72,
William Junr. 17, 21, 67, 72,
ROBERTS.
James 4,
ROGERS.
Mary 3, 17, 29, 39, 50, 65, 94.

RONALD.
William Esqr. 4, 17, 29, 39, 50, 65, 68, 72, 94.
ROSS.
David Esqr. 4, 17, 29, 38, 39, 50, 59, 68, 70, 73, 80, 88,
ROUNTREE.
Randal 50, 65, 75, 93,
Randolph 1, 17, 28, 39,
Samuel 1, 17, 28, 39, 50, 65, 70, 93,
Thomas 65, 82, 93,
William 39, 50, 63, 70, 82,
William's Estate 39, 50, 70, 82,
ROYSTER.
John 63, 82, 93.
John (Capt.) 50, 65, 76,
Thomas 2, 17, 29, 39, 50,
Thomas (Capt.) 65, 94.
William 2, (Gent.-17), 29, 39, 50, 65, 94.
RUTHERFORD.
William 6, 17, 29, 39, 50, 59, 88,

SADLER.
Benjamin 5, 17, 29, 40, 51,
William 51, 55, 60, 74, 78, 88,
SALMONDS / SALMONS
24,
Benjamin 7, 18, 60, 67, 71, 80, 88,
James 51, 60, 70, 89,
John 8, 18, 69.
SAMMONS.
James 40,
SAMPSON.
Charles's Estate 4, 17, 29, 40, 51, 65, 94.
Richard 3, 18, 29, 40, 51, 65, 94.
Stephen (Capt.) 3, 29, 40, 51, 60, 81, 89,
Stephen (Gent.) 34, 69,
Stephen (Sheriff) 42, 77,
William (Capt.) 60, 80, 89,
William (Dep. Sher.) 77,
SANDRIDGE.
William 94.
SAUNDERS.
George 89,
John 3, 17, 29, 40, 51, 65, 94.
Robert H. (Major) 40, 51, 65, 70, 94.
Stephen (Capt.) 17,
William 4, 17, 40, 51, 65, 75, 94.
SCOTT.
John 60, 80,
John (R.C.) 89,
SCRUGGS.
Edward 9, 18, 29, 40, 51, 78,
Edward (deced) 81,
James 51, 60, 74, 89,
Richard 60, 81, 89,

SEAY.
  Josiah 2, 17, 29, 40, 51, 65, 74, 94.
SHELTON.
  David 40, 51, 60, 70,
  David (Louisa) 89,
  John (Gent.) 5, 17, 29, 40, 51, 65, 68, 94.
  John (Hanover) 5, 17, 29, 70,
  Joseph 40, 51, 60, 89,
  Joseph (Capt.) 5, 17,
  Joseph (Capt.) (Louisa) 29,
  Joseph (Capt., deced) 70,
  Joseph Junr. 70,
  Robert (Glebe) 60, 80, 89,
  William 60, 81, 89,
SHOEMAKER.
  Thomas 1, 17, 29, 40, 51, 65, 94.
SLAYDEN.
  Arthur 5, 17, 29, 40, 51, 60,
  John 6, 18, 29, 40, 51, 60, 89,
SMITH.
  Robert 51, 60, 73,
  Robert (Capt.) 9,
  Robert (Cap.) (P.tan) 18, 29, 88,
  Robert's Estate (Capt., P.tan) 40, 70, 76,
  William Junr. (P.tan) 51, 76, 79,
  William S. or L. 7, 18, 29, 40, 51, 60, 81, 89,
  William S. (deced) 81,
SOUTHALL.
  Stephen (Major) 40, 51, 65, 70, 75, 94.
STAFFORD .
  Thomas 6,
STODGHILL.
  Elizabeth 1, 17, 29, 40, 51, 65, 94.
STRONG.
  John 8, 18, 29, 40, 51, 60, 89,
  Nathan 8, 29, 40, 51, 60, 89,
SYME.
  John (Colo., Hanover) 2, 17, 29, 40, 51, 65,
      82, 94.

TERRY.
  Thomas 60, 81, 89,
THACKER.
  Benjamin 18, 21, 30, 40, 51, 60, 89,
THOMAS
  James 9, 18, 30, 40, 51, 60, 89,
  Sarah 6, 17, 30, 40, 51, 60, 89,
THURSTON.
  Esther 8, 18, 30, 40, 51, 60, 89,
  John 8, 18, 30, 40, 51, 60, 89,
  Mary 60, 81, 89,
  Reuben 18, 21, 30, 40, 51, 81,
  William 8, 18, 30, 40, 51, 60, 61, 81, 89,
TIBBS./ TEBBS
  Sarah 40, 70,

TINSLEY.
  Philip 1, 18, 29, 40, 51, 65, 94.
TOURMAN.
  Thomas 94.
TOWLER.
  Cornelius 7, 18, 30, 40, 51, 56, 79,
  Japheth 8, 18, 68, 72,
  John 18, 30, 40, 51, 81,
  John's Estate 9,
  Mary 6, 18, 30, 40, 51, 60, 89,
TOWLES.
  Stockley (Capt.) 2, 18, 29, 40, 73,
  Thomas 2, (Esqr. -18), 29, 40, 51, 65, 94.
TUGGLE.
  Henry 8, 18, 30, 40, 73,
TURNER.
  Bartholomew 3, 18, 30, 40, 51, 65, 94.
  William 60, 81, 89,
TURPIN.
  Horatio 8, 18, 30, 40, 51, 59, 80,

UNDERWOOD.
  Elizabeth 4, 18, 30, 41, 52, 54, 94.
  George 5, 18, 30, 41, 52, 65, 94.
  James's Estate 30, 41, 52, 65, 68, 94.
  Thomas (Gent.) 5, 18, 30, 41, 52, 65, 94.
UTLEY.
  Ann 2, 18, 30, 40, 52, 65, 94,
  Hezekiah 2, 18, 30, 40, 52, 65, 94,
  John 2, 18, 30, 40, 52, 65, 94.
  Obadiah 2, 18, 30, 40, 52, 65, 94,
  William 2, 18, 21, 30, 40, 51, 65, 94,

VADEN /VARDER. / VAIDEN
  Jane 1, 18, 67, 71,
VAUGHAN
  James 1, 18, 30, 41, 52, 66,
  Matthew 1, (Gent.-18), 30, 41, 52, 65, 73, 94.
  Matthew (Dep. Sheriff) 20, 31,
  S. 60,
  Shadrach 7, 18, 30, 41, 52, 59, 60, 79-81, 89,

WADDELL.
  Charles 30, 68, 69,
WADE.
  Dabney 7, 19, 31, 42, 53, 61, 89,
  Daniel 1, 19, 30, 41, 52, 66, 73, 94.
  David 73,
  John 18, 30, 41, 52, 66, 95.
  Richard 1, 18, 30, 41, 52, 66, 73, 95.
  Robert 1, 18, 30, 41, 52, 66, 95.
  William's Estate 7, 19, 42, 53, 61, 89,
WAFFORD.
  Thomas 19, 31, 42, 52, 60, 73, 76, 87,

WALKER.
  John 5, 19, 31, 42, 53, 61, 89,
  Peter (Constable) 5, 19, 31, 41, 61, 75, 81, 90,
  Peter (Geneto) 3, 19, 31, 41, 52, 66, 74, 94.
  Shadrach 52, 66, 74, 95.
  William 6, 19, 31, 42, 52, 60, 73, 89,
WALMACK
  Henry 5, 19, 31, 41, 53, 61, 89,
  Richard 30, 41, 69, 76,
WARE.
  John (Capt.) 20, 21, 31, 42, 53, 61, 81, 90,
WATKINS.
  21,
  Benjamin 3, 31, 41, 52, 66. 95.
  Benjamin Junr. 4, 19, 31, 53, 66, 95.
  Dorothy 3, 19, 30, 41, 52, 66, 95.
  John 3, 19, 31, 52, 66, 95.
  Joseph (Little Creek) 19, 31, 41, 52, 66, 67, 71-73, 94.
  Thomas 3, 19, 31, 41, 52, 66, 68, 72, 95.
WEATHERSPOON.
  Reuben 52, 60, 75, 89,
WEBB.
  Foster Esqr. (New Kent) 30,
  Foster Senr. 68,
  John 72,
WEBBER.
  William 2, 3, 19, 31, 41,
  William (Preacher) 19, 30, 41, 52, 66, 95.
  William Senr. 52, 66. 92.
WEBSTER.
  David 2, 19, 30, 41, 52, 64, 66. 96.
  Nathaniel 2, 19, 30, 41, 52, 66, 75, 95.
WHITFIELD.
  39,
  William 9, 19, 31, 70,
WHITLOCK.
  Thomas 90,
  William 5, 19, 31,
WHITLOW.
  Henry Junr. 4, 19, 31, 41, 53, 66.
  Henry Senr. 4, 19, 31, 41, 53, 66.
WILBERN / WILBOURNE
  Lewis 7, 19, 31, 42, 53, 61, 89,
  William 8, 19, 31, 42, 53, 61, 89,
WILKINS.
  Joseph (Geneto) (Little Creek) 3,
WILLIAMS.
  Drury 31, 42, 53, 61, 68, 70, 72, 94.
  J. 43, 86,
  James 19, 21, 31, 42, 53,
  John 6, 9, 42, 73, 79,
  John (D.C.) 19, 31, 42, 52, 60, 72, 74, 81, 89,
  John Junr. 19, 31, 53,
  Philip 20, 21, 31, 42, 53, 61, 90,

WILLIAMS (contd.)
  Solomon 19, 21, 31, 42. 52, 61, 76, 81, 89,
  William 5, 31, 42, 53, 61, 68, 72, 74, 78, 81,
  William (deced) 19, 68, 72,
WILLIAMSON.
  John 19, 31, 42, 53, 61, 89,
WILLIS.
  Edward 2, 19, 30, 41, 52, 66. 95.
  Eleanor 2, 19, 30, 41, 52, 66, 95.
  Pleasant 19, 30, 41, 52, 64, 70, 82,
  William (of David) 4, 19, 31, 41,
WINGFIELD.
  Robert 2, 19, 30, 41, 52, 66, 95.
WINSTON.
  Isaac (Hanover) 5, 19, 31, 42, 53, 61, 89,
WITT.
  John 4, 19, 31, 41, 53, 66, 95.
WOOD.
  Henry 52, (Esqr.-60), 73, 81, 83, 84, 86, 87, 89,
  Lucy 60, 81, 89,
  Valentine 's Estate (Colo.) 6, 19, 31, 42, 53, 57, 58, 60, 68, 72, 79-81,
WOODALL.
  William 2, 19, 30, 41, 42, 52, 53, 66, 95.
WOODSON.
  24,
  Benjamin (Fluvanna) 3, 19, 31, 41, 52, 66, 95.
  J. 84,
  John (Colo.) 1, 30, 41, 52, 66. 94.
  John Gent. (Beaverdam, Ferry) 4, 19, 31, 41, 53, 61, 74, 89,
  John (Majr.) 1,
  John (Meadow) 7, 19, 42, 53, 61, 89,
  John's Estate 18,
  Joseph (Geneto) 41, 52, 66, 95.
  Joseph (Major) 18, 30, 41, 52, 66, 75,
  Joseph (of Tucker) 52, 61, 89,
  Joseph's Estate 41, 52, 66, 95.
  Joseph Junr. (Geneto) 3, 19, 30,
  Joseph Junr. (Major) 41,
  Joseph Senr. 3, 68,
  Joseph Senr., (Geneto, deced) 19, 30, 68, 72,
  Matthew 1, 18, 30, 41, 52, 66. 74, 76, 82, 94.
  Samuel (Capt.) 20, 21, 67, 71,
  Thomas 2, 19, 30, 41, 52, 66, 95.
  Tucker 4, 19, 31, 41, 53, 66, 95.
  William 95.
WOODWARD.
  John 66, 82, 95.
  Samuel 66, 82, 95.
  Susannah 1, 18, 30, 41, 52, 92,
  William 1, 18, 30, 41, 75,
YOUNGER.
  Ann 20, 21, 31, 42, 53, 61, 90,

Heritage Books by Ruth and Sam Sparacio:

*Abstracts of Account Books of Edward Dixon, Merchant of
Port Royal, Virginia, Volume I: 1743–1747*

*Abstracts of Account Books of Edward Dixon, Merchant of
Port Royal, Virginia, Volume II*

*Albemarle County, Virginia Deed and
Will Book Abstracts, 1748–1752*

Albemarle County, Virginia Deed Book Abstracts, 1758–1761

Albemarle County, Virginia Deed Book Abstracts, 1761–1764

Albemarle County, Virginia Deed Book Abstracts, 1764–1768

Albemarle County, Virginia Deed Book Abstracts, 1768–1770

Albemarle County, Virginia Deed Book Abstracts, 1776–1778

Albemarle County, Virginia Deed Book Abstracts, 1778–1780

Albemarle County, Virginia Deed Book Abstracts, 1780–1783

Albemarle County, Virginia Deed Book Abstracts, 1787–1790

Albemarle County, Virginia Deed Book Abstracts, 1790–1791

Albemarle County, Virginia Deed Book Abstracts, 1791–1793

Augusta County, Virginia Land Tax Books, 1782–1788

Augusta County, Virginia Land Tax Books, 1788–1790

Amherst County, Virginia Land Tax Books, 1789–1791

Caroline County, Virginia Appeals and Land Causes, 1787–1794

*Caroline County, Virginia Committee of Safety and
Early Surveys, 1729–1762 and 1774–1775*

Caroline County, Virginia Land Tax Book Alterations, 1782–1789

Caroline County, Virginia Land Tax Book Alterations, 1792–1795

Caroline County, Virginia Land Tax Book Alterations, 1795–1798

Caroline County, Virginia Order Book Abstracts, 1765

Caroline County, Virginia Order Book Abstracts, 1767–1768

Caroline County, Virginia Order Book Abstracts, 1768–1770

Caroline County, Virginia Order Book Abstracts, 1770–1771

Caroline County, Virginia Order Book, 1764

Caroline County, Virginia Order Book, 1765–1767

Caroline County, Virginia Order Book, 1771–1772

Caroline County, Virginia Order Book, 1772–1773

Caroline County, Virginia Order Book, 1773

Caroline County, Virginia Order Book, 1773–1774

Caroline County, Virginia Order Book, 1774–1778

Caroline County, Virginia Order Book, 1778–1781

Caroline County, Virginia Order Book, 1781–1783

Caroline County, Virginia Order Book, 1783–1784

Caroline County, Virginia Order Book, 1784–1785

Caroline County, Virginia Order Book, 1785–1786

Caroline County, Virginia Order Book, 1786–1787

Caroline County, Virginia Order Book, 1787, Part 1

Caroline County, Virginia Order Book, 1787, Part 2

Caroline County, Virginia Order Book, 1787–1788

Caroline County, Virginia Order Book, 1788

Culpeper County, Virginia Deed Book Abstracts, 1795–1796

Culpeper County, Virginia Land Tax Book, 1782–1786

Culpeper County, Virginia Land Tax Book, 1787–1789

Culpeper County, Virginia Minute Book, 1763–1764

*Digest of Family Relationships, 1650–1692, from
Virginia County Court Records*

*Digest of Family Relationships, 1720–1750, from
Virginia County Court Records*

*Digest of Family Relationships, 1750–1763,
from Virginia County Court Records*

*Digest of Family Relationships, 1764–1775, from
Virginia County Court Records*

Essex County, Virginia Deed and Will Abstracts, 1695–1697

Essex County, Virginia Deed and Will Abstracts, 1697–1699

Essex County, Virginia Deed and Will Abstracts, 1699–1701

Essex County, Virginia Deed and Will Abstracts, 1701–1703

Essex County, Virginia Deed and Will Abstracts, 1745–1749

Essex County, Virginia Deed and Will Book, 1692–1693

Essex County, Virginia Deed and Will Book, 1693–1694

Essex County, Virginia Deed and Will Book, 1694–1695

Essex County, Virginia Deed and Will Book, 1701–1704

*Essex County, Virginia Deed, 1753–1754
and Will Book 1750*

Essex County, Virginia Deed Abstracts, 1721–1724

Essex County, Virginia Deed Book, 1724–1728

Essex County, Virginia Deed Book, 1728–1733

Essex County, Virginia Deed Book, 1733–1738

Essex County, Virginia Deed Book, 1738–1742

Essex County, Virginia Deed Book, 1742–1745

Essex County, Virginia Deed Book, 1749–1751

Essex County, Virginia Deed Book, 1751–1753

*Essex County, Virginia Land Trials Abstracts,
1711–1716 and 1715–1741*

Essex County, Virginia Order Book Abstracts, 1695–1699

Essex County, Virginia Order Book Abstracts, 1699–1702

Essex County, Virginia Order Book Abstracts, 1716–1723, Part 1

Essex County, Virginia Order Book Abstracts, 1716–1723, Part 2

Essex County, Virginia Order Book Abstracts, 1716–1723, Part 3

Essex County, Virginia Order Book Abstracts, 1716–1723, Part 4

Essex County, Virginia Order Book Abstracts, 1723–1725, Part 1

Essex County, Virginia Order Book Abstracts, 1723–1725, Part 2

Essex County, Virginia Order Book Abstracts, 1725–1729, Part 1

Essex County, Virginia Order Book Abstracts, 1727–1729

Essex County, Virginia Order Book, 1695–1699

Essex County, Virginia Will Abstracts, 1730–1735

Essex County, Virginia Will Abstracts, 1735–1743

Essex County, Virginia Will Abstracts, 1745–1748

Fairfax County, Virginia Deed Abstracts, 1799–1800 and 1803–1804

Fairfax County, Virginia Deed Abstracts, 1804–1805

Fairfax County, Virginia Deed Book Abstracts, 1799

Fairfax County, Virginia Deed Book, 1798–1799

Fairfax County, Virginia Land Causes, 1788–1824

Fauquier County, Virginia Land Tax Book, 1783–1787

Fauquier County, Virginia Land Tax Book, 1787–1791

Fauquier County, Virginia Minute Book Abstracts, 1759–1761

Fauquier County, Virginia Minute Book Abstracts, 1761–1762

Fauquier County, Virginia Minute Book Abstracts, 1762–1763

Fauquier County, Virginia Minute Book Abstracts, 1763–1764

www.ingramcontent.com/pod-product-compliance
Lightning Source LLC
Chambersburg PA
CBHW080618270326
41928CB00016B/3112